ADVANCE PRAISE

"Feuerverger's search for a 'place of inner solace' is profoundly inspiring ... often rendered in poetically stirring prose. With affecting clarity, the author meditates on the ways in which trauma is transmitted generationally...This is a powerful story, conveyed with deep humanity and insight." –**Kirkus Reviews**

"With her parents' survival of the Holocaust a dark shadow in the background, Grace Feuerverger's moving memoir takes us into the sunlight. Her first discovery of crossing the border into another culture – that of French-speaking Canada – leads to a life of more languages, more borders crossed. Her description of how she joyfully introduced that wider world to her students made me wish I had been one of them." –**Adam Hochschild, Historian and Journalist (UC Berkeley) and author of** *American Midnight*

"In this profound work of poetic beauty Grace takes us from the minefields of the world's tragic past into the pale beauty of winter light streaming through windows etched in frost. This is a very personal story. The music of its words are filled with wisdom and courage and affection for the broken hearts innocently cast upon the shores we inhabit. We are privileged to share Grace's tears of joy and sadness and are the better and wiser for having done so." – **Roseann O'Reilly Runte, President and CEO of** *The Canada Foundation for Innovation*

"From the very first sentence to the very last this is a wonderfully written memoir. It shows the long shadow cast by the war and how while everyone's experience was essentially the same what really matters is that everyone's experience was essentially different." – **Daniel Finkelstein, Member, House of Lords, UK, and author of** *Two Roads Home: Hitler, Stalin and the Miraculous Survival of My Family*

"Feuerverger's memoir reminds us that the traumatic legacy of the Holocaust is varied and manifests in deeply personal ways across generations. Her unflinching and vulnerable story reveals truths about pain, self-preservation, and healing." –**Hannah Weisman, Executive Director, Magnes Museum of Jewish Art and Culture, Berkeley CA**

"Engrossing and spirited, Grace Feuerverger's memoir captures both the darkness that clings to a child of Holocaust survivors and the light of a fully realized life." –**Paula S. Fass, Professor Emerita (UC Berkeley) and author of** *Inheriting the Holocaust: A Second Generation Memoir*

"This is a heavenly book, enlightened and enlightening, deeply touching and deeply humanizing. It is much, much more than the memoir of the child of Holocaust survivors. In exquisitely descriptive language *Winter Light* takes you on a journey that opens new doors of understanding for what it means to be human." – **Evelin G. Lindner, Professor, University of Oslo and Director of** ***Human Dignity and Humiliation Studies Group*** **(Columbia University)**

"In *Winter Light* Grace Feuerverger depicts her bright, passionate younger self becoming a successful scholar, a happy wife, despite and because of her parents, whose lives remain deeply shadowed by the Holocaust. Her vivid writing, full of wit and warmth, makes even the darkest stories a pleasure. This is an eloquent, irresistible memoir." –**Margot Livesey, author of** *The Road from Belhaven*

"*Winter Light* is a frank, intelligent, and well-written memoir that charts the inner journey of a daughter of Holocaust survivors and her struggle to find a path forward for herself, from the darkness she inherited into the light of a meaningful, love-filled life. This book is a valuable addition to the literature on second generation Holocaust survivors, contributing thoughtfully to what is known about the struggles and triumphs of this particular population." – **Nora Gold, author of** *18: Jewish Stories Translated From 18 Languages* **and** *In Sickness and In Health/Yom Kippur in a Gym*

"*Winter Light* is a moving and lyrical memoir of how the author liberated herself from a bleak and traumatized world to find love, professional success, and joy in living." –**Frances Dinkelspiel, author of** *Towers of Gold: How One Jewish Immigrant Names Isaias Hellman Created California* **and co-founder of** *Berkeleyside*

"Feuerverger's brilliantly illuminating book excavates the enduring multigenerational struggles among human cultures and offers us a temporal image of a lifetime of growth as the human spirit fights for recognition and expression." –**Michael Connelly, Professor Emeritus, University of Toronto, author of** *Narrative and Experience* **and Founder of** *Journal of Narrative Inquiry*

"Écris tout lorsque tu seras prête à le faire, c'est ton devoir." –**the late Cardinal Jean-Marie Lustiger, Archbishop of Paris, and author of** *Le Choix de Dieu* **(in a private conversation)**

WINTER LIGHT

THE MEMOIR OF A CHILD OF HOLOCAUST SURVIVORS

GRACE FEUERVERGER

ISBN 9789493322615 (ebook)

ISBN 9789493322608 (paperback)

ISBN 9789493322622 (hardcover)

Publisher: Amsterdam Publishers, The Netherlands

info@amsterdampublishers.com

Winter Light is part of the series Holocaust Heritage

Copyright © Grace Feuerverger 2024

Cover image: The author at age six or seven.

CONTENTS

Do not be daunted by the enormity of the world's grief. Do justly, now. Love mercy now. Walk humbly, now. You are not obligated to complete the work, but neither are you free to abandon it.
    - The Talmud

Author's Note

This is a work of nonfiction. The names of some individuals and locations have been changed (and in some cases omitted) in order to protect their privacy.

For all children coming from places of trauma

PART I

1

IT BEGAN WITH FRANÇOISE

It was not the language and culture of my own people that saved me; it was the language and culture of strangers. When I discovered my French-Canadian neighbors in the east end of Montréal, they offered me the first glimpse of hope in this world. I will forever be grateful that I grew up in their midst.

Françoise Leduc lived on the top floor of an adjacent fourplex. She was around the same age as I when we met, almost four years old, but that is where any similarity between us ended. Her blue eyes shone with life and laughter. My brown eyes were always clouded with sorrow and shame. She had many relatives who would come over to her house and visit on Sundays after church. I sat alone on my stoop watching them hug and kiss one another on both cheeks (the French way), carrying pots and pans filled with deliciously smelling food. My mouth may have watered then, but my eyes never did. Tears came only many years later when as an adult I became healthy enough to face the pain. Back then, all I could do was watch and wait.

There is one black-and-white photo of me as a child of about that age. I am holding a skipping rope, wearing a wrinkled dress torn at the elbows. I am trying to smile but cannot quite. My eyes have dark circles under them. Then I see Françoise in my mind's eye who looks fresh, like a little princess with pink bows in her blond hair. Her bows were not necessarily all that new and neither were her clothes, yet they looked so much better than mine – at least that was my perception at the time. Most amazing was that it seemed Françoise liked me. I couldn't figure out why, and what surprised me more, was that somehow we were able to communicate even though I could not yet fully speak the language that rolled so easily off her tongue. I started to spend a great deal of time at her place.

My mother seemed relieved at this development. Looking back, I realize that it must have taken some of the everyday pressures and responsibilities off her mind. I now understand that she was imprisoned in her grief and guilt, alternating between crying hysterically and then weeping silently about her losses. She would cry about her two brothers who had been sent to the death camp at Treblinka. *She was supposed to have taken care of them.* How are you supposed to take care of someone in a Nazi concentration camp? Yet, those were the final words to her from her own mother as they stood gathered in the main square of their city, Częstochowa, in Poland, while being herded by the Nazis onto railway cattle cars: "*Take care of your brothers. Don't lose sight of them.*" Nobody could have understood then that this was to be an impossible demand.

Sometimes I felt that my ghostly uncles were more real to my mother than I was. Secretly I hated her for that, but I also hated myself for being so ungrateful. After everything she had suffered, how dare I expect her to be able to mother me? She needed someone to care for her. There was no space for the needs of an emotionally bereft little girl like me who rocked herself to sleep at night, terrified that Hitler might come and carry her off to the land of her parents' nightmares.

I always felt safe in Françoise's home. The lights seemed brighter there and no members of Hitler's Gestapo seemed to be hiding in or under any bed. I remember my first invitation for dinner. I was excited, yet also nervous that I might do or say something wrong and they would not want to see me again. When the moment arrived and I was seated at their Formica table with its

4

chrome trimming and their plastic padded chairs, I was able to relax. The soup on their stove bubbled just as it would in my house. Françoise's mother brought the big pot to the table holding each ear with bright green oven mitts, set it down and then dished out the thick yellow pea soup into our bowls with a ladle which looked a lot like the one my mother used. The soup smelled so hearty. Maybe it came from the same can of Campbell's Habitant Pea Soup/Soupe aux Pois with its bright yellow label that my mother bought.

It was as if it wrapped me in its simple warmth. The huge crusty bread on the table looked freshly baked. After the soup came a steamy round pie filled with meat that smelled like cinnamon along with other more mysterious spices. Madame Leduc cut the meat pie [tourtière] into wedges and gave me a bright smile when she noticed how my eyes fell upon it in anticipation. The radio played in the background and my ears picked up on that fancy language that the Leduc family all spoke around the table. It twirled and trilled and tossed "r"s around as if it were on a carousel.

Françoise had two older brothers, Jean-Louis and Paul, and one baby sister, Lisette. Jean-Louis and Paul were close in age, seven and eight years old. They loved woodworking, and were always hammering away at some project – not surprising, since their father was a carpenter and proud of his profession. Françoise's mother had a silky name, Gisèle. She was a petite and pretty woman with soft hazel eyes and light brown hair pulled back in a chignon; she worked as a receptionist in a men's clothing business downtown.

In the midst of all the savory food and the sounds of easy-going conversation, I could make out many of the words spoken: "La pauvre petite; ses pauvres parents; c'est pitoyable ce qui est passé aux Juifs là-bas; Quelle horreur; Seigneur, donnez-leur Votre misericorde." Even at that young age I realized they were pitying my family and asking the Lord to have mercy on our souls – us, the Jews. As I grew older I knew that I did not want to be pitied and that I did not want to feel abnormal, however at the time this family's genuine sadness about my situation and their gesture of human kindness comforted me. I remember too that they clasped hands at the beginning of the meal, bowed their heads and mumbled a prayer to the *Vièrge Marie.* A sense of being a traitor overcame me. These were *goyim.* And didn't their religion condemn the Jews for having killed somebody named Le Seigneur, somebody whom they loved very much? I felt that by being present I was doing something bad.

Sometime during the meal I looked up at the wall and saw an image of a half-naked man hanging on a wooden cross. He wore thorns in his hair and his head was slumped to one side. Was that a red gash in his rib? Was he dead? I understood in an instant that he was the one they loved so much; the one they accused the Jews of having killed. Many confusing thoughts ran through my young brain. This man whom they called Jésus had – like my parents and my other relatives – suffered terribly. Was there any connection? I was too afraid to ask. One thing was clear: if he had suffered so much then he *must* have been Jewish – and just looking at him up there on that cross it seemed clear that was the case. This was a startling revelation and yet I knew in my heart that it must be true. Maybe I had once heard my parents say this or maybe I had only dreamt it – I have no clue as to how this information had come to me. But I did know. And somehow, I was just as certain that Françoise had no idea that Jesus was in fact a Jew.

I guarded this secret carefully and began to feel closer to that poor man suspended there so sadly. Did he by any chance know any of my relatives who had also been killed in a terrible way? I was afraid to bring up this line of discussion with my parents. I understood that this would hurt them and that they could not take on any more pain.

Next to Jesus, high on a shelf, stood a statue of a woman in a long white robe, white veil, and a sky-blue cape. Her arms were outstretched and a halo of stars surrounded her head. How peaceful she appeared, although she had a faraway look in her eyes. My eyes were fixed on Jesus and on this woman all through the meal. After we all ate our fill, the Leduc family – except for baby Lisette – said their prayers and crossed themselves from the top of the head to the heart and then to each shoulder and up to the mouth. Madame Leduc then went over to that statue and crossed herself again. So this was the *Vièrge Marie*. For me on that warm July evening, only a few weeks before my fifth birthday, it was love at first sight. *Un coup de foudre*. This was the Holy Mother Mary. Françoise wore a lovely gold medallion around her neck with the face of this woman engraved on it. Earlier, when we had been playing hopscotch in the afternoon, I had asked her about her necklace.

My friend had a broad toothy smile with a dimple in her pink cheek as she held out the medallion for me to take a closer look. She explained that *La Sainte Mère* was the Mother of God and that she possessed great powers of healing for anyone who believed in Her. She could perform miracles and cures. She could ease the pain of even the most downtrodden. She would take you into her arms even if you had committed a sin. She would help you get back onto the right path. Mindful of those in deep suffering she was called by many other names: Our Lady of Sorrows, of Peace, of Miracles, of Charity, of the Sacred Heart, Queen of Heaven, Queen of Angels, and so on. Many churches in Montreal were named after Her, such as the magnificent Basilica in Old Montreal, the Notre Dame [Our Lady]. Françoise looked at me quite seriously and said, "She has *your* name too: *Notre Dame de Grâce.*"

I was taken aback. "How could that be?" We sat down on the grass and thought about it. Birds were chirping everywhere. Françoise was intrigued. "Maybe there is a Catholic in your family," she said, her eyes glittering at the possibility that perhaps I was a part of her religious world after all. Françoise surely had no awareness of the fact that the historical Mary was a devout Jewish woman. One fat robin hopped by as if he wanted to be part of the conversation. "I don't think so," I replied with conviction hugging my knees to my chest. Françoise did not seem convinced by my answer, while for my part I was fascinated that I had something special in common with this powerful woman – a name, a holy name – Grace. Salut *Marie, pleine de Grâce, priez pour nous*. [Hail Mary, full of Grace, pray for us.]

Mary, full of Grace. For perhaps the first time in my young life, a sense of hope overcame me and transported me out of the dreariness of my own family story. A thought tugged at a corner of my mind: Could Mother Mary be my Holy Mother too, even if I was Jewish? Could she take me and fold her arms around me in the stillness of night? Could she feed me with her love? Could she protect me?

I knew that my older brother had been born under the icon of the Black Madonna (the dark-faced Holy Mary) – the *Matka Boska* – at the monastery of the Jasna Góra in Częstochowa, my parents' hometown, immediately after the end of the war. A part of the monastery had been turned into a makeshift hospital at the time. My mother described how the other Polish women who were there having their babies whispered in hushed tones that my mother was a *Żydówka* [Jew] – as if she had come from some far-away planet. In a sense this was true: she really had come back from the dead. My brother may have the distinction of being the first and perhaps the only Jewish child to have been born at the Jasna Góra where the Black Madonna was "in attendance."

The *Matka Boska* story filled me with wonder and in my young mind I interpreted it to mean that Mary had saved my brother's life. I decided to adopt her. Nevertheless I didn't breathe a word of this to anyone. I felt as if I finally had an ally, a guardian angel, a powerful friend. I was taking my first tentative steps toward the life force and yet my heart oscillated between excitement and a guilt-ridden foreboding of punishment to come for so heinous a crime. I have been waiting for that thunderbolt to strike me ever since.

2

STRANGER IN BERKELEY

On an impossibly radiant day in May, I got off an Air Canada flight at the San Francisco international airport wearing a red and white polka-dot cotton mini-dress, black fishnet tights, and red open-toed sandals – propelled by a sense of adventure and false confidence. There he was at the bottom of an escalator waiting for me in a camel-brown suede jacket, soccer-strong legs and dark blond hair falling over his eyes. Honey-colored eyes, so gentle and so bright. He told me later that he fell for me the moment he saw my eyes, my long legs and my auburn hair which reached down to my waist. I had no idea then that I was about to lose my carefully contrived "persona," and plunge headlong into what I had been trying so desperately to escape. It was supposed to be a two-week holiday, but it turned instead into the journey of a lifetime.

Going west? That was definitely not me. Going east was my thing. Two years earlier, at the end of my second year at McGill University in Montréal, I was offered a scholarship to study Italian language and literature for six euphoric months in Perugia, Italy. During that time, I visited Paris and also spent five emotionally filled weeks in Israel. It was during those five weeks that I decided I would apply to a Masters program in Israel after graduation from McGill two years later. All went according to plan. I graduated from

McGill with Honors in French and Italian literature and received my anticipated scholarship to begin my studies in the Fall semester at the Hebrew University in Jerusalem. So what was I doing traveling in the opposite direction?

This journey west was not of my own making. I owe it to a friend of a friend who telephoned me and suggested that before leaving for Israel there was someone in Berkeley, California I should meet – someone he had known at McGill who was now pursuing a PhD in mathematics. "I just have this feeling that you both need to meet each other. So why not take a trip to Berkeley before you head off to Jerusalem? Let's get together and I can show you a photo of this guy if you'd like," he told me in a quite serious tone. It sounded hair-brained, yet I will admit the idea of visiting Berkeley, the hotbed of the counterculture then, was tantalizing. I did have the time and so I thought, *what could be wrong with going on a wacky adventure*? I had, after all, just graduated and felt at loose ends. And anyway, it was 1971, a crazy, wild moment in history. So, why not go on a blind date some 3,000 miles away?

During my adolescent years, I had managed to keep my childhood traumas more or less at bay thanks to the power of hormones: in my case, it was attraction to the opposite sex. Parties, dates, and a crush on my French professor who taught *La Littérature française du Vingtième Siècle* were all part of my bag of unconscious strategies for leaning toward the life force. It was not a bad trick, considering my family circumstances. On the surface, one might have thought I was a young person on the move, ready to take on the world. When this mutual friend and I met for coffee he took out his McGill yearbook of 1967 and showed me a black-and-white photo of the guy he had suggested I meet. The intelligence and the steadfastness on the face of this young man intrigued me. As I stared at the picture, the face looked strangely familiar. An odd feeling overcame me as if I had known him in another life. I wondered whether we had held each other close in some faraway land, outside of time, outside of space. The tenderness I saw in his eyes suggested the chance of a new beginning, a chance to heal and be healed.

We decided to have a long-distance phone call first. Our conversation turned out to stretch for several hours – in spite of costly long-distance calls. His voice felt like a warm touch on my cheek. We spoke about all manner of things under the sun. He too thought this idea was crazy, but what the heck. He suggested I send him a photo, however, I managed to talk him out of it. I am not the most photogenic person in the world; for some reason photos of me tend to come out awkwardly. As we continued to talk, it somehow began to feel like we were old friends finding one another after many years. And I discovered that, like me, he too was a child of Holocaust survivors. This somehow created an immediate bond, no matter how things would turn out. So I packed my bags and flew.

That first night we talked until dawn in his shiny white 1967 Mustang with its black leather seats. We drove up into the Berkeley hills overlooking the San Francisco Bay. The lights of San Francisco twinkled like shimmering stars. It was startlingly beautiful to see the Golden Gate Bridge clear and glowing red at sunrise. I also drank in the fresh ocean air as we rolled down the car windows still wet from the morning dew. All night long we compared notes about our experiences of being children of trauma. We also shared exhilarating conversations about the "mysteries" of the cosmos and the poetry of mathematics. I, who was (and still am) a total "mathphobe" worried that he might think I was a dodo. Instead, he patiently took my hand and told me about the exquisite world of mathematics, so pure, so fascinating – and I could sense that it was and always would be his holy place.

When he spoke, his hazel eyes gleamed and I felt incredibly special to be allowed a glimpse into that rarefied world. And he, on the other hand, admired how I chose to reach out to humanity through my love of languages and cultures. He was surprised by my view of Montréal. Even though he too had grown up in Montréal he had never had a chance to see it as the vibrant, cosmopolitan city that it was (the only such city in Canada when we were growing up there). He had been raised in a home with parents who had withdrawn from the world because of the brutality they had experienced in the Nazi death camps – their connection to a social life limited to enjoying long conversations with adoring customers in their little gift shop.

His name was Andrey. I loved the sound and spelling of that name. What had been clenched tight within each of us began to open. Words came forth like rivers of release and comfort – and also of endless sadness. I had never before been with someone who had felt that same particular sorrow as deeply. He told me he had never spoken about this to anyone before. We became lovers almost immediately and I moved into his sunny apartment on College Avenue. We created a fiction that I was living at International House on campus whenever I called home. My parents would not have been able to handle my living with a guy. And he did what my parents could not do: in the middle of the night when I felt haunted by my demons, he would grab at the air and "catch" those "bad things" and banish them. He held me tight and explained that if you didn't run from the demons, they couldn't do much harm. And he explained how his way to survive was by entering the world of logic and reason. He could enter the world of mathematics and leave everything behind. And I told him that I did it by entering the worlds of other people's languages and cultures. Day by day we began to invent our relationship, like orphans who would save each other's lives. Having the boldness to articulate our pain was extraordinary, though it also turned out to be overwhelming. Sometimes I fell apart and it scared him. Other times he broke down and it frightened me. Yet, we somehow both knew that there was no way out except through it, and *together*. So we hung on. I gave up my scholarship to the Hebrew University and stayed in Berkeley.

This may seem like a story about a knight in shining armor and a damsel in distress, each rescuing the other. And perhaps it is, but it's more complicated than that. The other side of the story is that I had been parachuted into this radical college town, a hive of political activism filled with any type of drugs you could imagine. Berkeley is one of the most socially, politically and aesthetically vibrant places on earth. Although when I first arrived that May, I was an emotionally shaky girl barely out of my teens, and in no way able to handle the tumult of the anti-Vietnam War protests, the uprisings, the tear gas, and the head-bashing by the National Guard. Riots occurred almost daily. Stores were looted. *Power to the People. Black Power.* Malcolm X, the Black Panthers and so on. I was an alien in a place of rebellion. At parties I was terrified that someone would drop LSD into my drink and I would have a bad trip and jump off the balcony of an apartment building as one of my neighbors there had done and she had died. I was petrified by the violence and the steely eyes of some of the street people who loitered along Telegraph Avenue, most of them in filthy tatters, some carrying even filthier babies.

One afternoon while I was walking down a street some guy high on something called out from a car that screeched to a halt: "Hey, girl. You're outta sight. Do you have an old man?" I ran for my life. I who had been so popular and upbeat in Montréal — and who two years earlier had hitch-hiked my way from Italy all the way to Istanbul — was terrified in this place. Berkeley forced me to peel away the layers of an existence I had painstakingly built over the years of my early life. My only moments of calm were when I was with Andrey, but he was deeply immersed in his PhD program and didn't fully understand my sense of dislocation.

Was I a witness, or a voyeur, or a cipher? Perhaps all of these. I was engulfed by the noise, by the screaming, by the turmoil. I was choking for air. I couldn't understand it fully at the time, but I had lived through similar hysteria throughout my childhood. And I didn't need more. Yet there was nowhere to run. Everyone else seemed connected, involved in their studies or stoked by the fires of resistance, of rebellion, and of revolt while I was left out, imprisoned in the distress of my anxieties, ready to freak out. It was excruciating to be in the midst of all that chaos and have no place to feel a sense of real belonging. What happened to all that European cultural loveliness that I had enjoyed a mere two years earlier? I was stunned at how it all went wrong.

I hated everything about Berkeley at that time. As I became more and more lost, I couldn't appreciate the breezy blue skies and the views of the San Francisco Bay and the Golden Gate Bridge. It would have been so simple to leave. But there was the matter of this young man with the soft suede jacket and his dreamy eyes and soccer legs – this beautiful soul whom I was convinced I had known in a previous life. A strange and desperate feeling overcame me: that this young man would ultimately be my salvation and that I would be his; and that we must – absolutely must – remain together. So I didn't leave.

I became a wanderer with no professional purpose. I had never considered Berkeley as an academic destination and it was too late to apply for scholarships. It had all happened so fast. Blinded by confusion, I thought that my only avenue was to take a secretarial course at a place called "The Polly Priest Academy" deep in the heart of Oakland, then the murder capital of the United States. I was the only white girl at Polly Priest and felt rather awkward. The woman at the reception desk did finally warm up to me a little bit after she found out that I was Canadian and not American. She even asked me to take care of the phones when she went for lunch and told me that if any creditors called, to say that I had no idea where she was. I returned each evening to Berkeley feeling like I had managed to survive another day in a war zone.

One day I got off the bus at the wrong stop in Oakland and suddenly was surrounded by a group of young Black guys who started whistling and asked if I had any dope for them. "What's in your bag, white girl? Ya gotta have somethin' for us," one of them said in a belligerent tone. I thought I saw the flash of a knife, and I turned the corner, with my heart knocking wildly against my chest and noticed a frail elderly Black man sitting on a bench at a bus stop. I stopped because I knew I couldn't outrun these boys and told this kindly looking man what had happened. He replied calmly: "Oh chile, they's just actin' tough. Stay with me. They won't hurt you." And sure enough when they saw me with this man they smiled feebly at him and then ignored me. It turned out one of the boys was his grandson.

I looked around and saw that neighborhood for the first time. The fog of poverty blanketed everything. Prostitutes looking wearily indifferent wore very short skirts and very high heels as they stood at street corners; young kids were making drug deals; wrinkled grandmothers with babies and toddlers in strollers were carrying such groceries as they could afford. They were all African-American. The streets were full of potholes. The tenement buildings were crumbling. I saw for the first time the tragedy of it all. At that moment fear was more powerful than compassion and I didn't have the inner resources then to confront the truth – that I too had come from poverty, a different kind of poverty to be sure: mine was a lack of any sense of emotional security.

The older man sat in a light-blue suit, crisp white shirt and red bowtie holding a cane. He moved his head to one side as if trying to figure out what I was doing there and said, "A pretty white girl like you could get into a lot of trouble here." I sat down at the bench next to him and began to weep. He touched my hand, and said, "We have time to talk, if you'd like." Everything around me turned into slow motion. The man told me that he was curious as to why a pretty, young white girl looked so unhappy. This was not something he would have figured on, he said. He told me that being white was all he had ever dreamed of: "I reckoned it was as close to Paradise as you can be on this earth."

We're talking about the early-1970s, and this man told me that he was 75 years old, which meant he had been born in the late-1800s. He had come from Florida as a young man with his wife during the Great Depression to make a better life; and to escape the Jim Crow laws of segregation, prejudice and inequality that were in full force at the time. He was the grandchild of slaves. I had never before spoken to an African-American about race in such an intimate way. Young children and adults, all Black, walked by, but nobody bothered us. It was as if they sensed we were in some divine space.

His name was Walter and I told him that mine was Grace. "You be blessed with a name like that, chile," he replied. And then I told him that he would have been my grandfathers' ages. "Are your grandpas alive?" he asked. "No, I'm Jewish and they were killed in Poland by the Nazis along with the rest of my parents' families," I said much too matter-of-factly. He looked at me for what seemed an eternity and his velvety brown eyes became even softer as he said, "Bein' Jewish is a burden worse than bein' Black, chile. Jews are God's chosen; that's a heavy trial. Jesus was Jewish and God's only Son and look what happened to Him." We both began to laugh. At that moment I felt like he was my kin. I had just tasted what it might have been like to have had a grandfather.

Again, I looked around. In some odd way, I began to feel that I might have been in worse shape than many of the folks here, even though on the surface it didn't look that way. They seemed to have strength and power, and a sort of inner defiance. It was growing dark and I knew I had to head back to Berkeley. I shook Walter's hand and thanked him for his kindness. My bus arrived and Walter's last words to me as I waved goodbye to him were: "Keep your head up, girl. You's stronger than you think. You got lots o' livin' to do. Keep a-goin'!"

I landed a job at department store City of Paris in San Francisco – hands down the greatest gig I, or anyone else, could possibly have ever imagined! The place was created by a French entrepreneur who had settled in San Francisco in the late 1800s. The building featured a domed roof with an impressive version of the Eiffel Tower perched on top. I was hired on account of my fluency in French. My main function was to walk around the different departments and chat with the Francophile shoppers who were mainly women from the city's "high society" looking for opportunities to practice the French they had learned at university, or during their junior year abroad in France. Part of my job was to take some of the shoppers to the in-store restaurant for tea and cakes and as we enjoyed un café au lait et un morceau de gâteau they would talk about their adventures in France using their halting French. I listened to them avidly. These women were la crème de la crème of San Franciscan society and I was fascinated by their stories.

I recall one woman in particular. She wore a green silk blazer and matching pleated skirt with a diamond brooch in the shape of a flower on her lapel. She had blond silky hair in a flip and soft green-gray eyes with delicate hands holding une tasse de café to her lips. Originally from New York City, her husband, a banker, had been transferred to San Francisco. Of course, she accompanied him and had to say goodbye to her life there. She confided in me in the best French she could muster that she very much missed Manhattan and her friends. Her eyes grew misty. When she spoke of her junior year in Paris in 1949-1950 (she had been at Smith College) she glowed with excitement. She told me that in Paris she had even been at a party which was also attended by Jacqueline Bouvier (well before Jackie married JFK). It looked like those years were long gone, yet this woman desperately held onto them. *"C'est formidable!"* was all I could voice in the face of such privilege. And I thought, *Wow, even the very wealthy have problems!*

It really was an incredible job and offered me an oasis away from my own troubles. At night though, I dreamt about the graduate program at the Hebrew University which I had thrown away. I would wake up in a sweat still feeling myself running to catch the plane to Jerusalem, always missing the flight by a few seconds. Anxiety stalked me in my waking as well as in my sleeping hours. In the months that followed I spiraled downward into a depression. My job at City of Paris had been "occasional," so when the season slowed down in winter, the job ended. I was devastated even though I always knew it was just a temporary position. All of my false personae were unraveling and I was left staring into a dark abyss. Andrey was alarmed by what was happening. He definitely wanted me to stay with him, but was very concerned about my unhappiness. This just added to my anguish. We were in two different worlds: his filled with purpose and promise, mine with emptiness and dread.

Looking back, I realize how powerless we both felt. I couldn't leave and yet I tormented myself that perhaps that would have been the best thing to do. I placed glossy travel brochures on the coffee table in our living room. Europe, Asia, Africa – anywhere but Berkeley. Andrey was afraid to ask why they were there while I never asked myself why I was placing such items on the table. Maybe our relationship would have survived over a long distance. Who knows? Remember: there were no cell phones then, no email.

And long-distance calls were very expensive. We were stymied by the personal, familial and societal pressures acting upon us at that time. One thing stood out in stark relief: I felt more intimately protected with this guy than I had ever felt before in my life. Never had I experienced such a sense of safety. Was it our destiny to meet? A Divine Force seemed to be in charge. I kept recalling the words that had come to my mind on that first night in Andrey's car: *that we would save each other's lives*. Where had those words come from? I clung to them as though I were hanging from a ledge by my fingernails.

We did have some fun in spite of it all. We ate at upscale restaurants whenever we could. There was some money for that. Andrey had worked at various part-time jobs in his undergrad years and held a graduate assistantship at Berkeley. I too had worked part-time during my McGill days. The seafood restaurant on stilts at the Berkeley Marina was one of our favorites. It was called Solomon Grundy's at the time. What a spectacular view it had of the bay and the Golden Gate Bridge – the waves lapping at the rocks by the shore. Then there were our late-night haunts in Oakland's Jack London Square where we read and chatted until the wee hours of the morning. We were such night owls. And our drives into San Francisco were truly joyful. Whenever I saw the freeway sign "SAN FRANCISCO" my heart rate speeded up. *"If you're going to San Francisco, be sure to wear some flowers in your hair"* (that song written by John Philips of "The Mamas and Papas" and sung by Scott Mackenzie) had seized the imagination of a whole generation, including me.

Many months passed. And then it was almost a year. My weekly phone calls to my parents in Montréal always made me feel like an ingrate. I continued saying that I was at International House. My mother's message was always the same: "Come home immediately." Her tone of voice was imperious and hysterical at the same time. How dare I run around in that crazy place? Was I going to end up being abducted by crazies? By the time I would get off the phone I felt my stomach cramping and my eyes burning with a sense of homesickness brought on by guilt.

One evening at one of our favorite restaurants in San Francisco, Biff's (which had the most amazing steak soup), we came to a clear understanding that we both wanted to be together no matter what and we decided to make that official by becoming engaged. There was something comforting about that step. We hoped that it would take the pressure off. Several months later we decided to take the further step and announced that we would get married.

We flew to Montréal to meet our future in-laws with a very small wedding in mind. My mother had definitely wanted something larger and more conventional, yet I insisted on having the wedding in my parents' home. She was not at all pleased because she had planned to fully take charge of the event: the dress I would wear, the hall, the guests, the seating arrangement, the menu, and so on. And my father, a gentle soul ravaged by rage and sorrow, allowed her to do whatever she wanted. My mother scowled with her eyes boring into me, and wringing her hands, "How can you not allow your mother to have the kind of wedding that everyone else has? Why do you have to be different?" I shrugged and told her that this was what we wanted. And I added, "In fact I was thinking of wearing a jeans skirt and peasant blouse with a garland of flowers in my hair. That's what they're doing in Berkeley." My mother's olive complexion turned sheet-white. She looked like she was about to have apoplexy. She finally had no choice, but to concede to a small wedding in her home although she didn't have the sense to consult with her future son-in-law's parents on any of this. They were left out of the discussions completely.

My future in-laws were quiet, dignified people and respected our privacy. Taken aback by my mother's heavy-handed behavior, they began to wonder whether their son was making the right decision. They spoke to him about their concerns and suggested that perhaps he should first complete his thesis and then see how he felt about me. Andrey told them firmly that I was the one. To go against his parents' quite rational wishes (given what they had seen of my mother's ways) speaks to the devotion he had for me right from the start. Somewhere deep down he must have known that when the time came, he would stand up and protect me from her. A few days later he presented me with a delicately designed engagement ring and a wedding band to match. His father who was a jeweler (an unsung artist) had designed it.

My mother planned to buy the wedding dress for me and I decided to go along with her wish. I was curious to see what she would choose. We went to a shop downtown which specialized in wedding apparel and as we entered, my eyes fell upon a simple, lacy-white floor-length dress with a hazy tulle veil that dropped to the shoulder. My mother had hurried over to some other rack of heavily beaded wedding gowns and was pointing to them.

"I like this one here," I uttered with conviction. This time I had promised myself I would choose an outfit which I liked. I tried on the dress of my choice and it fit perfectly. Then that look came upon her face: the one that had always frightened me as a child – the look that heralded either a high-pitched shriek or a strangled sob, both of which came from a profoundly tortured place in her soul. The saleswoman saved the day by announcing how the dress I was wearing suited me so well. My mother turned away, no emotion at all. I was rattled, feeling a bit dizzy. And terribly guilty.

Tables and chairs were rented for about 30 guests and small floral arrangements were placed unassumingly in the center of each table in the living room. I remember my about-to-be in-laws walking toward the *chuppa* [canopy] with a bleak expression on their faces. Only years later did I come to truly understand their deep fragility. My father accompanied my mother with a dazed look. We all settled ourselves under the canopy for the wedding ceremony. The veil covered my face and through the tulle I looked up at the young man who had already become my true family. A rabbi officiated. Andrey was wearing a gray suit with a mauve tie and looked not only handsome but also aristocratic. I remember his eyes shining as he recited the *Ani l'dodi v'dodi li* from the *Song of Songs* in the Hebrew Bible, one of the most beautiful love poems ever written. "I am my beloved's, and my beloved is mine." He then slipped the wedding band onto my finger. I repeated this recitation and placed a wedding band on his. We beamed at one another.

The wedding had gone well (what a relief!), however, I felt very concerned about returning to Berkeley. When I discussed my anxiety of non-belonging there, all our parents could say was that a wife needs to stay with her husband. None of our parents offered to lend us money for the out-of-state tuition for a Masters program at Cal – which was steep even then. The idea came up but they couldn't understand the value of it. To be fair, none of them were well-off financially although we promised to pay them back as soon as we could. The real problem was that being poor immigrants from small towns in Eastern Europe, they dismissed my feelings as inappropriate and unworthy of a wife.

How defeated I felt – I who had always won scholarships and awards had to beg for help to pay tuition because I never had expected to be in Berkeley and therefore missed the deadlines for application. The scholarship to the Hebrew University which I had given away rose up in my mind like an abandoned child. All I could do was turn my distress inward and become more depressed. We returned to Berkeley and I stumbled my way from one day to the next. My husband had agreed that we would return to Canada within a year when his thesis would be completed. We didn't have the proper visas to stay in the US anyway. My only desire at the time was to make it out of Berkeley alive, and never, ever to return. Had anyone told me then that Berkeley would end up playing a pivotal role later in my life, I would have thought them deranged.

Thinking back, I am amazed at how out-of-step I was with the 70s. I might as well have been living in a post-World War II Displaced Persons (DP) camp trying to piece together my shattered life. There were the Civil Rights and the Black Movements, Women's Liberation, Ethnic Studies, free love, going off to live in caves in Greece, or to India to learn about Eastern philosophy, not to mention the Peace Corps. Who wanted to hear about the psychological problems of a child who had grown up with Holocaust survivor parents? I was not yet fully conscious of the straitjacket I was in and of how it affected my every step. And to make matters worse, Berkeley was such an alienating place at that time for anyone not immersed in a university program or in radical politics, and I was involved in neither. But "in a dark place one begins to see," wrote the poet Theodore Roethke. From that moment on, Berkeley became a mirror for me, cracked and broken – yet alive with the power to see what could be salvaged from the shambles in which I found myself.

I woke up one morning and the fog in my head began to lift. I took a baby step toward taking charge of my life by the decision to at least *audit* graduate courses at Berkeley – in Italian literature, psycholinguistics, and multicultural education which I was able to do at no cost. All I needed was permission from the professors at Cal and they offered this happily. So I finally ended up on campus. And remarkably one course turned out to transform my life: a graduate seminar on language learning and bilingual education taught by Professor Robert Ruddell at Tolman Hall in the Graduate Department of Education. Ruddell's seminar spoke directly to my multicultural experience growing up in Montréal. I remember how much effort I put into the final oral assignment for the class documenting my bilingual schooling both in elementary school and in high school. The course offered me my first entry into ethnographic research although I was at that time unaware of any purposeful direction to which this would lead. After all, I was only auditing this course while legitimately I was still enrolled at The Polly Priest Academy. I never breathed a word of the secretarial course to anyone on campus. They would have thought me mad.

On the last day of classes, Professor Ruddell invited our class to his home up in the Berkeley Hills. We all sat on deck chairs on his large cozy verandah. My body began to unwind as I stared out at the Golden Gate Bridge and at the sailboats floating about on the azure-blue bay, a glass of Napa White Zinfandel in hand. After the lecture part of that class was over, our professor spoke to each of his students individually in his study, a sort of glorified office hour. When my turn came, he asked me what I wanted to do next. I never told him about my lost scholarship or about any other aspect of the emotional wreckage that Berkeley represented for me at the time. I quietly responded that I was planning to return to Canada and that I wasn't sure of my next step.

Searching my face for a clue to my inner feelings, he spoke to me prophetically, "You should go into teaching. You're a natural and it sounds like you could do a lot for multicultural education in Canada. Why don't you try the classroom for a while? Your students would be so lucky!" I was surprised at how much he had paid attention to me in his classes.

What I couldn't know then was that "angels of mercy" were waiting for me on the other side of the border – back in Canada – prepared to patch me up and make me whole. And that, many years later, I would fall in love with Berkeley and see it with very different eyes.

3

LOOKING BACK

My early life was shaped by experiences that I didn't live personally. My survivor parents and three-year-old brother arrived in Montréal in 1948 – penniless refugees carrying all the ghosts of their murdered relatives with them. I was born several years later. Those years were fragmented, filled with demons and ghosts. Snippets of stories swirled around me like dark snowflakes in a storm.

My parents were beyond my grasp. They lived in a no-man's land of self-recrimination, guilt, blame, and rage, even as they soldiered on. It took great effort for them to create a new life in Canada. In the aftermath of the war everyone wanted to rebuild. This was a duty, if not a desire. Having children was a must. My mother had one too soon. Her first child, a boy, had been unplanned and was born at the end of the war. Becoming pregnant in a concentration camp does defy imagination, but it happened.

The message of the 1950s was that a family should have at least a second child as a sibling for the first. My mother had wished for a girl in their new life in Montréal. However, the little girl she bore was not the child she had hoped for – too small, too fair, too fragile.

So many years later, I am in my study at home grading my graduate students' essays and suddenly I remember that some photographs from my childhood are right next to me in the drawer of my cherry-wood desk where I had placed them decades ago when my husband and I first moved into our house. I open the drawer and slip the photographs out of an envelope. I arrange them on my desk and turn on the lamp as shadows begin to form outside in the twilight. The photos are not arranged in any particular order.

I pick up a little picture of me (I must have been about one year old) being held by my father. The black-and-white photo is out of focus and overexposed so it looks gray and blurry. I have a head full of light brown hair and big dark eyes and am wearing a thick sweater and pants. It must have been winter. I'm not smiling. I'm clutching my father's shirt collar. I don't want to ever let go of him. His eyes are wide and much lighter than my own, and he is valiantly trying to look happy. I know that his first job was as a dishwasher. Later on, he took on jobs as a bookkeeper in different places. He shuffled through these way stations, longing for the "real" life that had been denied him. I look more closely at the photo. There is an otherworldliness about the picture: a gentleness, a touch of the divine. Two lost souls hanging onto each other.

I look at myself at six about to turn seven – the date is printed on the edge. I am holding a skipping rope in one hand and a lollipop in the other. I'm wearing a sweater with the bottom button missing and a wrinkled skirt. My hair is pulled back into a ponytail and I'm smiling, but the smile looks forced. Did every child look this disheveled?

Then there is me at about eight years old in a swimsuit leaning against a summer chaise longue where my mother is proudly holding my baby sister whose olive complexion and wavy black hair are just like hers. Finally, she had the little girl she wanted! It's as if the photo is irrevocably torn in some gaping space between me and my mother and sister. Why didn't my mother have her arm around me as well? I am staring at the camera trying to look happy. For the first time I can see how out-of-place I felt. I look down at another snapshot of me in a baby in a carriage wearing a frilly bonnet and woolen jacket, and covered with a blanket. I am sleeping deeply and it looks as if I never want to wake up. I am safe in that carriage, safe with my dreams and far from any glare of reality.

I was told that as a baby I did not have a good appetite and supposedly it was difficult to feed me. I slept so noiselessly that my mother was always anxious that I would stop breathing. As I stare at the photo I wonder whether I was hovering between life and death, trying to decide whether or not it was worth living. Perhaps I had already figured out that something noxious was in the air around me and could suffocate me. Perhaps I was already dreaming of escape.

Although my mother tried to be a good housekeeper, after her own fashion, she was plagued by severe emotional ups and downs. She could be optimistic and positive one moment, and then plunge into dark worlds. I was terrified at such emotional "seesaws" and tried to hide out of sight. The devil was never far away and he could choose to torment my poor mother at any time of the day by reminding her of how she had lost track of her two brothers in the concentration camp. She was the sole survivor of her nuclear and extended family. I know little of what happened to my grandparents before the war. Only that they had come from impoverished backgrounds. What about their emotional lives, their family lives before the war? So many stories, untold and unheard, hung in the airless atmosphere of our home. Maybe my parents really had nothing to cling onto. Maybe that was why they could move forward only haltingly. How could they find any meaning for their losses?

The bottom line was that my parents' loyalties were given fully over to those who had been murdered, although my older brother had special status on the grounds that he had suffered along with them as a baby. The authority of the Holocaust had to be worshipped and I accepted this without question. After they exhausted all their emotional energies for the dead, there wasn't much left for their children. Who was I to point fingers after what they suffered?

Perhaps the most dangerous idea my parents instilled in me was that I might one day vanish into thin air, that all was shifting and shiftless, that the world was a cauldron of doubt and anxiety and that – most of all – the devil was *always* lurking around the corner. Yes, there were moments of laughter and respite, yet these were fleeting. The message was that everything could dissolve into a pool of destruction at the whim of a bad memory or, even worse, of a bad decision. That one misstep could bring down the whole house of cards. And that all must be lost in the end.

But must it?

I look up from my desk for a moment. Souvenirs I purchased in market stalls from past conference venues from around the world are lovingly arranged on the shelves above me. I run my fingers across the ones on the first shelf: a statue of the monkey god Hanuman from India; a bronze Buddha from Vietnam; a porcelain Guan Yin (Goddess of Mercy) from China. This Bodhisattva wears a crown on her head and she is in the Lotus position with her first finger touching her thumb. I fiddle with the pearl buttons on my sweater as the sapphire ring from a pilgrimage town at the mouth of the Ganges River in Northern India shines from the third finger of my left hand.

I look down again, this time at a photo of myself at around age ten pretending to dance, trying hard to look happy – again. It lies quietly on my desk. So many spaces open in my mind, so many memories seep toward the surface. I begin to realize that I look much younger now than I did in that photo. I pick up a steaming cup of tea with lemon, ginger and honey and take a long sip. The aroma of roast garlic chicken, vegetables and potatoes baking in the oven for dinner are wafting from the kitchen up the stairs into my study. I am away far enough from that time in my childhood that it seems safe to let the memories unfold.

My first memory of family life is of standing in a crib sprinkled with broken glass, hot blood flowing from my leg and spreading over the mattress. All around there is shrieking. I am alone in this commotion and have only the bars of the crib to hang onto. My tummy heaves as if I'm on the high seas. I'm about two years old. A drinking glass had fallen to the floor near my crib and a large shard landed on the railing of the crib. Was I told that I picked it up and it skittered across my arm? Someone must have patched me up as there are no scars on my arm now. I don't know if my mother was the one who took care of the wound, or my father. Or perhaps a neighbor intervened.

Suddenly I feel as if I am back to when I was three or four years old, before school age. My mother would have been about 30. I was watching her stare at a wall in the living room of our apartment in Montréal. She was speaking with her brothers who had died in the furnaces of Treblinka. Tears streamed down her face. I can't remember whether she was speaking to them in Polish or Yiddish. By that time I could understand both languages. What I can remember is the soothing tone of her voice. I had never heard that gentleness from her. The voice I had heard up until then was always laced with anxiety and hysterical weeping. I could not understand this transformation nor why she was speaking to the dead as if they were right beside her while she didn't notice me at all, alive, and in the room. A vacant look in her large black eyes made me feel invisible. I crept away and went to my own room where I rocked myself to sleep.

One time I screwed up the courage to try to help her by saying, "Mama, they aren't really here; don't worry, they are in heaven and are safe now." In response to what I had said to her, my mother fixed her blazing eyes on me. "They are here! Don't ever say such a thing again," she shouted. I wished I could have hugged her but she was not in the room with me. She was far away in that place where they stole her brothers and she couldn't stop them. I clung to my dolly really tight. I felt cold and alone.

Another recollection surfaces: I hadn't begun school yet. It was an early morning and I had just gotten up and walked into the kitchen of our crowded apartment to get a glass of water when a shimmering light called to me through windowpanes, the sun glowing against the bright-blue sky and on the freshly fallen snow of a bitter cold winter day in Montréal. From what place did it come? The brilliance startled me. I was unable to make sense of this light. And especially that it could be shining upon *me*.

Everything was as it had always been. My father always got up around 5:30 a.m. to get to his first job as bookkeeper in a fur factory far from our apartment. He juggled two jobs to make ends meet. He had been gone for hours by the time I woke up. The yellow and orange oilcloth that covered the kitchen table held my father's glass of cold tea with a leftover wedge of lemon. A plate with the remains of rye toast, scrambled eggs and herring sat next to the glass. My mother was elsewhere helping my brother get ready for school – he was in grade five. I stood alone in our small kitchen. The light beckoned as I peered outside. I heard its whisper: "You belong in this light, you will find your place in it; just follow the light."

From that moment on, I became a regular at our kitchen window and at our other windows as well. My eyes would fix on the Jack Frost patterns that formed on the windowpanes. The patterns spoke of mountains and valleys, of rivers and oceans, of birds and other animals: shapes that seemed to glimmer like crystal. Over and over I would stare at the designs and trace them with my index finger. Those designs seemed like images of faraway territories. What I could not know then was that I would one day travel to many such places for research projects as a university professor.

Then a jagged shard rips into my mind: When I was four or five years old, my mother would nervously rush across busy streets on our way to the supermarket. The devil seemed to be in charge during such excursions. "We can't make it across the street before the light changes; what should we do?" I would cry. I hung on as best I could. Each crossing was a harrowing event. Who was the child? Who was the mother? When would we be able to stop running? Running from whom? Running from where? When we got to the supermarket my mother had to sit down in a seat near the entrance, sweat pouring from her face. I put my head near her shoulder as she breathed in and out. Sometimes she had to rush to the washroom and I waited outside hoping she wouldn't disappear. I didn't even know the telephone number of where my father worked. I wouldn't have wanted to bother him anyway because he had a mean boss who could fire him at any time. I did know the name of the school my brother attended. He was a lot older than me and could have come to get me if necessary.

I also remember waking up in the dark of night jolted by a dream in which Hitler was about to break through our apartment door and take us away to the land of my parents' nightmares – Poland. I awoke screaming. I must have been around nine years old. My parents rushed into the room. My mother's thick hair tangled around her face. She wore a shapeless cotton nightgown over her plump body. My father's eyes peered out from under dark blond hair that fell over his pale face. He had on an undershirt and pajama pants over his slim body. I told them about my bad dream, no doubt hoping for comfort. Instead, they began gesticulating, hands clutching their faces, and uttered the unutterable: a *dybbuk* must have entered my body. Their panic stunned me into silence.

The concept of a *dybbuk* was murky to me at that tender age although I knew that a *dybbuk* was a powerful and undesirable supernatural entity. I could feel my pajamas become soaked with sweat. Then I thought I caught a glimpse of a shadowy figure lurking in the background. Was this the *dybbuk*? It more looked like a monster with shiny black Nazi boots. It was holding a long black iron hook that could collar any child who might try to escape its clutches. I had the sensation that I was floating above the heads of my parents. I looked down at them as they continued to discuss the calamity of my having been invaded by a *dybbuk*.

I made a decision then and there. "Go back to bed," I said calmly. "I'm fine now." I don't know where those words came from. In my mind, I floated down from the ceiling and back into my bed. My parents were inconsolable as they returned to their room, never seeming to realize that all I had needed was a hug. Usually, it was my father who had nightmares that woke him up with a sharp scream. There were no hugs for anyone. The shadowy figure with its long iron hook saw to that. It stood like a sentinel at the door. Maybe I had dreamed it. Maybe I imagined it. It doesn't matter. That figure was real to me and I knew it could do me great harm. The superstition that held sway over my parents had taken hold of me. I pulled the blanket over my head and somehow lulled myself back to sleep.

The following morning I awoke to sunshine. I ate breakfast, rye bread, scrambled eggs with sliced tomatoes, onions and herring, and got ready for school. I put on my school uniform with white blouse and navy pleated tunic, white socks and black oxford shoes. No one said a word about what had taken place in the middle of the night. Nobody ever talked about my father's screaming nightmares either.

4

THE POLAND THEY KNEW

My parents never had a chance. The Holocaust saw to that. And they never had a chance even before then, impoverished as they were by the economic and social circumstances of their families in Poland in the decades leading up to World War II. They lived in a godforsaken time and in a godforsaken place, probably the absolute worst place to be at that time if you were a Jew – and especially if you were a Jew without the means to get out. That was my parents' lot. I will not write about the horrors they had to endure. Instead I will try and piece together what little I know about their lives from their whispered conversations, choked thoughts, endless emptiness.

What do I know about their lives in Poland? Not much – and yet perhaps too much. My mother seemed to have placed a spell on her husband. He was intoxicated by her. She was dark and expressive, wild as the wind, and almost a decade younger. He was fair and reserved, an intellectual. They were opposite ends of a spectrum. Whereas she exuded emotional intensity, he was afraid to show his feelings. She was afraid not to. They could have been protagonists in a novel by Flaubert or Tolstoy.

I know that they never had a wedding on account of the war.

They almost didn't get engaged either, but that wasn't Hitler's fault. My father's parents did not want him to marry my mother. She came from a lower social background, and was not at all cultured. His parents had picked out a girl from a well-to-do family. Being an obedient son, the youngest in his family, he wanted to please them, to make things better. Times were tough; the Depression, poverty, and the more the economy got worse, the more virulent the antisemitism became in Poland. My father had to find whatever work he could to bring in money in order to put food on the table. His father was already very ill with heart disease.

My father got engaged to the girl who had been chosen for him. He must have been heartbroken at having had to give up his true love and settle for this dull girl. At least that's what my mother told me. She must have felt jilted, devastated. Her mother, a tyrannical woman, was livid. Then my father's father died of a heart attack at age 49. Perhaps the shock of this brought him to his senses. He broke the engagement to the other girl and went back to his sweetheart asking her for forgiveness on bended knee. He told her that life would mean nothing without her at his side.

First, he had to get past my mother's mother who no longer wanted anything to do with him or his family. Not only did he love my mother, but she also loved him – or, at the least, she needed him. This time she did not let him get away, regardless of how her mother felt. Young love triumphed and they became engaged, not a trifling matter in those days. My father had to formally annul his engagement to the other girl under the auspices of the local rabbi. His family and the girl's family had to sign a formal religious document to annul the engagement. There must have been shame and humiliation for this girl and her family.

My parents' engagement took place in an increasingly dangerous time, the beginning of 1939. The Nazis were already in power in Germany, already stripping Jews and anybody else who opposed them of any civil rights. They also loved to round up Jews and force them to clean streets with toothbrushes. If the streets were still dirty, they were beaten to death. The Nazis had occupied

Czechoslovakia, renamed "Sudetenland" and Austria had been annexed. Soon Hitler would invade Poland and the war would begin. Life as they knew it would end for the Jews. They were forced into filthy, overcrowded ghettos and many died of disease or starvation.

On September 23, 1942 the Jews of Częstochowa, the city in which my parents' families had lived for centuries, were all deported to various concentration camps. It was Yom Kippur, the holiest day in the Judaic tradition, a day of fasting and reflection. As a child I tried to picture them being herded by the Nazis, confused and bewildered by the blaring of megaphones, shocked at the brutality. Jews were killed for not standing up straight enough or for standing too straight, for not looking "properly" at the Nazis or avoiding their gaze, or for not listening carefully enough to instructions. My mother, still a teenager, stood with her family clutching a valise. My father and his family were there, too. They had been rounded up in the same crowded ghetto.

In the midst of all that madness and chaos and cruelty my father made a monumental decision: he and my mother would go together, as if husband and wife (they were only engaged) to wherever they were to be sent. He was going to be with her for as long as possible. Because my father and mother (as well as her brothers) had been young and able-bodied, they were sent to a prison that had been converted into a forced labor ammunitions factory/concentration camp called HASAG (an acronym for Hugo Schneider AG, or *Hugo Schneider Aktiengesellschaft Metallwarenfabrik*) in Częstochowa. By 1939, HASAG had become one of the biggest arms manufacturers in Germany. During the war, HASAG had factories in eight German cities and three Polish ones. The forced laborers lived under heavy police surveillance in barracks near the factories.

With meager food rations, with lice and rat infestation everywhere, disease was rampant. Many people in that camp died of typhus. When anyone looked ill, they were either shot or transported to the death camp, Treblinka. My mother was grief-stricken when she found that her two brothers were gone. They must have been sent almost immediately to the gas chambers at Treblinka. She was supposed to have taken care of them. She never recovered from this loss. Her brothers were lost forever – *verschwunden*.

Verschwunden, a word which in Yiddish means lost, disappeared, swept away. That word smells of burnt flesh and the blood-soaked fields of the bleak, windswept landscapes in a killing field called Treblinka. The blood of my relatives still lies in the earth there. I am told that the fields at Auschwitz/Birkenau, Treblinka, Maidanek, Sobibor, and all the other concentration camps are fertile now. I am told birds sing there and fields are covered in flowers.

As a child I wondered what became of the children's toys as they suffocated in the gas chambers. I couldn't understand what had happened to God. Had He been kidnapped by the Nazis? I had to believe that He had been turned into one of those suffering children by some wicked witch who worked for Hitler. But this didn't make any sense to me because if God was all-powerful, then why couldn't He escape? And if He was supposed to be loving, then how could He have allowed those children to suffer?

My father was determined to keep my mother alive. He was a man on a mission; this was his response to the insanity around him. A piece of good fortune was handed to him in that forced labor camp. The Nazi guard who oversaw my father's unit took a liking to him. Indeed, years later my father would say that under more normal circumstances they might have been friends. It seems there was something they saw in each other, some subtle connection which had to remain hidden. This guard brought my father extra food and cigarettes, and promised him that he would keep an eye out for my mother, who was in a unit for women. My father was a good worker and so it must have been easy for this guard to rationalize his usefulness in this labor camp.

The guard made it possible for my father and mother to meet in the camp, often at nighttime. He had to be careful, as he had superiors to whom he was accountable. If his commanding officers discovered what was going on, the three of them, my mother, my father, and the guard as well, might have been summarily shot. So for three long years, my father and mother hung on. Throughout all of this time, inmates were sent off to Treblinka with bureaucratic regularity. My father witnessed unspeakable brutality and he himself was the victim of cruel beatings, but he *had* to save my mother's life. Everything could be borne, as long as he had her.

One day he lost track of her. His guard had not been able to stop a higher ranking official, the *Überkommandant* [chief officer] from placing her in one of the line-ups for the box cars to Treblinka. "That horrible man had it in for me right from the start," my mother told me years later. "He always smirked and shouted: You'll be on the next transport, you dark beauty!" And he finally made good his threat. When my father heard what had happened to my mother, he demanded to be told where this line-up was located. The guard told him. My father, a quiet man, then did something that even a reckless person would never have contemplated. He rushed over to the area where the line-up was taking place. There were Nazis everywhere, shouting, pointing guns, standing erect in their crisp uniforms and black boots. My father saw my mother amidst this cacophony looking dazed, already gone. He decided that he didn't care then whether he lived or died, he wanted to be with her. He ran towards the line and literally pulled her out. "For some unfathomable reason," he would later tell, "they didn't shoot me. Maybe they didn't notice, or maybe for that one moment they just couldn't be bothered."

The sympathetic guard helped my parents hide in an obscure part of the camp as many of the other inmates were pushed into the cattle cars for Treblinka over the next several days. The Soviet troops were advancing and the Nazis should have cleared out immediately, but couldn't resist sending more Jews to their deaths, thus slowing their own retreat. "The din grew louder," my father would tell us. "We heard bombs exploding, and the skies were dark with smoke. I don't know how long we were in our hiding place; something eerie yet comforting encouraged us." At long last the

36

guard hurried over and told them that the Nazis were fleeing. "The Soviets are a few miles away, we have to go. You will be all right. They will liberate you." As he rushed off my father yelled to him in the tumult, "Where in Germany do you live? Maybe we can meet each other after the war? But the guard did not hear me; he was running too fast. There was the sound of more shooting."

"I don't know how long afterward it was that a quiet descended upon the concentration camp. An eerie calm. Your mother and I clung to each other," my father told us. When the Soviet troops appeared on January 16, 1945 in their weather beaten uniforms they wore smiles on their faces. "You are free," they proclaimed in Russian. My father said of that moment: "We were so weak from hunger. I understood Russian, but I could hardly register the words. I learned later that the Russians had shot the retreating Nazis just outside the perimeter of the camp. I have never forgotten that guard. He was tall and lanky and had the face of a smart young man, with sandy hair and green eyes that didn't miss anything."

The Russian soldiers fed them and gave them fresh clothes. It took a little time before they had recovered enough strength to leave, although the hardest part of their journey still lay ahead: the long road toward rebuilding their lives. Yet, the miracle had happened. My father had delivered on his promise to save my mother's life. They did not know it then, but they soon discovered that a life was growing inside my mother, my older brother, who was born six months after their liberation from the camp. I guess you could call this a love story. This story is as close as I can get to what seems real to me about my father: a fierce determination and courage against all odds. Although this story makes it seem as if my father was Superman, there is another side to the story. I was told that my father collapsed into a deep depression. But that happened later.

My parents' first step after leaving the concentration camp was to return to their homes in Częstochowa to try to find surviving relatives. There they found that their apartments had been given to Poles after the Jews had been forced to vacate and to move into the ghetto. They had knocked on the door of my father's apartment and a man with a bottle of vodka in his hand yelled that if they didn't leave he would kill them. They ended up boarding somewhere in town. They searched for news of their relatives, but there was nobody left. No siblings, no parents, no grandparents, no aunts, no uncles, no cousins. Not one member from their immediate or extended families, other than themselves, had survived. Only a few distant relatives. Only a few neighbors and friends also searching for kin. They had to go on; there was no other choice. And there was a baby coming. This was the last thing they needed, given their situation, but there it was. The modest remnant of survivors started pairing off as soon as possible, trying to "normalize" their situation. My parents were the only ones from their circle who had survived as an intact couple from before the war.

After my brother was born in the summer of 1945, my parents stayed in Częstochowa for more than a year. They still planned to leave Poland, as there was nothing left for them there. There was one glimmer of light. My father's oldest sister – the oldest of his seven siblings – my *ciocia* [Aunt] Helenka had left Poland in 1927 and settled in Montréal with her husband and their one-year-old child. My father was 12 years old when *ciocia* Helenka left Poland. Now he was 33 and she was 48. They wanted to be reunited. That meant my parents and brother would have to leave Soviet-occupied Poland, which was illegal. In any case, they felt that they should stay put until their baby was old enough to handle the difficult journey ahead.

A year later on July 4, 1946 the unthinkable happened. A pogrom broke out against the Jews in the town of Kielce, a small town in Central Poland. During the Kielce incident, a mob of Polish soldiers, police officers, and civilians murdered at least 42 Jews and injured over 40 others in one of the worst outbursts of anti-Jewish violence in postwar Poland. The Jews were blamed for having started the war. And now they were being blamed for the Communist take-over of Poland. My mother told me years later that her first reaction upon liberation was to think that the monstrous acts of the Holocaust would finally force everyone on earth to understand the horrors of hatred and prejudice, and that the concept of war would be eradicated. Instead, hatred lurked in the hearts of people who wanted the few remaining Jews to be dead. Even the devil might have been shocked – and perhaps ashamed – by such a realization. It became clear that it was not safe to remain in Poland. Weary as they were, survivors began to discuss their plans of departure. But how, and to where? They were devastated, emotional rubble. Everyone was malnourished. And now with the Soviet take-over, emigration was forbidden.

My parents and brother somehow managed to escape through the heavily patrolled border into the American controlled zone in Germany. It was nighttime and my mother explained how they had to cover my brother's mouth because he was uttering sounds as he pointed to the big white moon against the black sky. They had to keep him quiet. It was a matter of life or death, again. They made it out: a young mother, a protective father, and a baby son born into an impossible circumstance: a broken trinity. Food was scarce. They always said that it was a miracle my brother didn't starve to death. My mother was so malnourished that she didn't have enough milk for her child. On one train ride, things looked so bleak that a woman sitting near them began to shriek: "That baby will die on this train. What will we do with the body?" Once again my father rose to the occasion. "Because of this child," he said, "we were saved. He will not die." He spoke with determination, as if he had some personal lifeline to God. The woman bowed her head and made the sign of the cross. She wasn't in great shape either. She told my parents that she had lost her husband during the bombing of Warsaw. Still, she understood the difference between their experiences. This woman had not been in a concentration camp; she had not been hunted like an animal. The woman offered my brother juice and a little porridge which magically appeared from a container within her cloth bag. My father remembered that a smile came forth on the baby's ancient, wizened face.

When they were finally safe in a DP camp in the American-controlled zone of what became West Germany, my father broke down, his fabled energies vanished. He was told by a doctor to chop wood, or do anything to keep himself busy. Maybe he wasn't able to wake up in the morning and believe that the war was behind him. What kind of victory could these survivors celebrate? What did they have left to look forward to? The idea of having to begin again must have seemed insurmountable. Suddenly my father wasn't Superman anymore, just a destitute survivor. Something complicated was unfolding: the unambiguous urgency of the need to save my mother's life from the ever-present dangers of the slave labor camp was gone. He must have felt alive and useful during those years. Now he was a refugee, an orphan, a nobody. Before the Holocaust, all he had known was poverty and deprivation growing up in Poland. How much kindness had my father known before the war? And how much professional accomplishment? What was it that he was now supposed to rebuild?

When I was a child, my father mentioned a silver cigarette case which survived the war with him. It was battered, but had made it through. My father never said so in words, yet the glitter in his eyes when he showed us this mysterious silver case reflected some kindness that he cherished deeply. I believe that it was given to him by the guard who daily placed a handful of cigarettes into it.

Eventually word came that my father's sister, the one who had left for Montréal, would be able to sponsor them and bring them to Canada. My *ciocia* Helenka had tried hard to get them out of Poland in the years leading up to World War II, but was thwarted by the antisemitic Liberal government of William Lyon Mackenzie King. Under a new Prime Minister, Louis St-Laurent, my aunt was at long last given legal permission to sponsor my parents and my brother to emigrate to Canada in 1948 My father said he tried to imagine a new life in a country called Canada. He found out about my aunt's constant trips to Ottawa, Canada's capital city, to plead with officials for the visas needed to get her brother and his family out of Poland before the war. She was a blood relative; that wasn't good enough. Canada's doors were shut tight against Jews.[1]

In the spring of 1948 my parents and brother, who by then was three years old, arrived in Canada after a long ship journey and then a train ride from Halifax to Montréal. However, they didn't arrive with only my brother; they also brought with them all of the ghosts of their relatives. The reunion scene was devastating. My mother let out a gasp. She thought she was seeing my father's mother. My aunt was much older than my father and many years had passed, so that my aunt was now about the same age my father's mother would have been at the time of the deportations. That had been the last time my father and mother had seen her.

5

THE NEIGHBORHOOD

When I was growing up in Montréal, it was one of the most cosmopolitan cities in the world. The Paris of the New World, *Le Paris du Nouveau Monde*. Elegant and exciting, it will always be the city of my heart. I remember the joy I felt the first time I heard the sounds of French coming out of the radio. Different, enticing, unknown. The voices of the announcers rang with clarity. Their words were elegant as if dressed up in finery and the songs in French were bursting with life. The very notion of being part of a world immersed in the pleasures of living stunned me. I developed a passion for this beauty and vitality. Imperfect as this connection was, I felt a sense of life, a glimpse of *élan!* Of *joie de vivre!* We lived in a working-class area in the east end of Montréal – one quarter immigrant and the rest French-Canadian. Although these early years were a time of emotional distress and economic difficulties for my family, they were also a time of wonder for me surrounded by our French-Canadian neighbors. The immigrants were mostly from Eastern and Central Europe, and nearly all, including my parents, had been in DP camps after the war before arriving in Canada. My parents happened to be the only Jewish immigrants in the immediate neighborhood.

I was always searching for shelter and must have known from

the beginning that my home was the last place on earth where I would find it. No wonder then that I was so mesmerized by my neighbor Françoise and grateful to be her friend. This was in the early-1950s and Maurice Duplessis, an ultra-conservative, populist premier was in power in the province of Québec. He was not interested in the cosmopolitan nature of Montréal or in the influx of immigrants and refugees from World War II who were arriving with languages and cultures foreign to Québec. Who were these people arriving with so little material baggage and so much pain? Duplessis was French-Canadian, but it was the "Anglostocracy" (the English Canadian elite) who were really in charge of Montréal and they simply ignored us. We must have seemed quite the bedraggled beings to some, and like poor souls to others.

We lived on the second floor of a fourplex, sandwiched in by the Jolys, a family of seven, on the first floor, and the Beaudrys, a family of six, on the third floor, as well as an elderly couple, Madame et Monsieur Tremblay, on the top floor. Monsieur Joly, a jovial man who always had a smile on his face, worked as a machinist. Madame Joly, who seemed to wear a different hat every time I saw her, was a saleswoman at Eaton's, a popular downtown department store. She worked in the hat and glove department. The Jolys were hard-working folks and everything about them was neat and generous. They brought my family gifts at Christmastime, and I would play hopscotch and skip rope with their twin girls who were two years younger than me. The older three children were boys, and so were out-of-bounds. Nevertheless it was fun watching them and the other boys of the neighborhood play hockey on the sheet of ice in the laneway.

The boys all wore the red, white and blue sweaters of the *Montréal Canadiens* team with the number 9 of the most famous player of the National Hockey League, Maurice Richard, emblazoned on their backs. In those days nobody could beat the Habs (short for "habitants," the French word for the settlers who had come from France to settle what became New France and later Québec). All of us Montrealers – whether French-Canadian or not – reveled in the celebrity of the Habs.

On the third floor directly on top of us lived Monsieur Beaudry, an unemployed alcoholic, and his wife who cleaned homes in the upper class English-Canadian neighborhood of Westmount. Monsieur Beaudry was a tall, dark-haired man with bloodshot eyes and a gaunt face. Their four children always had a hard look in their eyes which were often surrounded by bruises. The youngest child was almost three, a pretty little thing with golden ringlets – still wobbly on her feet, afraid to go too far. There were two older boys, nine and eleven, both dark-haired like their father. They stared at you in a way that made you feel uncomfortable. The eldest, a girl, was 12 and already looked ancient with tired dark blond hair. Madame Beaudry, petite, slender and attractive, had permed hair and a creamy complexion. Her eyes were a green color which could sparkle when the light was just right. But there were mornings when I would see bruises on her neck before she hurriedly wrapped around a scarf as she left for work. Her eyes didn't sparkle then. I instinctively knew that I was not meant to see those black-and-blue marks. Everyone else in the neighborhood also pretended not to notice.

It was more difficult (especially in the late evenings) to ignore the screaming and the sounds of glass crashing against walls that emanated from that third-floor apartment. My parents always worried that this man could do serious harm, however, they were also keenly aware that we were the only ones in the immediate area who were Jewish and were afraid to call the police for fear of stirring up antisemitic sentiment.

Madame et Monsieur Tremblay, an elderly couple, lived on the top floor and were extremely quiet. They did call the police when Monsieur Beaudry's shouting became intolerable yet nothing ever changed. One hardly ever saw the Tremblays, but whenever they were outside they held hands while Monsieur Tremblay smoked a pipe. I loved the vanilla scent, and I often wondered what it is that they did inside their apartment all day. I heard that Madame Tremblay had been an excellent seamstress when she was young, so maybe she sewed. I used to admire the lace curtains that covered their windows. On Sundays their five daughters and sons-in-law visited, as well as a throng of grandchildren. They all trooped out to church for morning Mass and returned to enjoy a midday meal filled with the aroma of roasted pork or chicken and sizzling *frites* as well as *tarte aux pommes* or *tarte au sucre*.

I often saw Madame Beaudry together with her children when they were on their way to church – I never saw Monsieur Beaudry with them on those occasions. As time passed, the Beaudry children began to droop as they walked, appearing more and more defeated. Monsieur Beaudry looked like he had been defeated a long time ago. But his wife soldiered on, resembling one of the statues of martyred saints atop the church a few blocks away. Sometimes her husband walked by me on the street carrying a brown bag that held a bottle of dark liquid from which he drank. I soon learned that it was whiskey and that that's what I smelled on his breath and that made him lose control and beat his family. I did always wonder what he might have been like as a child. What was it that happened to him that he turned out to be so nasty? Where did that vacant expression in his eyes come from? It seemed as though the brown liquid in the bottle in the paper bag was meant to choke back something scary inside him.

I remember the first time it dawned on me that the Beaudry boys were likely heading in the same sullen direction as their father. It was as though some invisible force had them all in a terrible grip from which they couldn't cut loose. A powerful force seemed to be in charge of my family too, but in a different way. The Beaudry boys took pleasure in calling me "*maudit juif*" (dirty Jew) whenever I passed them on the street. I was relieved that their assaults never went further than words. They never physically hurt me, perhaps because I was a girl. Instead, they tried to get into fights with my older brother. He did his best to steer clear of them nevertheless he did end up in plenty of brawls. A variety of bullies often hid at the back of my favorite candy store as I walked to and from school. Every so often the owner of the candy store, a frail old man, would emerge to break up a scuffle waving his finger at the bullies, calling them *vauriens* [good-for-nothings]. I felt superior to those boys. They too came from homes harboring much suffering, but I was disgusted at the way in which they chose to act out their misery. It never would have entered my mind that humiliating someone who is different from you could be a remedy to assuage your own battered psyche.

It was always an event to go shopping with my mother (or more often with Françoise and her mother) on Boulevard St-Denis, the main street near where we lived. The shops were modest, but there was always a bustling energy on that street and a great deal of bargaining took place in the stores with voices rising and falling in accordance with the negotiations. The storekeepers knew the regular shoppers and items were often bought on a lay-away plan. I could always tell who was a French-Canadian woman and who was an immigrant. All were poor yet somehow the French-Canadian women had a flair for fashion. It was the way they comported themselves, confident in their looks, even if their faces were plain. Hats would be tilted on their heads at just the right angle and they knew how to drape a shawl around their coats in a way that immediately dressed up their outfit. They made sure that their hair was styled, and they added accessories, such as earrings or belts or bracelets. How they could make this all happen with so little money was a mystery. The immigrant women, my mother included, couldn't get it together quite like that. They huddled in shapeless dresses and coats and hats as they hurriedly went about their shopping. This isn't to say that they didn't dress up on certain occasions, but for the French-Canadian women every outing seemed to be an opportunity to look attractive.

On weekends people piled into the cafés and restaurants, indoors during winter and outdoors as soon as the snow melted. This was not the gentrified boulevard that it is today. It was shabby, down-at-the-heels, filled with people barely scraping together a living. The women were constantly trying to make ends meet. Men were all but absent outside during the week, working in low-paying jobs, and often more than one. They left early in the morning and came back late at night. My father was one of those men. Even if a man was unemployed and had time on his hands, he would scarcely have shown himself on the street during a weekday – it would have been considered a disgrace.

As far as antisemitic incidents went, it seemed easier to deal with the French-Canadian approach on account of its simple openness. Being called *maudit juif* was not pleasant, however, at least it was aboveboard. The antisemitism of the English-Canadians I found more hurtful. My first direct encounter with it shocked me because it had come from what seemed to have been an unlikely source. On my way to the English-Protestant elementary school I attended (non-Catholics were not permitted to attend the French schools in those days) anti-Jewish epithets were hurled at me on a regular basis from an old lady at the (English) Home for the Aged situated close to my school. This woman seemed to have found out that most of the children of immigrant parents attending my school were Jewish because the majority of the other immigrant children were attending the Catholic school. In her mind, the less well-dressed children on their way to my school were therefore Jewish. A frail, ancient-looking woman in a wheelchair, all prim and proper, would sit on her balcony and shout at the top of her surprisingly strong lungs when I walked by: "Goddamn dirty Jew. Hitler didn't do a good enough job, because you are still here!" I hurried by as quickly as I could.

To my young mind, this was the same evil force that had made people in far-off Europe become so vicious and end up killing Jews. My father said that this could never happen in Canada. But in the dead of night I sometimes woke up terrified that the devil who had mesmerized so many people in Europe would one day find his way over to Canada.

6

LANGUAGE AS HOME

Languages swirled about both inside and out; in the private world of my home as well as in the public world of my neighborhood. The languages inside my home, Polish and Yiddish, both floated into my ears, and offered sustenance, like fluttering angels. Polish and Yiddish – sweet, melodious, soothing. Words became sentences which I began to understand. I felt that I could count on their meaning and their intent. They nourished me in ways that my poor parents never could. I soon learned to listen for the soft as well as sonorous cadences of more and more words each morning and later on I began to parrot them. In my hunger for love, I grabbed hold of them and made them my own. These words were filled with abundance. They made me forget about the bad things that seemed to creep around my house and that could pounce on my parents in those moments and make them be so frightened or angry or mean. As I grew older, I noticed that Polish was spoken between my parents as their language of communication. It had a lyrical sound, and even today when I hear Polish it feels to me like a silken garment. This turned out to be a stolen pleasure.

I learned early on that the realm of Polish within my childhood home was reserved exclusively for my parents' use. There seemed to be a fence around it, which we as children were not permitted to penetrate. They did not want us to learn that language. As a child I didn't make an issue of this; it just was the way it was. Polish was the adults' exclusive domain and all I wanted at the time was to try to figure out what it was that they were saying to each other.

Although I cracked their code early on, I knew that my knowledge of that language would have to remain passive. Something was wrong with it and only later did I discover exactly what it was. I knew that this wasn't a mere matter of communicating. My parents were able to discuss anything using that language as their medium. They read and wrote in Polish. My father especially enjoyed literature and poetry in Polish. And I loved to hear my mother speak on the telephone with her friends in Polish and to listen to radio during the Polish hour. She had such a lilting voice in Polish, so flowing and free. Not like the way she hobbled through her words in English. Eventually I understood that my parents were ambivalent about using Polish with us even though it had been their everyday language in mainstream society. They had been schooled in Polish, but in their homes they had spoken Yiddish. They also took Yiddish and Hebrew lessons at *Cheder*. These were afternoon educational programs which focused on Yiddish literacy as well as the learning of Hebrew and Torah studies.

There was another, much more powerful, thing that I sensed well before my parents put it into words: *Polish and Yiddish were not friends with one another.* This tension between the two languages was oppressive. They inhabited the same space in my home, but strong, invisible borders held them apart. Only by means of listening could I transcend those borders and enjoy the dangerous presence of Polish at my home. I learned as I grew older that it was dangerous because it symbolized the antisemitism in Poland. Even after the Poles themselves were subjugated by the Nazis, some took out their rage on an even weaker victim, the Jews.

So Yiddish was deemed to be the proper medium of communication between parents and children in our home. Yiddish was *our* language, that of the Jewish people of Eastern Europe. It was a gentle and expressive language, however Yiddish was a bird with a broken wing. It had barely survived an unspeakable catastrophe. This is how I came to know that Yiddish was not merely a language, but also the reservoir of Eastern European Jewish hopes and dreams and sorrows. The same was true for Polish although it was in the reservoir for the Polish Catholic people who had their own hopes and dreams and who also felt a deep sense of vulnerability about their identity. Poland had been invaded over and over again for countless centuries.

Language was a *culture*. A language can be blessed or cursed; it can be created or destroyed, it can be magical or morose. All of this depends on the experiences of its people and the places in which they found themselves historically, socially, economically, religiously. Although the two cultures, Jewish and Polish, had lived side by side for many centuries in Poland, there was an unease between them. Many Jewish people in Poland could speak both languages; this did not mean that they had been accepted fully in both cultures. There may have been a strange intimacy between the two languages, Polish and Yiddish – but not a healthy one. Often, bits and pieces of them collided and then scattered quickly away. I instinctively understood that the notion of identity was omnipresent in this duality and that it mattered. So who was I? And where, if anywhere, did I belong?

My mother and father knew all about antisemitism in Poland even before the Nazis arrived. They knew that it was not unusual for priests to deliver vociferous anti-Jewish sermons on Sundays blaming Jews for all the ills that plagued the Poles, whether political, economic, social or personal. Stones were frequently thrown at Jewish shops or apartment windows, especially in the poorer parts of town where my parents lived. Częstochowa was home to the Monastery of the *Jasna Gora*, an important Catholic pilgrimage site. The *Matka Boska* was the "Queen of Poland," and religious fervor could easily get out of hand during times of pilgrimage.

Many of my parents' non-Jewish neighbors openly considered Jews to be Christ-killers. I remember this story my mother told me. It took place in the mid-1930s. I was well before school age when my mother recounted what happened to her little brother (later to be killed in the death camp Treblinka) while walking home from school one day. He was eight years old and wore glasses. Suddenly, a group of older boys overwhelmed him and beat him unconscious, all the while yelling that he was the anti-Christ. His eyeglasses shattered. Mother's family was so poor that they didn't have the money needed to replace them, and so he had to miss school.

My mother had no understanding of what was and was not appropriate to tell a small child. She hammered her hysterical anxieties into my young brain. When I got my own first pair of glasses in grade four at the age of nine, I felt excited. The frames were a soft shade of blue, and I felt quite grown-up walking out of the optometrist's store. Then I remembered the story about my mother's little brother and his broken glasses. Guilt overcame me like a tsunami. How could I possibly enjoy my new glasses given what had happened to my uncle? In that instant all my excitement vanished. A few years later, when I was twelve, I saw the Alfred Hitchcock film "The Birds" on TV. The scene in which the birds attacked the children on their way home from school was terrifying. What frightened me most was the moment when one boy's glasses were knocked off his face and shattered amidst the chaos. To me he wasn't just a young actor in a horror film; he was my uncle. I felt like I was suffocating.

I attended Yiddish classes starting at age eight. They took place twice a week after the regular elementary school day. These classes might as well have taken place on another planet for how alien and insignificant they seemed within Canadian mainstream society. There was no such thing as "heritage/international language education" in those days. I remember children making fun of me while waiting for the bus that would take me to the run-down community center in another part of the neighborhood. They knew where I was headed and taunted me; I pretended not to hear them. At the community center and in the classroom, there was never any sense of community. A dark, cold place, the pipes would hiss and sputter as we recited mindless sentences in Yiddish with our coats, hats and mittens on.

The Yiddish teacher, ancient and exhausted, did not capture any of our attention as we stared out the window at children playing in the street. There might as well have been bars across those windows. The books were old, torn and gray. The only fun we had in class was when the more creative boys would sling erasers through the air – a carnival of rubber snowballs. We could then imagine that we were playing outside. Once an eraser hit the teacher in the face. Dead silence. She sat down at her desk and began to cry. I remember how sorry I felt for her – and also disgusted. How could anyone allow themselves to be humiliated so? I compared her against the exciting French teacher at my "real" school and decided not be a party to such a sham. Even then I had more respect for language learning than that.

A more ominous thought took hold during those Yiddish classes. As if to make it more holy or at least more meaningful, our teacher told us that many children in Russia and Poland before the Holocaust had read the same children's book that we were struggling to read now. But I knew what had happened to most of them. This was never discussed. I felt that I had to get out of that classroom before being stifled. I had to run far away from Yiddish all those years ago. I had to escape the clutches of my mother tongue. I couldn't bear the dead-end-ness and the finality of it. My teacher discussed the loss of Yiddish caused by the loss of its people. I couldn't bear the thought that I was one of the last (non-religious) speakers of this jewel of a language. It took me more than four decades to begin to retrieve my long-lost love for Yiddish. I always knew, deep down, that I would one day have to go back and try to make my peace with it, to search for this lost child...

One evening my father brought home a mysterious object. It looked like a boxy piece of furniture with a dark screen and several knobs. I turned the knobs expecting to hear words as I had from our radio. Instead something incredible happened. There were moving pictures on the screen and I could *see* the images actually *speaking*. A television! There were shows with cartoons and puppets and dolls as well as shows with live people. How did they all get into the box? There was Channel Six for English and *Canal Deux* for French, but where else in the world in the mid-1950s (other than in Montréal and in its environs) could you turn on a television and discover the amazing Channel Seven, *Canal Sept*, which offered programs in French for several hours each day and then magically transformed itself and offered programs in English. You didn't even have to turn any of the knobs; it happened all by itself!

I will never forget the sense of adventure as I would turn to that channel and wonder which language and culture would greet me. The whole experience had a mysterious feel to it and I watched those programs intensively. My love affair with French began the moment I heard its sounds over the radio, and not long afterward it swept me off my feet in the fantasy which Channel Seven offered: a new world of more than one language and more than one culture – "*un nouveau monde.*" How did I recognize this? Perhaps we are all hardwired to recognize works of art in whatever shape or form they come to us. Or maybe we have to be willing to reach out for them. Maybe we have to make a choice, the choice to be alive, to become alive, to remain alive. The beauty of the French language which I heard so early on in childhood offered me an unexpected freedom to imagine what life could be like outside my home. It gave permission for desires to grow, for wounds to heal.

I ran into the arms of the French-Canadian language and culture like an orphan child seeking warmth and shelter. I knew that I had found my foster home. I believed in French just as a devout Roman Catholic might believe in salvation. I became a joyful traveler, a "border-crosser" into the territory of the French language not only through radio or television, but also on account of living in a French-Canadian neighborhood. How effortlessly I could traverse from one culture into another and (somehow hope) to be accepted by both. My longing to be accepted in the French-Canadian milieu became an act of devotion so complete that it offered me the promise of restoration.

7

FIASCO IN KINDERGARTEN

I was one of those children who couldn't wait to start school, but I almost didn't make it to my first day of school. There had been so many children of kindergarten age that enrollment had to be cut off by date of birth, and July 1 became the divisor. Since I was born after that date it was decided that I would not be admitted that year. The haze of memory has not dulled the rupture in my heart when I first learned of this news. Then, a few weeks into the school term, as I was moping around at home I heard the telephone ring and my mother repeating words that were being told to her: a boy was having trouble in class and needed to be taken out of school; I was next on the waiting list. To this day I have faith in waiting lists.

School was my ticket out of a loneliness that haunted all the corners of my childhood. But the route was not a straight one. My first disappointment came when I found out that I would not be allowed to attend the same school as Françoise. This came as a shock to me. The reasons for it shaped my future personal and professional life. In those days, the English- and French-Canadians of Montréal lived in their two "solitudes" while immigrant communities struggled to learn English in order to be able to survive economically. Without question English Canadians held the purse strings. I desperately wanted to go to the French-speaking

Catholic school around the corner with Françoise. That option was not permitted. I had to attend the Protestant English-speaking school.[1]

I remember trudging off to my first day at school as if I were traveling to a different planet. It seemed like a terrible injustice, in my child's mind, to have been denied access into their educational system. I was probably the only non-French-Canadian who adored the Francophone world in complete innocence. Indeed this was symbolic of the historical struggle between English- and French-Canadians, a struggle which still holds Canadians hostage to this day.

When I entered the inner sanctum of the kindergarten classroom on that first day, I believed that all would be well with the world from now on – the hope of a child who had placed her gambling chips on a fantasy world called *School*. Yes, there was the disappointment that *School* would have to be the English one which was many blocks away and not the French one which was just around the corner and where all of my friends were going. But in the end school was SCHOOL, be it Protestant or be it Catholic. I somehow must have sensed that education could become my road to liberation. I felt my heart beating as I was shown to my seat in the long row. It was intimidating to land in an English environment although I was not fully conscious of what I was feeling at the time. All I knew was that all that had been familiar to me was now gone.

I was quiet as a mouse when the teacher began the roll call. I wasn't the most confident of children to begin with. And then came a sense of foreboding. Family names rolled easily off my teacher's tongue. Those were "Canadian" names: names easy for the teacher to pronounce, names that were part of the same club. Some names were slightly different, but those she could handle. I felt dread rising within me with each passing letter of the alphabet. She finally came to my clunky Polish name – a perfect name of not-belonging, a label of outsiderness. Still, I was unprepared for the cruelty to follow. As the teacher stumbled over the multiple consonants in a row, her face became red. I wished that she would have asked me how to pronounce my name. That would have ended her agony at once. As I was about to speak my name, she threw the list down on her desk, glared and said: *"When you immigrants come to this country, why can't you just shorten your names to make it easier for us Canadians?"*

I wanted the floor to open up in front of me so that I could disappear. Instead, a sea of faces stared at me: some were smirking, others were as just as frightened as I was. They too had strange names; it was just that mine came toward the end of the alphabet and by then the teacher had lost whatever little patience she may have had. I took some comfort in the realization that I was not the only immigrant child in the class. There were other children of displaced persons from the war. Playing in the schoolyard during recess meant being immersed in a multitude of languages and cultures from Eastern and Central Europe. Multiculturalism was as natural there as breathing.

In Canada there was a name for our immigrant parents: greenhorns. We often felt ashamed when our parents spoke to us in Yiddish (or Polish or Hungarian or Romanian or Italian or Russian or Ukrainian or Slovenian or Latvian, the list goes on) when we were in public. We wanted them to speak in English and without an accent. I knew that even though I was their child and constantly listened to their accent, I didn't have one. I puzzled over that. I noticed that my classmates from "foreign" homes didn't speak with accents either. Even at that young age I knew that in Montréal, English had power and that French had less. The languages of immigrants had no power at all. Those of us who were "different" formed an immediate and unspoken alliance which would carry us through difficult times.

When I got home that evening I approached my father and, trying to sound nonchalant, I asked him whether we could shorten our family name. He looked genuinely puzzled for a moment and then asked me whether it was my teacher who had suggested this to me. I nodded and burst into tears. Although my father was usually a prisoner to his silent rage about the war, once in a while a ray of sunshine would pierce his sorrow and I could witness what he might have been. And this was one such moment. Stepping outside of his woundedness, my father put me on his knee and gave me a hug. "You tell your teacher," he said, "that our name is as good as anybody else's and we're not going to change it." This act of defiance gave me back my dignity, and when I walked into class the following day I told my teacher exactly what he had said. She looked annoyed, but never bothered me about my name again. I tell this story for all children who understand how easy it is for a teacher or for others to steal their sense of self with careless indifference. An action doesn't have to be monstrous to end up being an injustice.

Sometimes a "bad" teacher" can teach you as much or more than a "good" teacher. On that first day of kindergarten I came to understand that a name is a sacred thing. In spite of occasional negative messages from teachers about our immigrant status, School still was a place of refuge. There was order and quiet, and there were toys and books. I remember how happy I felt when I was chosen to play cymbals in the band – like being chosen to be a film star. And I discovered that I enjoyed singing. We learned the Protestant hymns and recited the Lord's Prayer first thing in the morning and sang "God Save the Queen." My voice rang out each day. Somehow I knew that it was okay to do all of those things as long as I didn't say the name "Jesus," and so whenever the word "Jesus" or "Christ" or "Savior" came up in the hymns, I held silent for that moment. There were a few other Jewish children in the class, and they did the same. Had we discussed this amongst ourselves? I don't think so – we knew that we were each other's allies. The hymn "Onward Christian Soldiers" had an ominous ring.

I learned early on that well before the Holocaust, Jewish blood had been spilled throughout the millennia, all in the name of Christianity. By not saying "Jesus" or "Christ" or "Savior" I knew I was holding steadfast to my Jewishness and this gave me strength. I had nothing personally against Jesus himself who, as I had gathered from my father, was a brilliant teacher and healer and strove to fight the poverty and misery caused by the Romans who were in control of where Jesus lived at the time. According to what I had heard in my religion, the Messiah had not yet arrived and only God the Father was considered to be divine.

I enjoyed playing skip rope with my classmates on the playground at recess. When the bell rang we all rushed into line and stood straight and silent as the teacher-on-duty would pass by us toward the school door to lead us back into class. The shuffling of our shoes on the pavement and the scrunching of papers were pleasurable sounds. But walking to and from school was an anxiety-provoking activity. I had to cross several busy streets, sometimes with classmates, often alone. The trek was fraught with the noises of cars and trucks and police sirens. I always felt relief as the street where I lived came into view.

It started with terrible guilt over a new friendship I was forming in class. She was a tall, boisterous and free-wheeling girl – a tomboy, and I was immediately drawn to her. She spoke what was on her mind and didn't seem to be afraid of anybody. But when she thought nobody was looking, her face evidenced a bruised expression. I could see the fragility beyond her tough exterior and was intrigued. I already admired, even at that young age, anyone who could hide her feelings and put on a good act. Her name was Marianne and it turned out that she lived in an apartment building not far from my place. Her father was the janitor of their building. His job offered him a wage as well as a rent-free basement apartment for his family. On the third day of our friendship I found out that her parents came from Germany and that they had also arrived in Canada after the war. When I discovered this, I was heartbroken. She was the "enemy." How could I possibly become her friend? I felt a weight descend upon me as I began to devise ways of avoiding her. She didn't understand what was happening. I hadn't told her that I was Jewish – I only told her that my parents had come from Poland. The hurt look in her olive-green eyes followed me. The joys of school suddenly vanished and that was too much; school was the only hope I had and I couldn't afford to lose it.

Once again I decided to confide in my father and tell him about this conundrum. Tears ran down my cheeks as I explained my quandary to him one evening before bedtime. I was prepared for any sort of disapproval or even for punishment, however what actually happened was that he looked at me for a time and simply asked: "Is she a nice girl? Do you like her?" I answered: "Yes, I do. But she is German." Then my father looked at me in a way I had not seen before. He quietly told me that no matter what had happened during the war, we have to see one another as individuals. If Marianne is someone I wanted to play with then that was okay. He told me that her father had in fact been a soldier in the German army and that he didn't have anything to do with humiliating or killing Jews. He went on to explain that Marianne's father had spent the war on the Eastern Front in Russia and had been badly wounded there. Finally, I understood the reason for this man's severe limp. That is the way my father was: someone who could look beyond stereotypes even in the most horrific of circumstances, and go straight to the heart of the matter. Today he would have been considered an advocate for social justice and intercultural harmony. Then he was just a human being who longed for peace and who respected humanity in all its glory and frailty.

8

DICK AND JANE

The *Dick and Jane* primer was the first book I ever owned. My grade one teacher Miss Robertson introduced me to this English language basal reading series and it seemed to me that windows had blown open in my brain allowing in the kind of fresh air you feel on a windy day. Each pupil was given his or her own crisp new copy of the book. I held it as if it were a priceless work of art. There was also a baby sister named Sally with curly blonde hair, her well-loved teddy bear named Tim, a dog named Spot who was a black-and-white Springer spaniel, and Puff, an orange marmalade cat.

The series used phrases like, "*Oh, see. Oh, see Jane. Funny, funny Jane.*" Thinking about them now I know that these were not the most fascinating stories on the planet, but whenever I opened my reader in first grade I could pretend that I lived like Dick and Jane. I could pretend that I was carefree and wore pretty clothes like theirs. That I too had parents who felt comfortable where they were. And I could pretend that I had grandparents. I knew that Dick and Jane didn't look like me, and that their family's situation bore little resemblance to my own. They were white, Anglo-Saxon, and Protestant. They were always well-dressed, successful, and having a fine time. Their father held a respectable job and their mother enjoyed her role as a homemaker and, I imagine, was a member of the PTA and did volunteer work. She was slim and pretty and dependable.

What would I not have given to jump into those pictures and never return to the shabbiness that was my own life. They all lived on Pleasant Street in a quiet neighborhood of single-family dwellings that had white picket fences and green lawns with flowers and shrubs. A shiny red wagon carried their plentiful toys. When it rained, they all wore shiny boots and raincoats and they unfurled yellow umbrellas and enjoyed playing in the puddles. In summer they visited their grandparents who lived on a farm and there they played with all the barnyard animals.

Grandparents! This was unthinkable. Everything about their family life was peaceful and cheery. I doubt that they would have wanted to know me: a forlorn child in a secondhand dress, afraid of life. A little girl who at much too young an age knew that her world was a dangerous place – a place where Hitler and his Gestapo lurked always in the shadows. *"Don't turn around, even if your shoelaces are undone. Keep running with your coloring book and crayons and your Dick and Jane reader. Even if your heart is beating fast. Just keep running."*

I longed for the normalcy which my teacher, Miss Robertson, possessed. She represented the life of Dick and Jane and I watched her carefully. She had softly curled light brown hair which framed her heart-shaped face and sparkling blue eyes. Crisp blouse collars adorned her long creamy neck and her blazers and skirts were always perfectly tailored. I remember how acutely aware I was of how different her family circumstance must have been from mine. Did she ever reflect about the world I had come from? Did she understand how sitting in her classroom and learning to read was the greatest gift that the Universe could offer? Each word, each gesture, each lesson, each story was saturated with meaning.

I knew when Miss Robertson read to us there was something trying to reach me – an interesting phrase, a joyous message, a lesson to be learned from one of the characters in those stories. I shall always remember her melodious voice as she read us those stories and how delicately she turned the pages of the books pointing to the illustrations. I became a little wayfarer waiting for the words of these stories to lift me onto a rock and give me restful shelter there. For me that rock was School. Fielding School became that place where heaven and earth would meet and shed light onto my darkness. I paid attention to everything that happened there. I was mindful of what was expected of me, and of what it *looked like* to be *normal*.

Albert Einstein famously pointed out that imagination is more important than knowledge. I had to re-imagine my story and lift it up from the defiled into the sacred. It is impossible to explain how much defilement, how much desecration there is in the shock of knowing that your relatives are a mountain of naked corpses. To be confronted with such horror at so young an age is to be in danger of losing sight of the sacred beauty in life.

Losing sight. I was terrified of going blind. I was terrified of the light going out and yet I could sit in darkness for hours rocking myself for comfort. That fear followed me like a curse. One autumn Saturday morning when I was seven years old, I was riding my bike. My father had recently taught me how to ride and I felt proud. I even allowed my hands to leave the handlebars for a moment. A taste of freedom. Suddenly, I felt something hovering over my head. I looked up. A fuzzy, blurry cloud began to chase me. I rode faster but it followed me faster still. I careened down a steep hill, hands clammy, my heart pounding. And then the impossible: the blurry blob blocked my field of vision, robbing me of the way forward. I couldn't see; I could hardly breathe. I lost my balance. I fell off the bike and got the wind knocked out of me. I lay sprawled on the ground, catching my breath. The palms of my hands were sore and my knees were bleeding. As I limped all the way home pushing the bike, I shuddered at the thought that the *dybbuk*, that scary ghost which often menaced me at night was planning to take away my sight. My sleek blue Schwinn bicycle (second-hand, majestic all the same) looked dazed and wounded.

I parked the bike downstairs and entered my apartment from the fire escape and tiptoed into the bathroom to clean away the blood and smear iodine on the tangle of raw red lines that crisscrossed my knees. Then I bandaged them. My mother was on the phone in the kitchen having a conversation with a friend alternating between Polish and Yiddish. I crept into my bedroom and changed from shorts to long pants to cover up what had happened. I lay down and fell asleep. The last thing I wanted was my mother scolding me for riding so fast on my bike.

The following Monday morning all the children in my class went to the nurse's office to get their eyes examined. When my turn came, I guessed at the squiggly letters on the chart. Just as I had been doing with the words on the blackboard in the classroom. The nurse told me I needed glasses. I never connected what the nurse said with the incident on the bike. I finally did get a pair of prescription glasses, but that didn't stop the evil force (maybe it was the *dybbuk*?) from lurking all around. Yet I knew I had to keep going. I endlessly sang the songs I learned at school. There was one hymn that I sang over and over again as I sat on our living room chair. The lilting soprano voice of my teacher Miss Robertson who played the hymn at the piano in class floated in my ears.

Standing at the portal of the opening year
Words of comfort meet us
Hushing every fear,
Spoken through the silence
By Our Father's voice.

Sometimes panic would overpower me at school. My breath would become ragged and come in gasps; my hands would turn clammy. *Did I catch a glimpse of the devil's iron hook? Would he finally collar me?* I always felt so weak when I would lift my hand to tell the teacher I was not feeling well. Miss Robertson would take me out of the classroom into the hallway and then her sleek arms folded around me in a warm embrace. Tears would well up in my eyes as the teacher whispered: "It will be all right. You will be back here tomorrow." She also said, in a hesitant voice: "Your mother will come to take you home."

I didn't want to let go of my teacher. I felt that she didn't want to let go of me either. Miss Robertson gave me a stricken look and, waving goodbye, she was barely able to utter: "Don't worry," as I shakily walked toward my mother who was waiting at the entranceway with that upset, gruff look on her face. At home I sat in the armchair in the living room singing quietly and rocking back and forth. The "orphan" of an orphan.

Here is the letter I might have written to Miss Robertson if I had been able to articulate then what I am able to express now.

Dear Miss Robertson,

I am just a small child, but I want so much for you to understand me. I live on parallel tracks: one path leads to Auschwitz or Treblinka where my relatives were put to death; the other leads to school and life. I must stay on the second track, no matter how much I am being pushed to get back onto the first.

Miss Robertson, I like it when you smile at me. I love your soft voice. It makes me feel calm. You will never have to worry about heaps of corpses and their smoke curling up from chimneys of the ovens. No, you are lucky. Thank you, Miss Robertson, for teaching me how to read and write English.

9

THE GIRL IN THE HOLY COMMUNION DRESS

An apparition came to me as I awoke one spring morning. A little girl about the same age as I, around seven or eight years old. I rubbed my eyes. When I reopened them, she was still there, long chestnut hair cascading down her back, adorned with an organza veil of baby's breath flowers and pearls. A white satin dress hugged her little body with its puffy short sleeves and delicate embroidered piping. She wore shiny white patent leather shoes, white socks and white gloves, and she was holding a bouquet of bright yellow roses. It was early in the morning and nobody else was awake. I could hear birds singing outside my window. I could hear the clock ticking in my parents' bedroom. My sister was sound asleep in her crib on the other side of my room.

The image in the white dress stayed there at the foot of my bed, waiting. Waiting for what? I looked at her more closely. Why was she here? What did she want of me? She looked familiar yet I couldn't recognize her. I wondered if I might still be asleep but, no, I felt too alive for that to be the case. I remained in bed, afraid that if I moved she would disappear. Suddenly, a wondrous thought entered my mind: this girl in white might be an angel who had come to gather me up and take me away. I could hardly breathe. I was worried that somebody might wake up and spoil this moment. Everything remained calm. I didn't know where she had come from, but I knew that today was the day of First Holy Communion for many of the children in my neighborhood. It was Palm Sunday, the beginning of Holy Week, *La Semaine Sainte*, the week leading up to Good Friday and Easter Sunday. And it was to be the First Holy Communion for my dear friend Françoise.

Several weeks earlier on a glorious springtime day I had been invited to go shopping with Françoise and her mother for a dress and veil on Boulevard St-Denis. I delighted in the displays of all those First Communion dresses with ribbons and bows in immaculate white taffeta or lace, or satin, and the floral headpieces and sheer tulle veils displayed in the windows of the children's clothes shop. We combed through the racks of dresses in several stores. Françoise tried them on in front of large mirrors as her mother and the sales women fussed over her. Finally, after some haggling about the price, a taffeta meringue-like dress was chosen with a veil that had a floral tiara. Françoise looked like a fairy princess. What an alluring ceremony this First Holy Communion was that allowed little girls to dress up as brides. Bat mitzvahs, the Jewish religious coming of age for girls, were not yet in vogue when I was a child. I held onto the radiance of the First Holy Communion concept with a guilt that nearly eradicated all my joy of the occasion. This didn't stop me from going to Françoise's First Holy Communion ceremony at Eglise St- Sauveur which was several blocks away, in the direction of Mont-Royal. The church featured a magnificent gold dome, and stained-glass windows all along its walls depicting the Stations of the Cross as well as other Bible stories. I shared a pew with Françoise's parents, siblings, grandparents, aunts, uncles, and cousins. I did wish that I could be in the ceremony and felt a ragged sense of guilt at even thinking that thought.

I watched the scene just as the conscientious cultural anthropologist I later became in my professional life. I looked intently at the children standing in line, excited and nervous, waiting for the communion wafer to be dropped into their mouths by the priest. *"Corpus Christi,"* he murmured each time making the sign of the cross. Each girl looked like Snow White and each boy was Prince Charming. And so when the imaginary little girl in the white dress stood at the foot of my bed and held out her gloved hand to me, I took it.

10

RETURN TO FIELDING SCHOOL

It had happened unexpectedly. During a trip to Montréal one December, I visited my elementary school. I hadn't been back since I was a little girl, even though I had been a university professor for many years by that time. I had been to a conference in Ottawa on "Immigration and Diversity" that fall, and by chance I had sat down next to an older woman at lunch the first day and we began to talk. I told her about a multicultural literacy project for immigrant and refugee students which I was conducting in Toronto. The woman, who was a Catholic nun, said she knew of a school in Montréal in which a similar project was taking place. Soeur Marie Monette is the director of a social organization serving newly arrived families in Montréal and works with immigrant school populations. I asked her which school this was and she answered: "Ecole Fielding." I was quite unprepared for this answer, and she herself seemed startled when I told her that I had gone to that same school as a child of refugees. We looked at one another for a few moments and she then declared in a decisive tone: "*You must go back. I can arrange it for you.*" And so began my journey back to an ancient time.

I was staying at a small hotel near the Université de Montréal where my husband had some research commitments. I had slept in and awoke to the sublime beauty of a Montréal snowstorm. In the distance, from the window, I spied a silvery church spire, ubiquitous in the Montréal of my childhood. The Oratoire St-Joseph, the largest church in Canada, sat high on the slope with its huge dome and its 99 outside steps which the devout climb on their knees to the entrance. I dressed in my warm black Persian wool coat with its comfy down inner lining, bright red scarf and red beret and went outside and into a *librairie-bistro* next door, as glamorous as any in Paris. I browsed the shelves of books and sat down in a chair thumbing through a few of them. As people flowed in for lunch, taking off wet coats, hugging and kissing one another on both cheeks in the French custom, I realized I'd better grab a seat in the bistro. Many of these get-togethers were related to the Christmas season and many of the tables had *Réservé* signs.

I sat down at a small corner table and surveyed the scene. The waiter was a young, good-looking French-Canadian guy. I was immediately drawn back into my childhood fantasies. Who knows – maybe Françoise, my first best friend, was one of the people sitting at one of the other tables. As far as I could make out, these patrons were connected with the *Université de Montréal* – either as faculty, students or staff. Nobody could see behind my facade of a well-dressed woman, ordering a meal of quiche aux épinards and soupe à l'ognion, and of course café au lait. I seemed like a person with an air of confidence. How could anyone possibly tell that I was about to embark on a pilgrimage to my beloved refuge: *School.*

I left the bistro after my meal and began walking, block after block after block in the swirling snow, trying from memory to retrace my childhood steps. It was a time for wandering, a moment for returning, alone, to a shadowy past. I had forgotten the school's exact location but I was determined to find the place just as a lost child might have done. And I needed to see *her*, and to *be* that little girl once again. I needed to ask her to forgive me for leaving her behind. After a while the street signs began to look familiar. I stopped to ask a taxi driver who was waiting at a red light. He told me that I was on the right track, that there were several more blocks to go. He offered me a lift but I told him I needed to walk. A look of sheer confusion passed over his face. He must have thought I was crazy to refuse a ride in such a snowstorm.

I passed the hospital where I was born. The Jewish General Hospital which, when it opened its doors in 1934, was founded as a general hospital open to all patients regardless of race, religion, language or ethnic background. A group of interlocking buildings made of brown brick with many wide curtained windows, it is situated at the corner of two busy intersections, Rue Côte des Neiges and Chemin de la Côte-Sainte-Catherine in the center of the city on the western slope of Mont-Royal. This neighborhood has always been flamboyantly multicultural and multilingual, filled with a mosaic of restaurants and other shops owned by people who come from around the world.

There were a lot of comings and goings at a nearby bus stop; I was anonymous to these commuters, a passer-by in the snow-white landscape. People were slip-sliding about on the icy sidewalks. I had to be careful not to fall because I was now heading downhill. At a corner, stood a Salvation Army officer in a black army uniform with the red crest on the coat lapel ringing a bell for donations next to the familiar kettle on stilts with the sign *Armée Du Salut* [Salvation Army]. Nearby a little boy, also in uniform, was playing a recorder in accompaniment to three uniformed women who were singing Christmas carols in English, French and Haitian Creole. Their combined breath floated upward in the frigid air.

I trod gingerly during this *promenade* – as I had done as a child whose heart was always stronger than her feet. The more I walked, the closer the loneliness came, my old companion. I passed young mothers of all colors, with children in strollers, all bundled up. Black and Brown, Yellow and White. So many languages twirled in my ears. Suddenly, I found myself back in a land of immigrants and refugees. The snow-crunched ground seemed to have remembered me, but this time I looked Canadian. "What does it mean to look like a Canadian?" an international student in one of my university classes once asked. "Maybe you have to look like you belong, even if you don't feel it," I had responded.

The snow was now falling fast and hard. The last few steps were treacherous – ground so icy that I practically ended up on hands and knees to descend the staircase leading onto the school's playground. (The ice was so fresh that the janitor probably hadn't yet had time to throw salt on the ground.) The area was deserted. I must have just missed recess. I felt that I was on sacred territory. I stared silently at the building in front of me. I was about to begin my research project here. It was late December, a Thursday, the day before the school term was to end. Fielding School – what was I doing returning here, so many years after I had said goodbye to this place – my school, my shelter, my refuge? In my mind's eye, I saw my younger self who was waiting silently at the side of the building, in a corner where she once used to hover. I moved toward her and reached out to embrace her. To tell her that she was alone no longer, that she was an outsider no more. To snatch her away from this place of hiding, into the light of second chances. The brick school building before me was exactly the same as I remembered it. I stood there not really wanting to move, wanting the moment to last forever. I knew the time had come for me to re-enter this lost world.

Lost once and now found. One might say that I was returning in a triumphant manner – but that is overstating the case. I had left this place many years ago, as a child of Holocaust survivors, almost as weary and as wounded by *that war* as my parents had been. Many memories greeted me while I stood there. I set them aside as I briskly entered the school looking for the office of Geneviève Durocher, the coordinator of the literacy program for the school, who was waiting to meet me. The familiarity of the surroundings, the walls, the hallways, the smells, the sounds surprised me. After so many years Fielding School looked almost exactly the same! As teachers and students strode past me, what they saw was a professional woman carrying a dark brown leather briefcase (I had bought it in a bazaar (*shuk*) while at a conference in Morocco a year earlier). Could any of them really understand that what they were seeing was a phantom who had returned from another era, from a time long ago? No, they would not be able to guess it. I fooled them just as I could now fool anyone. I looked like a well-dressed professional, a visitor with a purpose. I felt my feet carrying me toward the office and in my daze I sensed a woman extending her hand toward me. This, I thought, must be Geneviève.

Geneviève! How many times did I use exactly that name when I wrote my make-belief stories about French-Canadian families who were enjoying life and who had relatives and who celebrated Christmases and birthdays and summer holidays. I wrote those stories when I was a pupil at this school, trying desperately to hold onto the life raft of the French-Canadian fantasy that I had manufactured and had woven into my shattered life. Those blessed stories of make-belief saved me. I wish I had kept them; in my heart they will always be there. And now, here I was, shaking hands with an adult version of the French-Canadian girl whom I had then longed to be. Sometimes, in the darkness of night, I also wrote little stories about the end of War. I tried to hide from the suffering of my parents through the medium of my stories, which always featured people of different cultures and different religions living happily together. I was terrified of losing contact with humanity. Nightmares haunted me regularly in which Hitler's henchmen found me in hiding, an orphaned child, and threw my body, splashing it against a bloodied barbed wire fence. I see other little children, carrying tattered dolls and teddy bears, being marched to gas chambers. Such scenes haunt me still.

Geneviève escorted me into her office and introduced me to her colleagues. I was the professor of Education from l'Université de Toronto. Did the ghost of my former self understand that I had come back today to reclaim her? Did she know that I had not yielded to the demons of despair? Did she know that I had survived in spite of the bleakness of my family life? Was she surprised to see me now looking confident, poised and professional? How could such a transformation have happened? Geneviève brought me to the *classe d'accueil* [reception class for newly arrived immigrant children] where a visible diversity of children aged eight, nine, and ten were working on a lesson in arithmetic with their teacher. She introduced me to the teacher whose face radiated good intentions. Her name was Sylvie and she was *d'ancien souche*, a descendant of the original French settlers to New France in the 1600s. *Sylvie* – another name from out of my childhood stories!

I had been invited to speak to her class, and the first thing I told the children was that I had been a pupil in this same school when I was the same age that they were now. They looked surprised at this. And it was indeed a surprising piece of news – hard to believe. What was I doing there? The students seemed to sense that there was something unusual – and yet familiar – about me. I felt that they knew instinctively that we all had something important in common. They sat up ramrod straight in their seats. I also told them that at that time we spoke English in this school and not French. (Of course, it would not have been appropriate then for me to go into any of the history of the Separatist movement and how the *Parti Québecois* who were voted into power in 1976 transformed the social, political and linguistic landscape of Québec forever.) I sat as an observer at the back of Sylvie's class next to a brown bunny rabbit, the class's mascot, who hopped around in its cage. Looking out of the large windows which lined the far wall of the classroom, I could see the old brick apartment buildings across the street. How many times had I drawn pictures of those same rundown apartment buildings imagining children sitting on the balconies and flowers on the entrance lawns?

The pure snow continued falling softly outside. In turns the children stole glances at me. Some of them smiled, and I smiled back. While they were working on their arithmetic, the teacher came over to tell me that some of the black children spoke French patois and were from Haiti. Others were from Ghana, Guyana, Somalia, the Sudan, Sri Lanka, Rwanda, and the Congo. Some of the children looked Slavic. I found out that they were from parts of the former Yugoslavia – Bosnia, Croatia and Serbia. One was from Romania. There were also some children from China, others from Iraq, Iran and Afghanistan. One boy, sitting a little apart from the others, was from Russia and had lived in Israel for several years. What were their stories? They probably wondered about mine. One thing was clear: We were all children who had come from the Land of War. Some had never been to a school before. Some had never had enough to eat before. And some of them were trying hard to look "normal," to hide any wounds. I knew something about that; I've been trying to hide from trauma all my life. It was in Fielding School that I had written in my diary: *"Put a smile on your face. Try to look as 'normal' as you can. Try to look like you belong. Maybe one day you will."* When I was at school I was surrounded by other children (both Jewish and non-Jewish) some of whose parents had also been through World War II. This gave us a bond of camaraderie. We never talked about it. We didn't have to. It was comforting to know that we were not alone.

Later that same day at the school I interviewed two little girls from Afghanistan named Fariba and Leila. Their eyes carried haunted expressions which spoke of war and death. Fariba's dark eyes darted around the room, perhaps searching for an escape route. Her mouth twitched. Leila, who was smaller and fairer looked like she was hiding behind her classmate. They both sat mute. I understood their anxiety. Who was I, after all? Part of some trick? You cannot trust others after you have seen one of your own parents shot in front of your eyes, as Fariba had. She was only nine years old at the time, and got out with her mother and sisters – a miraculous event. Then they lived in a refugee camp for 15 months before being able to emigrate to Montréal. In a little alcove off the main classroom there were Christmas decorations on the wall. It was a cheerful room, but Fariba seemed distracted. She was in Montréal and at the same time in Kabul seeing her father's body disintegrate. She was polite towards me, completely silent. Leila, the smaller child, looked frightened, with a thick strand of her light brown wavy hair in her mouth. I decided to read them a story instead of talking. I read *A Time for Toys* by Margaret Wild and Julie Vivas, a magnificently sensitive book about children in a Nazi concentration camp and about the older women around them who wanted, in spite of the degradation and loss all around, to create some makeshift toys with any scraps they might find. One older girl in that story remembers the pretty toys that she used to have before the war. She remembers the Friday night Sabbath dinners and Passover Seders when her relatives would all gather together to recite the "Haggadah," which in Hebrew simply means the "Telling" – the story about the Exodus of the Jewish People from Egypt.

Then I told Fariba and Leila that my cousins and aunts were just like these girls and women in the book and that they did not survive. Only my mother, father and brother survived. And they ended up in Montréal because my father had one sister, his oldest, who had come to Canada long before the war and had sponsored my parents and brother when they were in DP camps after the war.

"What is a DP camp?" I was startled to hear Fariba's voice. I had been speaking incessantly, having accepted her and Leila's silence. "It is a refugee camp. They called it a Displaced Persons (DP) camp then." Fariba nodded with understanding. "I was in one of those. There are lots of people and it's hot and sometimes you get sick and lonely. There aren't many nice things there, but at least there is something to eat. And nobody is shooting your family or friends. How old was your brother then?" I told her, "He was a little baby and luckily he didn't die." Fariba's big velvet brown eyes became larger still as she stated after much thought, "Yes, he was lucky, and you were lucky that he or your parents didn't die."

I wanted to hug this sweet child, but I reminded myself that I was a researcher and that this might overstep boundaries. I squeezed her tiny hand instead and said, "War is horrible, isn't it?"

"Yes," she answered. "War is awful. It happens because some people hate others and they want to kill them. They killed my father. They killed so many. I wish they would stop. How do you make them stop doing that? It's in many places too, not just Afghanistan." Perhaps Fariba decided to speak to me because she realized that in some way I was a kindred spirit who also had been witness to such evil.

"Do you like school?" I asked her. "School is really nice." A big smile glowed on her face. "It makes me feel better." I understood exactly what she meant. "Maybe good things will happen to you in school. You know, school changed my life – it gave me a new life."

"I hope that will happen to me too. I couldn't go to school in Kabul because I was a girl. We were locked up in our house the whole day," Fariba's eyes opened wide. "School is my chance now." For a little girl of ten she was wise beyond her years, an old soul. A child like this can remind a teacher that education has deep meaning and purpose and that sometimes school is the safest place children know.

What can I take away from this encounter with Fariba and little Leila who sat almost mesmerized by the conversation? Their wounds were so much more immediate than mine. There was an intimacy we shared. We became comrades-in-arms. I had read them the story A Time for Toys so as to open a door to hope. The children and women of this (true) story were saved by British soldiers. Theirs was a happy ending, so to speak. They had held onto a thread leading to freedom and were lucky. Their brothers, sisters, fathers and mothers were not.

War for Fariba and Leila; memories of war for me. Nobody carries these realities without some part remaining in agony forever. How clearly I remember, as an elementary school teacher, the valiant effort of many of my students to hide their sufferings of family abuse or other misfortunes. After a time I thanked the teacher and said goodbye to all the students and then went to the main office and said goodbye to Geneviève. As I walked out into the crisp cold air after leaving the school that afternoon amidst the falling crystalline snowflakes, my mind wandered back to that time of my own childhood family struggles.

11

ALICE IN WONDERLAND

The incident I am about to tell took place in grade 4. I remember we had just finished our arithmetic lesson when two well-dressed women entered and shook the teacher's hand. They spoke quietly to her for a few moments. My teacher had an expectant smile on her face and I couldn't figure out why at the time. Then she announced to the class that these women were interested in having us audition for their play based on Lewis Carroll's *Alice in Wonderland* to be performed on stage. Audition. It sounded so grown-up. They explained that they would sit on the stage in the gymnasium and listen to us, one-by-one, read a section from the story. I had no idea that they planned a really large performance. I didn't know they came from a well-respected children's drama troupe in the city. I didn't know that they planned for the performance to be held at the ultra-chic Ritz-Carlton Hotel downtown on Sherbrooke Street and that it was to be televised! All I could think of was how I had loved reading that book. Such a fast-moving story full of mystery and adventure. I had read it twice. Alice had become as lost in the tale as I was in life. Nothing made sense, and with this I could certainly identify. The rabbit hole into which Alice fell distorted reality and opened up strange and fascinating adventures which offered intriguing new possibilities. I loved the White Rabbit and I felt that he was my friend in spite of his unusual mannerisms. I put up my hand to volunteer.

My turn came to go to the gym to audition. The women pretended not to notice the patches in my tights. I wasn't even embarrassed by this – it was just a part of my everyday life. I read for them the section of "Pig and Pepper" and about the peculiar logic of the Duchess who was nursing her child (who was really just a little pig). I read several pages for them and I loved the part of Alice with Humpty Dumpty, the one with the conversation about names: *"My name is Alice,"* – *"It's a stupid name enough!"* *Humpty Dumpty interrupted impatiently. "What does it mean?"* My hands went high up in the air with a gesture of impatience as I read this aloud. *"Must a name mean something?"* *Alice asked doubtfully.* My eyes narrowed as I read. *"Of course it must," Humpty Dumpty said with a short laugh: "My name means the shape I am – and a good handsome shape it is too. With a name like yours, you might be any shape, almost.* I nodded my head emphatically. I could understand Humpty Dumpty's thesis about the importance of a name and the sense of pride he possessed in his identity. It's as if he spoke to me directly. The two women looked at each other, their faces glowing. They nodded their heads. I guessed that they liked that section too.

"You have the part of Alice," my teacher told me the following day, her face beaming and her voice sunny. I was startled. How could this possibly be? It was all as in a dream. The rehearsals were fun – something I could count on every day for months. In those rehearsals a family of child actors was born. I never seemed to forget any of my lines, sailing through all of the rehearsals with ease. Then the big day of the performance arrived. I remember the sheer exhilaration of being on stage in front of so many people. There was such innocence about the play and in the performance. Onstage *all* was possible. Our faces shone with such faith that it seems as if God himself must have been somewhere in the audience that evening. I knew I had it in me to perform and had tasted my first success.

As I ran toward my mother afterwards, I noticed the emptiness in her eyes. I knew that she had been in the audience but her expression was as if she hadn't seen me at all. She had come with a friend. Words of praise came out of my mother's mouth yet they were totally incongruent with what I saw in her eyes. A crushing disappointment descended upon me. Had I done something wrong? How dare I have had such a good time up there on stage! Who did I think I was to want this and to have performed in this way? When I went backstage I peeled off the pink chiffon dress with its shimmering crinoline and I delicately hung it on the clothes hanger. I felt myself shrink just as Alice had when she drank the potion. Where was the drink that would make me grow tall again? Afterwards, all the children in the play were treated to huge ice cream sundaes in the luxurious dining room of the Ritz-Carlton Hotel. I couldn't taste the dessert. All the fun had evaporated. I could no longer aspire to be *Alice in Wonderland*.

Did anyone find out what happened to the little girl who played Alice so spectacularly one year then flubbed her audition for a part in another play the following year? This second time up there auditioning on stage holding the script I felt nervous and unhinged as a voice inside me uttered: "Don't you dare! Just don't." I stumbled over the words on the page as I hustled through the text. The two women (the same ones as the year before) looked at each other in shock. One of them said kindly, "Are you feeling well? Try again, dear. There is no hurry."

"I'm okay," I muttered without making eye contact. I wanted to escape, to disappear. A monstrous force held me in its thrall. My tongue had turned into lead. My stomach churned, my heart thudded and I broke out into a sweat. My throat was parched and the room was spinning. My whole body ached. I hated myself. These women had been so proud of me a year earlier. How could I let them down this way?

"Are you sure we can't help, dear?" one of them wanted to know. She had a stricken look on her face. "May I please go back to my class?" my voice quivered. The women felt as helpless as I did. They put down their scripts, took off their reading glasses and looked genuinely bewildered. They thanked me and I hurried off the stage feeling nauseous. A riptide of anxiety grabbed me by the throat and the knot in my stomach didn't go away for hours. I entered that foggy place again, empty and alone. Something had betrayed me, or I had betrayed myself. Confusion raged through my brain. All I knew was that I had messed up and it was my fault.

Years later, as a university student, I saw a similar magical dress on a dancer from the New York City Ballet at Zellerbach Hall on the Berkeley campus. I cried and cried in my seat. When the lights went up after the performance people near me in the audience could not understand what had happened. I would not step back on stage until more than 30 years later.

12

ALL MY DESIRES

My mother's smoldering black eyes were missiles that never missed their target. Too dark, too intense, they held an arsenal of grief and fury that could be unleashed upon me at any moment. There was never any telling when she would pick up her invisible hammer and knock it on my head with its message of death and suffering. It could happen at any time, usually when I was alone with her after I came home from school. She would corner me with her shrieking stories about the concentration camp; I would run to the bathroom and vomit out all the evil. I would sit on the toilet and let my mind go blank while outside the door my mother continued to scream.

She became a mystery I was endlessly trying to solve – like a small Sherlock Holmes with a magnifying glass, constantly asking myself questions that could not be resolved. It seemed that she was chasing after dreams that could never materialize for her but which she longed for interminably. What was it my mother was so desperately searching for? Was it some fantasy of being part of a loving and happy family in Poland? She said her parents doted upon her as the favored only girl, amidst two brothers; that they showered endless attention upon her. I heard that story over and over again, however it never rang true. If she had been as much loved in her family as she claimed to have been, why then was she so rough with me?

I tried really hard to be a model daughter. If only my mother could have taken pleasure when I brought home stellar report cards, or when I received prizes for public speaking. Or when I had been chosen to play the lead in *Alice in Wonderland*. Why did my mother turn away from me at such times? And why didn't she send me to the drama group created by a Russian actress who had come to Montréal after the war to organize Yiddish Theater for children, many of whom were children of survivors? And why did my mother criticize me for being so "skinny" whenever we went shopping for clothes? Those trips were an ordeal. "You look like a herring in everything you try on," she would blame me in a voice that made even the saleswomen head for cover. They may not have understood the Yiddish but they could feel the scathing disappointment in my mother's tone. Perhaps it was an affront to my mother to have such a thin child when she had almost starved to death in the concentration camp. Perhaps she was afraid that I would get sick and die.

Another memory has just sprung forth. It was a frigid December afternoon and I had just returned from school. Something about that peculiar blank look on my mother's face and her voice which seemed more out-of-control than ever made me even more frightened than usual. As usual I ran into the safety of the bathroom. This time the walls of the bathroom seemed to be moving, and were about to smother me. I made my get-away when my mother finally walked away from the bathroom door and into the kitchen to stir the soup. I gingerly opened the bathroom door, tiptoed out, grabbed my coat, scarf and boots from the closet and raced into the apartment building hallway. My heart was pounding as I ran down the flights of stairs like an Olympic champion. Then I stuffed my feet into my boots and flung the coat and scarf onto my shoulders. I forgot my hat and gloves. Just as I was turning the handle to the entrance door of the apartment building I heard the screaming again. "Come back! Where are you going? I need you." I flew away like an ace pilot.

Out on the street where it was cold and crisp I was relieved to see my best friend Françoise carrying a grocery bag to her home. I tried so many times to explain my mother's tantrums but Françoise always said it's the child who should have tantrums, not the mother. I tried to explain that my mother was not like most mothers. She was a little girl who lost her own mother and father when all of them were forced away from their house in that scary place far away. When Françoise saw my face that afternoon she quickly gave me a piece of candy cane. She also noticed I didn't have a hat or gloves on. It was almost the last day of school before the Christmas holidays, already pitch dark at 4:30 pm – and it was freezing. "Why don't you come into my apartment and play?" Françoise put her gloved hand onto mine and we both trod quietly over the crunchy snow. It was a scene that had become familiar to us both. However, this was the first time it was taking place just a few days before Christmas.

I noticed the colored lights and wreaths on many of the apartment windows. The snow banks glistened in the yellow light of the street lamps. So much snow made the world grow silent. It was dreamy to watch my breath flowing into the crisp air. We entered Françoise's building and hiked up the four flights of stairs to her home. Her mother opened the door and took the bag of groceries from her daughter. I stepped over the threshold and knew that now I was safe. Françoise's *maman* helped us take off our wet boots and brought fluffy slippers for us both. We entered the brightness of the kitchen where baby Lisette was sitting in a highchair with a large spoon in her chubby hand. Her mouth looked like it was painted with chocolate pudding. Françoise's *maman* put two bowls of hot chocolate pudding in front of us as we sat down at the table. Such a rich aroma. Only then did I realize how cold I was. The pudding slid down my throat like velvet.

After we had finished our chocolate pudding, Françoise led me into the living room. What a stunning sight met my eyes. A glittering pine tree with all manner of decorations hanging from its branches, candy canes, tiny reindeer and a small Santa with elves and miniature dancing bears, kittens, puppies, banjoes, guitars and many different colored balls, and sparkling silver tinsel, little glass fishes of all shapes and sizes – but most extraordinary of all – a golden angel with a shiny halo sitting proudly on top of the huge tree.

I had seen Christmas trees in the windows of shops, never before in a home. I tiptoed toward Françoise and touched the branches. Yes, this was real and the tree was much taller than we were. The smell of the pine exuded a clean freshness. Françoise handed me a bright green bauble and I slid its loop onto a branch of the tree just the way she was doing with other ornaments. She gave me a toy Santa and I slid it onto another branch. The pine needles felt prickly. We both threw more silver tinsel over the branches. I might as well have been at a royal ball.

Something about seeing that Christmas tree close-up brought me to a stunning revelation: that it was not wrong to want things, to have desires. It wasn't about the Christmas tree *per se*; it's what it represented. Joy, desire, caring, celebration, a little fun. Love. It woke me up to the little things I had wanted yet felt guilty to ask my mother for. The satisfaction on Françoise's face as she handed me some ornaments to dress the tree and the glorious smile on her *maman*'s face were riveting. Maybe I could help my own mother to unveil that emotion which Françoise's *maman* had on her face that bright evening. At the time I wouldn't have been able to put into words what that smile meant but I knew it was good and right. At the same time a sharp feeling of loneliness stabbed at the most tender part of my heart. I wanted to cry nevertheless I stopped myself. What lightened my mood was allowing myself to think about those desires I had hidden deep in that little heart of mine.

First and foremost, I deeply desired a nurse's kit which had a crisp white uniform and a white cap with navy-blue stripes as well as a shiny stethoscope. I had seen it in the window of a toy store in our neighborhood and dreamed of the intriguing adventures of being a nurse, helping people who were sick. How smart and professional and grown-up I would look in that outfit! I mentioned the kit to my mother many times but the request was ignored. She was too involved in silent weeping and speaking to her dead relatives. Maybe if I wore that nurse's uniform I would be able to care for my grieving mother.

One blustery day in late autumn almost a year after that "Christmas tree" evening at Francoise's, I happened to again pass the toy store with my mother. This time I finally worked up the courage to stop in front of the store and ask for the item in quite a determined way. My mother was annoyed although she followed me into the store. Maybe I had worn her down because finally I held the longed-for prize in my hand, a moment of exultation. Unfortunately, the clasp on the box had not been fastened properly and somehow the toy had not been wrapped carefully. When we stepped outdoors the kit blew open in the fierce wind and all its contents went flying along with the last leaves from the trees. The elegant nurse's cap shot high into the air. The white uniform and navy-blue cape and the silvery stethoscope were strewn around on the cold ground far down the block. My mother scolded me. "See what happens when you keep bothering me like that?" She yanked me away before there was a chance to run over and scoop up the remnants. All that was left in my hand was an empty box.

Time passed. I fell in love with the idea of taking ballet lessons. I adored the round pink ballet cases some of my classmates carried, their pink leotards and gauzy white tutus inside. And how beguiling were those delicate pink slippers! I wanted to glide in the air like Odette, the princess who was turned into a swan by an evil sorcerer's curse in *Swan Lake*. I had not seen the performance but had heard classmates talking about the recital in which they performed this ballet. Enchanted with the idea that things could come alive on stage, I asked my mother for the hundredth time about taking ballet lessons. She finally gave in, however the look on her face showed disdain for such frivolous desires. Eventually she handed me a secondhand black leotard whose broken zipper was held together by a safety pin. I was eight years old. Dread accosted me as I walked into the studio for ballet class. Some of the children began to snicker. Even the ballet teacher seemed shocked. If you listened hard, you would have heard the devil cackling with delight. I never went back.

One afternoon after I had gotten home from school my little sister had attached chewed up gum onto our brother's bedspread and it got embedded into the fabric. (What was my little sister doing with gum anyway?) Our mother went into a rampage. "Who did this?" She rushed into the kitchen and began yelling at me, sitting at the table doing my homework and eating an apple. My sister, also at the table, confessed to the deed. Didn't my mother hear her? Instead, she glared in my direction, looked at the apple core on the table and shrieked: "Why didn't you throw this away?" She picked up the apple core and, in a fury, tried to ram it down my throat. I gasped for air, hands flailing. She finally let go, as if suddenly released by an invisible demon.

I seemed to be on the wrong side of everything. My strivings for the life force were a crime against the order of things, a crime against the cramped vision of my mother's world. I challenged the tyranny that reigned supreme. How dare I want things when my mother's whole family had been murdered? How dare I ask for what my mother had been so deprived of when she herself was a child?

Several years earlier, when my mother became pregnant with my sister, she would bring home books about baby care from the doctor. I peered at the pictures and knew that this was not something I wanted. When I became a teenager that feeling did not change. Society's norms, however, trumpeted the sanctity of motherhood, and I began to feel an ambivalence which only grew stronger when I married. I was expected to have children. "When will I have my first grandchild?" my mother would demand incessantly as the years went by. In my heart I knew that becoming a mother, having a child, would be like going straight to prison. It is a fact that one aspect of having children involves reliving one's own childhood. A terrifying prospect. And how could I protect my child from my mother's voracious need for control?

Life in the New World went on. My mother did love to sing. I adored her bright soprano voice. She sang as she did housework, songs from when she was a small girl, in Yiddish and in Polish. She'd also sing songs she heard on the radio. Popular songs like: *How Much is that Doggie in the Window?* by Patti Page or *Tammy* by Debbie Reynolds, or *Hey There* by Rosemary Clooney. Listening to her sing was as close as I could get to the gentleness trapped somewhere deep within her. The songs had a delicate texture that could caress me in a way that my mother never could. She was always too preoccupied with her lost family. Perhaps if she had had a chance to sing more fully, she might have been happier.

13

GATINEAU LIBRARY

My father was a paradox – perplexing, although interesting. He tormented himself with business ventures that went awry, the "missed opportunities," as he called them. A look of utter despair would cloud his eyes. Perhaps he knew that he had the intellectual ability to be a professor or a journalist or even a politician – and yet he also knew that he would never get there. Some of his peers, who didn't have such lofty ambitions, did much better than he on the professional front. They had an easier time overcoming the sense of desperation that permeated my father's daily activities. I imbibed his sorrow and it became my own. I knew he could have been more successful, had he only believed in himself. That kind of inner strength would have had to come from his family life in Poland before the war.

He worshipped my mother above all else. She could not worship him in return. She needed him but never understood his sensibility which was subtle and nuanced. She was not a complex thinker, rather an untamed woman with serious emotional problems that likely had ruled her life from the start of her existence. She never understood how insignificant her husband felt, how afraid he was of failure. I sensed his predicament better than my mother did. And yet, my father's allegiance to his wife was absolute. Perhaps that was all he had to go on as he trudged from one day to the next. And he did not see – or did not want to see – how little my mother tended to my needs. He never stepped in to say: "Let go of this child. Choose someone else to devour." Was he that afraid of losing her? Terrified of losing her to the demons that ruled her –and him?

Thankfully, my father was able to show affection when I was young. Maybe that saved me. I felt his hugs and heard his words: "*Du bist a zisse neshama, mayn shepsele*" [You are a sweet soul, my little lamb.] I loved the twinkle in his gray-blue eyes and the scent of his aftershave lotion. His tone was like an oasis in the desert. It didn't last. When my younger sister was born a few weeks after I turned five, behold, she looked *exactly* like my mother – a chubby, dark-haired baby. Finally, my mother had the daughter that she had always craved. "*Sie is a lalke*" [She is a doll], my mother would insist euphorically. My father began to ignore me. I would dance in front of him in the living room and he turned away. When my baby sister came crawling in, he would suddenly become animated and make a fuss over her. I became an expert at being abandoned. My father who had been my inspiration became my desperation. About a year after my sister was born, the family moved to a larger apartment a few blocks away. In all the moving of furniture and all the comings and goings, I was left behind in the dark. A neighbor found me sitting in the empty living room, alone on the floor, rocking back and forth.

———

My father shared his love of books with me. It was as if he could return to me, as long as we were out of my mother's territory. I shall always cherish my first visit to Montréal's Gatineau Library. With my hand in his I sensed there that I was treading on holy ground. Suddenly, my father became dazzling. As if he were wearing a top hat and swinging a cane as he high stepped through conversations with me about characters we met in books. In these moments I could witness his charm, a razzle-dazzle which could cover up all anxiety and despair – in the magical space of a library.

A rainbow of posters plastered the walls, and books. *Books everywhere*! Stacked high on shelves. People lounged at long tables reading. My father took me to the Children's Section. The small chairs and tables and the books reminded me of school. I was proud that I knew all about reading by then. But I hadn't yet known about the troubles and triumphs of Cinderella, or the transformation of the Ugly Duckling, or the sufferings of Hansel and Gretel. These books spoke directly to me and I devoured them. Their messages transcended all languages, cultures, religions, and races. They gave me the greatest gift – a sense of belonging to the family of humankind and a sense of *community*. I could commiserate with the characters no matter their places of origin. They were my friends.

Nobody lied in the fairy tales I read. That's what I appreciated most: that I was not being falsely reassured. The authors were not afraid to tell how desperate things were, and it was comforting to read the truth. Fairy tales offered strength and courage and hope in the face of adversity. They suggested that, in spite of the terrors of the darkness, you could transform your sadness into something that would lift you out of the ashes. When Hansel and Gretel were abandoned by their parents and forced to live in the forest at the mercy of a witch, I sighed with relief when I realized that they too felt pain and confusion and anxiety and hopelessness. That was something with which I was familiar. In short, they, too, were forced to wander in labyrinths and their trials and tribulations were *real*. In the depths of misery they whispered: "We can make it out of this hell; let us find a way together." Hansel and Gretel overcame their existential crisis by their wits and labors. If they could do it then perhaps so could I.

These stories spoke about universal issues. They spoke about displacement, about wandering, about fleeing from hardship, about violence, loss, death, acts of kindness, and friendship and courage. They offered me a faith in the knowledge that, in spite of terrors and injustices, humanity does exist and that I too was a part of it.

The stories revealed that there were connections to life even in the midst of chaos and destruction. And how else could I have made any sense out of my family story? These books offered me the world and a lifeboat. The realization that reading could be a liberating force overwhelmed me. I was hooked forever.

The greatest thing about the library was that they allowed you to take the books home. This was an amazing concept and I was struck by this great good fortune. The slim lady at the desk sported a crisp white blouse and blue skirt. Gold-rimmed glasses hung over her smiling eyes, her graying hair tucked into a bun. She took a rubber stamp and stamped the back pages of my books. I loved to watch this ritual. There appeared a date, and I was told that I had to return the books by then.

On weekdays my father worked late. On Saturdays he came home at 12 noon and we all had lunch with him. It always felt festive. After the meal, he would take his current book from the little sideboard in the dining room and place it under his arm and sit in his favorite chair in the living room. I loved to sit near him and bring my own book over, my father and I reading side by side. Sometimes he would peer into my book and ask questions. And I asked him about his bigger and more impressive looking book. When I was older I would be reading books like his, yet he respected my books as much as he did the ones that he was reading. He told me: "Each book has a special message. Each one has an important lesson about Life." "You learn more about yourself when you read about others. How lucky we are to live in a city where language and culture are so important. How I envy the French-Canadians for their *joie de vivre* but they and the English-Canadians don't get along. It's a big problem."

Those conversations with my father were the closest thing I knew to sheer bliss. He read all the history books about World War II that he could get his hands on. He had a keen intelligence and an insatiable desire to learn about the war within its larger political and military perspectives. My father read in English as well as in Polish, Hebrew and Yiddish. His English was good, having taken English classes from a then unknown young poet named Irving Layton (who later became poet laureate of Canada). One thing was clear: that reading allowed my father to escape the drabness of his life and I said to myself: "If reading can make him fly away to somewhere else, then I want to read the way he does." From that moment on, books became my intimate companions for life.

At such moments the house was peaceful, as my mother would be out with the baby buying items at a nearby grocery store for dinner and my brother was involved in his social world. I loved the fluttering sound of pages turning and the tapping of my father's pen on the pad of paper on which he wrote notes. Sometimes during those moments with my father, he would look at me and tell me that I reminded him of one of his sisters, the second eldest, named Karolina. This sister was 13 years older than he and she used to read stories to him when he was a child in Poland. *Ciocia* Helenka had also told me how pretty and intelligent Karolina had been, and that I resembled her. She would say, "*Wyglądasz jak Karolinka, która była tak piękna i delikatna*" [You look like dear Karolina, who was so lovely and delicate]. To look like this gentle, charming sister of my father's and aunt's! I may not have looked like my mother, but I could hold onto the image of a *piękna i delikatna* aunt named Karolina.

One particular fairy tale stands out forever. It was late November. The light was fading fast. I opened a book from the Golden Book fairy tale series which I had collected with 'green stamps' from the local grocery store offered each time my mother paid for food items at the cash. I sat next to my father in the usual place in the living room. A sense of tranquility enveloped us. I began reading and lost track of where I was. Suddenly, I was with *The Little Match Girl* who lay like a ghost on an icy patch of snow with a handful of shiny matches which nobody wanted to buy. She was slumped somewhere outside of where the world should be. She wanted only to survive and to live like other children. She would have enjoyed a fine meal or a dolly. Or a mother and a father who could care for her. But their hearts had been broken a long time ago in a place far away called "concentration camp;" so how could they possibly have been able to hear her? People rushed past her, coming and going, carrying brightly colored packages in their arms. It was Christmas Eve. A tree sparkled through the window of a house across the street.

Where had she come from? Where was her family? Did she have a name? I knew her only as *The Little Match Girl* and I knew that once upon a time there had been a grandmother who had loved her dearly. As the hours fell away and it became dark, she began to light the matches, her last hope. They shone brightly, warming her heart, however their light didn't last long and she was soon thrown back into darkness. Yet she could hear the singing from children caroling in the streets and she could smell the rich aromas of Christmas dinners being prepared.

I stared at the pictures on the pages of the storybook. I hid my tears because I didn't want my father to feel sad. Inside my heart raged. The world should show kindness to a little girl who is alone and hungry and who had never hurt anyone in her life. I hated that I couldn't help her. I hated that she was found in the morning, frozen and dead. Dead, like all my relatives. She was burned by the extreme cold, while they had been burned in the ovens of Treblinka.

The Little Match Girl could have been one of my cousins, from "over there," from the land of my nightmares. *But she did find her grandmother and lived with her in Heaven.* Those final words of her story soothed me because I knew that I too might one day meet my grandmother and grandfather and all of my relatives – including my dear aunt Karolina.

14

GRACE'S SUMMER LANGUAGE PLAY SCHOOL

The first time I began to share my love of languages and cultures was when I was almost ten years old. It was the beginning of summer. My parents didn't have the resources to send me to camp, so I was left to my own devices. Montréal in the summer can be hot and muggy, and for a child, the prospect of an endless chain of stifling days is like seeing infinity without any of the excitement. Had there been a circus in town I might surely have run away with the clowns. My father was juggling two jobs while my mother was preoccupied with my little sister. My brother was in his teens and his social life was well beyond my ken.

There was a slight chance that we might all go up north to Val Morin in the Laurentian mountains – *Les Laurentides* – and rent a couple of rooms in a house owned by two spinster sisters, supposedly very eccentric. The idea intrigued me. My parents had originally found out about these two women by word of mouth. Financially, things were precarious and there was little money for such a luxury. In the end, my parents and Mesdemoiselles Desrosiers negotiated a sum that was acceptable for all concerned – for they too had little. However, that would not happen until August. That was weeks away.

I longed for something to do immediately. I could read but that was solitary activity and I needed to play. My classmates had all disappeared into their holidays (a magical word!) or visits to relatives. One hazy afternoon, thick with the promise of thunderstorms, I was hurrying back from a nearby bakery where I had been sent to buy fresh bread and milk. As it happens, my favorite lemon cupcakes [*tartelettes au citron*] were featured in the window and I was able to buy one. My spirits soared as my tongue reveled in the tangy lemon cream. As the winds were coming up I overheard one woman say to another as they passed: "*If only there was a playschool in the neighborhood where I could send my three-year old for a few hours a week, it would be a godsend. My baby is a handful.*" The other woman nodded in agreement. "*I am in the same boat.*"

I almost dropped what remained of my cupcake. A *playschool!* This was Divine Intervention. I loved school and I surely could share my books with younger children. I could be a *play teacher.* Images of my teacher danced before my eyes. I could read to the little kids! My young mind went into overdrive and I hardly noticed the first heavy raindrops that were starting to fall. I ran home as lightning began to tear through the darkening skies. I pushed through the door utterly drenched, changed into dry clothing, sat down at our kitchen table, and began to print up signs in both French and English with colorful crayons on sheets of paper:

To Parents with Little Children
Aux Parents Avec des Petits Enfants
Grace's <u>Summer Play School</u> begins on Monday July 7!!
In her Home *** Avenue Durocher.
Grace has many Books to share with Young Children.
Grace has colored Chalk and a Blackboard.
Paper, Pencils and Crayons are included.
If You are interested please call *********.

Then I watched Nature's spectacular show of sound and light taking place outside our kitchen window. The storm was so fierce that the electricity went out and I had to finish my posters by candlelight.

In the sunlight of the following morning I began to post my hand-made signs. I posted one in the nearby bakery, and I dropped others through mail slots of homes in the vicinity of my home. I kept my fingers crossed. That same afternoon I received responses. Three different neighbors called and asked me how much I was charging. I hadn't even though about money! By the following afternoon I had recruited five pre-schoolers. For whatever reason, my mother didn't mind. She just wanted me to promise there would be no mess. They sat outside with me on the gallery off our kitchen. With chalk in hand I wrote my name on my blackboard. The children weren't impressed and were getting restless. Suddenly, I understood that they couldn't read yet. So I hurried to my bedroom and brought out one of the fairy tales from my collection and began to read to them. It was *The Little Match Girl*.

A wondrous thing happened when I read this story aloud that first time to my "pupils." Suddenly, I found solace in a most unexpected place – in a kitchen magically converted to a classroom. I confided to the children that my grandmother too was in Heaven and that maybe she was not as far away as I had thought. Maybe she was looking down at us at that moment. They nodded at me, gravely. There was no sugarcoating in the story. We recognized the starkness out there but we gained comfort from knowing that *The Little Match Girl* was able to connect with us, and that she embodied a powerful message: that even in the worst of times there is always a way out, a way to see a solution. Then we drew pictures about the characters, and acted out skits based on them.

When the mothers came by in the late afternoon to pick up their children, the little ones gave them their carefully drawn pictures of *The Little Match Girl* along with their impassioned oral narratives. And I made some pocket money which allowed me to frequent my favorite bakery and purchase those delicious lemon cupcakes a little more often.

15

L'AIR DU TEMPS

My aunt Helenka, my father's only surviving sibling, became a career woman well before it was considered "correct" for a middle-class married woman in Canada to work outside the home. But since she had already broken the rules by leaving her husband, she had nothing to lose. And she would not have left her husband had it not been for the fact that, during one of their altercations, he picked up a kitchen knife and threatened her. They never divorced; they separated forever.

In the late-1950s what my aunt did was taboo. The notion of domestic violence was hardly on the radar. It was assumed that if a husband was angry with his wife then she must have done something to deserve it. Some of her friends stopped seeing her. She could have become a pariah – in fact she became its opposite. This woman had gumption. She re-invented herself. She had been taught to be a seamstress in Poland, and so she found work in a ladieswear store in an upper-class part of Montréal. Had she been born during a later era, she could have been a highly successful fashion designer.

Dear, sweet *ciocia* Helenka. She offered more than I could have understood at the time – a counterpoint to my mother. She was born in 1900, the eldest of seven children. (My father was the youngest among his siblings, born almost two decades later.) She had married an elegant and well-off man in Poland in the early-1920s. He had, on their first outing, picked her up in a carriage [*droshky*]. He was tall and good-looking but temperamental. They left Poland well before the war, on a grand adventure to visit the Great White North and fell in love with Montréal. After their tour, back in Poland, they kept dreaming of Canada and finally decided to make it their home. They could not know that this move would save their lives.

They lived comfortably in Montréal during the first few years, however with the stock market crash of 1929 their lifestyle deteriorated. They had to move into a less desirable neighborhood and sell off some of their silverware and some pieces of jewelry that had been a wedding gift from her in-laws. But my aunt was well aware that much worse circumstances were taking place in Poland. Taxation was cruelly high there and her family, like so many poor families in Poland, barely escaped eviction.

As the clouds of war swept over Europe the futility of my aunt's efforts to bring her family out of Poland depressed her greatly. She once told me that she had sensed something sinister behind the government officials' continual refusal to grant permission for her to sponsor my father (a blood relative) to immigrate to Canada. He had wished desperately to get out of Poland.

After the war, when my parents and brother did finally arrive in Canada, my aunt looked forward to reuniting with the one surviving member of her family. But her husband's behavior became more temperamental and erratic. As his moods worsened, their relationship broke down into terrible rows. He seemed convinced that his wife was seeing other men although there was no shred of truth to it. It was a terrible let-down for my parents that their interaction with their brother-in-law became so strained and that my aunt was cornered into an intolerable situation. The incident with the kitchen knife was the last straw. So she had to leave him fearing for her life. She came to live first with my family then later with her married daughter with whom she lived the rest of her life.

When *ciocia* Helenka went to work at *Chez Madeleine*, both English- and French-Canadian women whose husbands were successful professionals came to shop there. This store offered ready-to-wear as well as made-to-order apparel. Dazzling dresses and gowns on mannequins glittered in its window. The shop's owner, a shrewd businesswoman, soon discovered that not only was my aunt an excellent seamstress, she also had a talent for designing women's clothes. To her credit, this woman encouraged *ciocia* Helenka to develop this gift. My aunt began to draw captivating sketches of lovely outfits.

Sometimes I came with her to the store and she showed me her sketches as well as the finished products. I was delighted by the different materials and the exquisite designs in a variety of colors on all of the finished dresses and gowns. Shimmering sequins, smooth silks, and glimmering pearls for evening wear. Tailored wool suits for daywear. Starched cotton for daytime or soft silk outfits for evening parties. Sometimes I touched the fabrics of the blouses and skirts that were meant to feel like they could flow off the wearer's body. I felt special just by touching them. She eventually became the manager of the store.

Ciocia Helenka would waltz into our home for dinner on Sunday nights and regale the family with stories of high society. Names of the rich and powerful of Montréal floated in the air like presents wrapped in silk and chiffon bows. When she described some of the wives of the most famous businessmen and politicians in Québec (and some of their mistresses), I could almost touch their creamy white skin and sleek figures wearing my aunt's sartorial inventions. In my imagination, they winked at me holding out their arms nestled in long gloves up past their elbows, the ultimate in elegance at that time. Sometimes my mother brought me back down to earth by asking me sharply to help her in the kitchen.

"When will you stop being such a dreamer?" she threw up her arms in exasperation. That didn't change anything. In my mind's eye, I just kept seeing those women who looked like the extraordinary mannequins in the window of *Chez Madeleine. Ciocia*

Helenka spoke with her clients about the different events they attended and what types of dresses and other accessories would suit for which occasion. She measured them carefully and created the most intricate pieces for them. Many even invited her to be their confidante.

How extraordinary: my aunt, so close to such exciting women! And she herself was exciting. I adored the parade of outfits that she wore week after week to our Sunday dinners. Her delightful perfume filled the air. Her silky medium blond hair was always elegantly coiffed, a dash of turquoise eye shadow made her gray-blue eyes sparkle. She was as charming as any actress. She was my personal celebrity. My mother criticized her behavior endlessly. I figured out that my *ciocia* was too "modern' for my mother and thus a threat. Whenever I did something that displeased my mother, she would say, "You're selfish, just like your *ciocia* Helenka." And I would say to myself, "Thank goodness! Because I want to be just like her and not like you."

On my birthdays *ciocia* Helenka would take me out for a cherry sundae and would bring a gift, sometimes a personally designed blouse or skirt or dress with scarf or hat to match, a charm bracelet and, when I was a little older, different pairs of earrings. She would call me her *młoda dziewczynka* [*mademoiselle*]. This aunt (the only living one I had) offered a dynamic role model, a different way of being a woman in the world. A lucky break.

There is one piece of information that she quietly shared with me during one of these birthday outings. I was either eleven or twelve, because we talked about my leaving elementary school and beginning high school. She knew how much I was suffering at home.

"Why is my mother so mean to me?" I cried and cried in her tender arms as she patted my hair with her slender fingers and held me tight. I breathed in the aroma of her peachy-woodsy French perfume *L'Air du Temps* (by Nina Ricci) as if it were a healing tonic.

My aunt answered in a sad voice, "She doesn't know what to do with you, my dear. You seem so foreign to her. She is perhaps afraid of what you might become. I know this is strange to say, but she must feel that you will overtake her and it scares her. I'm afraid that you must remind her of all that she wanted and never received." I looked up through watery-clouded eyes at my aunt and wailed, "I wish you could have been my mother."

My aunt's eyes became misty like an overcast day. "I want to tell you something, but never tell your mother that you know this. I knew your mother's family back in Poland before I married and left for Canada. They lived in a neighborhood not that far away from my family's. One thing I can't forget is this: when your mother's mother would walk by on the sidewalk, you could feel like the ground was shaking. She always had a harsh cold look on her face. I can't imagine how she must have treated your mother as a child." [*Zawsze miała ostry, zimny wyraz twarzy. Nie mogę sobie wyobrazić, jak musiała traktować twoją matkę jak dziecko.*] Pain slashed across my aunt's delicate face for a moment. I was deeply struck by this piece of information. I tucked it away in my mind and it gave me solace. Only now do I realize how much this conversation must have helped me to bear the weight of my mother's family circumstance. Nevertheless, there was a limit as to how much *ciocia* Helenka could intervene on my behalf. My mother simply would not allow it.

My mind wanders back to the first time I saw the perfume bottle of *L'Air du Temps* in my aunt's office at the store. The bottle was graced by a frosted glass dove on the top. *Ciocia* Helenka opened it up and let me inhale that flowery-spicy bouquet. I was almost drunk on its scent. With a big smile, she dabbed a drop behind each of my ears. She eventually presented me with a bottle as a gift for one of my birthdays when I was in high school. What a precious jewel had been bestowed on me. I placed in on my dresser and it was always the last thing I saw before I closed my eyes at night and the first thing when I woke up in the morning. Even now when I go to the perfume counter of a store I seek out *L'Air du Temps* and breathe in its scent from a tester. And I see my darling aunt again as if she were standing right next to me holding out her arms. No darkness is wholly without light.

16

ENGLISH-CANADIANS

Lenore MacPherson could have been a poster child for the *Dick and Jane* series – ivory white skin, turquoise eyes, caramel-colored ringlets which were always decorated with some fancy barrette or bow. I adored the tailored coats and hats she wore. I first met her in my grade three classroom. She sat at a desk in a row adjacent to mine and noticed a book *The Story About Ping* on my desk one morning. We had hardly spoken to each other until that morning during recess when she asked me about my book. I told her I would be talking about it at the Show-And-Tell that afternoon. As she was curious, I showed it to her right then. To my great surprise, we began a friendship based on sharing books.

I learned about the *Cat in the Hat* series from Lenore during recess. On first glance I thought it was babyish, but as she read the book to me I could see that there were hidden messages. Dr. Seuss asked what we would do if our mothers left us alone at home on a rainy day and upon returning at the end of the day wanted to know what we had done. We knew that we had experienced an amazing adventure with this mischievous and totally original Cat who made our lives exciting and unruly and then cleaned up and disappeared just before Mother returned. Would we tell her? She had specifically told us not to get into trouble or make a mess. This brought forth a subversive idea: You do not have to tell Mother everything! Lenore and I went back and forth about what was right and proper. Finally, both of us came to the same conclusion – that sometimes it's best to leave things unsaid as long as the secret doesn't hurt anybody.

———

I was invited to Lenore's place one weekend afternoon as the leaves were beginning to show off their fall colors. It was the first of many visits. Her father came to pick me up in his car, a green and white four-door sedan with what looked like fins at the back. The word "Laurentian" was engraved at the bottom of the hood. I remember this because it had the same name as the Laurentian mountains in the countryside north of Montréal. The car was roomy with green patterned cloth seats and a plush carpet on the floor.

My French-Canadian neighbors sitting on their balconies stared down at Lenore's father – and especially the car – and wondered if I was going over to the "other side." They sat on their balconies pretending to be knitting or eating or chatting, although I knew they must have been wary of this man who was taking me away to his English-Canadian home in order for me to play with his daughter.

At first, Françoise thought I was breaking a sacred allegiance and that I would abandon her. She acted as if she had been jilted, and I was consumed with guilt over this. She meant the world to me and I couldn't afford to lose her. So I explained again and again how I had met Lenore in the *école anglaise* and that in spite of my entry into the world of *les Anglais,* I was not about to leave her. I was truly desperate for her to understand that I was not a turncoat. We crossed each other's hearts and I swore to *Le Bon Dieu* that she was my best friend, *ma meilleure copine!*

That day marked the beginning of my understanding of the wall that existed between French and English in Québec. It was not as dramatic as the chasm between Polish and Yiddish, but it was palpable. I had to figure out some way to navigate between the two sides of that wall – a big job for a little girl. I waved goodbye to Françoise while Lenore's father drove me away from my first true place of community.

Lenore lived a few blocks away in a much more upscale neighborhood than my own, one where mostly everyone spoke English. I was surprised to see single family dwellings with manicured lawns full of well-tended flowers and perfectly arranged shrubbery. I thought I had landed in Dick and Jane's neighborhood. As I walked through the door of their home, a vision of order and social tradition assailed me. I spied a mahogany dining room in the distance as I took off my shoes in the vestibule. Even the vestibule was adorned with a bench made of imposing dark wood and had hooks on the side to hang coats and scarves. What impressed me most was that the pungent aroma of food cooking on a stovetop or in an oven was oddly missing. Also, everything was much quieter.

Lenore seemed grateful to me for listening to her read aloud. I knew that she recognized that I was superior to her in reading but I recognized that she was endowed with the social graces I lacked. One might have called our friendship a match of convenience as well as a bid toward upward mobility. Lenore could gain a literacy advantage through me, and I could learn how better to maneuver in the English-Canadian world. It turned out that it was Lenore's mother who was the instigator of this arrangement. I learned later on that Lenore had told her mother about my love for books. Her mother, who wanted Lenore's grades to improve, took note. She was a pleasant looking woman smartly dressed in a cotton eyelet blouse and a pleated skirt with a pattern of blue and red boxes (which I later learned were the tartan colors for the MacPherson clan) took me aside right away and asked if I believed in God.

I was taken aback. Was this some kind of test? I told her the truth: that I definitely believed in God. She began to relax but she was still not completely satisfied. "What about Heaven and Hell?

Do you believe in them?" I knew there was a Heaven; that's where my dead relatives were and God was taking care of them. I wasn't quite as sure about Hell. I remember Lenore telling me once that she might go to Hell because she thought bad things about her little brother. In Hell you burned to a crisp while the Devil kept poking at you with a pitchfork.

Jewish people didn't make such a big deal about Hell although we did worry about sinful behavior. We were afraid that God would punish us if we did bad things. We wanted God to be proud of us. And this is what I told Lenore's mother. She allowed me to continue to come and play in their home. The MacPhersons were not Catholic like my French-Canadian friends. They were Protestant like the hymns in my school. I didn't fully understand the difference at the time. I knew that they were both Christian and that they both believed in Jesus as the Messiah but Protestants didn't have statues of Jesus and Mary and Joseph or other saints in their homes. There were no crosses on the walls in Lenore's home.

Catholics and Protestants believed in Jesus as Savior in different ways; Lenore explained it all to me. Their crosses in church were empty, no Jesus nailed to them. He had gone up to Heaven. The Protestants thought it better to concentrate on the "going up to Heaven" part than on the "suffering on the Cross" element. When Jesus was suffering on the cross, He was being crucified. When He was off the cross, He was being resurrected and rose to Heaven to be with His Father. Lenore told me He had promised to return one day, in the Second Coming, and that then He would free people from their misery. Then I remembered that in the Jewish religion the Messiah still hadn't come but that when he did arrive, the dead would rise again and we would all live in peace. It sounded to me like the Christians had copied that story and changed it into their Jesus story.

The key conflict seemed to be about whether Jesus was the Messiah or not. This whole Messiah issue was baffling. It seemed impossible to be Jewish and Christian at the same time. Not if the Christians thought that Jesus was the Messiah, and if the Jews thought that the Messiah had not yet come. You just couldn't get around these opposites. And then to make matters impossible, one day I was informed by some of my friends on my street that the Jews had *killed* Jesus, but that they would forgive me personally because I wasn't that kind of Jew. Stunned, I was drenched with a growing dread. My stomach began to churn and my knees went wobbly. At least they hadn't decided to stop being my friends. From that moment on I knew I would always be an outsider looking in through the windows at their bright lights and blessed laughter.

Again, I turned to my father for an explanation. He told me in a sad but firm voice that Jesus was a Jew and that it was the Romans who had killed him. I eventually told two of my neighborhood friends (both girls were Catholic, one was French-Canadian and one was Ukrainian) exactly that as we were playing outside one afternoon after school. They said they had learned in Catechism class that Jews were Christ-killers and that the Church could not be wrong. This dialogue went on for a while when from a place in my mind I never had known came these words: "Because you are blaming Jews for having killed Jesus, all of my relatives were killed." My heart raced as I spoke and my face got hot. The two girls looked aghast. They were sweet children and didn't want to continue this dangerous conversation. Neither did I. So we resumed playing hopscotch and skip rope.

When I played with Lenore, I tried to explain that my relatives had suffered like Jesus, not on a cross, but in concentration camps that were just as horrifying and maybe even worse because it took longer to die. I confided to Lenore that sometimes I was afraid that Hitler would come in the middle of the night and drag me away to those awful places. "He did it to my parents and to my relatives, so maybe he will find me as well."

Lenore tried to comfort me but I felt uneasy when she said, "Maybe if you would believe in Jesus as the Messiah you'd be safe."

"The Messiah hasn't arrived yet in the Jewish religion. I've already told you that."

Lenore whispered: "Don't tell my mother. She might get upset and then I won't be able to play with you." We made a pact entwining our little fingers.

How can I ever forget Lenore's dollhouse. I was never terribly enamored of dolls, but I desperately had longed for a doll's house, perhaps because it could be construed as a "home." However, dollhouses were expensive, so I was ecstatic to be able to play with hers. This dollhouse was furnished with miniature chairs and sofas and buffets in the living/dining room and a kitchen complete with cabinets, sink and fridge and stove and table and chairs, a bathroom with shining faucets and gleaming sink and bath and toilet and a bedroom with children's bed and tiny toys on a wood dresser. When I picked up these items it was as if I was handling treasures.

Lenore and I also wrote stories and drew pictures together. I drew apartment buildings with individual units furnished with rich wood bedroom sets and high bookshelves lined with books and kitchen tables with bright tablecloths and chairs as well as white lace curtains with frills for the windows and pots with flowers of all types for the balconies, soft pink or flaming red roses, orange and yellow lilies (the stylized lily being the emblem of Québec, *le fleur de lis)*: some vibrant, some dainty (depending on my mood). And I always included a garden with a medley of maple, oak, or beech – and of course tall pine trees because they afforded color in winter. I was determined to draw only cheerful places and I wrote even more cheerful stories. Often in the drawings there would appear the face of a little girl at one of the windows looking out at the big world wondering if and when she would get to go to some of the holiday places that her classmates had mentioned in class. Sadly, none of those drawings are in my possession because my mother threw out the boxes of my personal effects when they moved away from my childhood home. She never asked whether I wanted to keep them.

Even though there were no crosses in Lenore's home, nor any religious statues, Lenore owned a book called Children's Bible Stories, full of stories about Jesus' life. Her mother told her to show me that book. I loved the pictures of Jesus as a shepherd surrounded by children and wished I could have been one of those children. Lenore didn't have to wish that for herself; she felt secure that Jesus loved her. She didn't talk much about Mary who was so important to my Catholic friends, and I never told Lenore about how much Mother Mary meant to me. She would have insisted that I should be saying this about Jesus.

17

OF CHRISTMAS AND NOËL

During Christmas I was invited to Françoise's home as well as to Lenore's. Both had Christmas trees, and both waited for Santa Claus (or *Père Noël* in French) to slide down the chimney on Christmas Eve and bring presents. The big difference was that the main celebration in Françoise's home took place on Christmas Eve (*le réveillon*) when they returned from midnight mass. Lenore and her family went to church earlier in the evening, and their big meal was at lunchtime on the following day. This way I got to go to both celebrations.

The French-Canadian *Noël* was boisterous, rambunctious, loads of fun. Not to mention mouthwatering. Pots and pans of all sizes and shapes graced the dining room table that sported a bright red tablecloth with lime green napkins and shiny silverware and snow-white plates. The aromas that emanated from them could knock a person over. One of Françoise's cousins, Annemarie, would mischievously jump up on a chair and take off the lids of two of the huge pots and the air would become sweet with the smell of roasted turkey and also a beef *tourtière*. The steam from platters laden with cooked vegetables, green beans, cauliflower, carrots, broccoli rose up into the air. Alongside these platters sat other dishes, the color of Père Noël's red suit, filled with salads and sizzling *patates frites* (the best French fries I've ever tasted to date) and freshly baked bread. Piping hot pea soup – *la soupe aux pois* – bubbled in a huge red pot with a green ladle. The grown-ups buzzed like honeybees in conversation, men on one side, women on the other. Many bottles of wine, beer and liquor perched extravagantly on a sideboard. I was ensconced with Françoise and the other children at the far end of the living room on a folding chair near an open window that allowed fresh air to float into this crowded, warm atmosphere.

Later we all trooped into the parlor adjacent to the dining room and which housed the splendid Christmas tree. Underneath it sat piles of gifts wrapped in glowing paper. Françoise and her siblings and cousins tore open their presents while their parents, grandparents, aunts and uncles glowed with satisfaction. And there was a present for me too! Astonished, I unwrapped the bright-green bow and tried hard to be tidy about the wrapping paper covered with stickers of Santa and snowmen. Even the wrapping paper seemed precious. A toy piano peeked out from the box. A tiny grand piano in black lacquer. I ran my fingers against its shiny surface not daring to touch the keys but Françoise's mother encouraged me to do just that. I started to plink out a few tunes that I had learned at another friend's home. Everybody clapped. I was on top of the world.

On Christmas Day, I would go to Lenore's house for their holiday meal at noon. The two events could hardly have been more different. It was as if I were transported from one world to another. There was also an exquisitely decorated tree in the living room, but that is where the similarity ended. Lenore's Christmas meal was a much more subdued affair with everyone seated around the polished mahogany dining room table and matching chairs. A fire crackled in the fireplace. There were much fewer people. Lenore's grandmother was the only other guest. She was Lenore's mother's mother, a prim and proper woman in a wool navy-blue dress with robin's egg colored trim. She had silver-gray permed hair, shining blue eyes and off-white skin – and a distinctly Scottish accent (I didn't know it was Scottish then).

How dignified she seemed. Just like the exquisite place settings on the table. English bone china designed with tiny pink flowers and green and brown leaves, crystal cut glasses and water decanter, and sterling silver cutlery all gleamed in the sunlight. I might as well have been invited by Queen Elizabeth to her palace. Lenore's grandmother also reminded me of the Queen Mother.

Immigrant children like me enjoyed the Royal Family, and much had been made in our school of the Queen's visit to open the St. Lawrence Seaway. We were given special commemorative coins to honor this event. The Queen was a young monarch then and I was impressed by her composed appearance. Perhaps this was what Lenore's family was trying to emulate. How lucky for them, I thought, to be just like Dick and Jane's family. And as we were seated at the table before the food arrived we listened to the Queen's Christmas message on the radio. She spoke with such poise. Each syllable was clear as a bell. It was in many ways just as attractive as the Parisian French accent (of my French teacher Madame Simon). Afterward, the grown-ups discussed the message and thought that *Her Majesty* (they used those words) had done an excellent job. The pride in their voices was unmistakable. She was *their* Queen in a deeply personal way – Great Britain was where they originally hailed from, and Canada was still a colony, as far as they were concerned. It reminded me of what our geography teacher once declared: "What's red on the map is ours!" I knew that my French-Canadian neighbors were less enamored with the monarchy. To say the least.

Then we said grace. I folded my hands as Lenore's family did and said Amen when they did. It was a simple prayer. It turned out that Lenore's grandmother's middle name also was Grace and she told me so with a smile. It brought me a little bit closer to all of them. The food arrived on platters and Lenore's mother dished out portions to each of us using a ladle with a Wedgwood handle. The gravy boat was trimmed with a deep blue border and had yellow and orange butterflies painted on it. I didn't know about Wedgwood bone china then. I remember how, many years later, the Christmas meal at Lenore's returned vividly to my mind when I was in a shop selecting a Wedgwood tea set for a friend's wedding party.

The food had a very different aroma from that of Françoise's home. It felt very "sit up straight," like the Queen. What astounded me was the English trifle. My tongue lolled around in the fruity, creamy concoction. It was as tasty as the Gâteau St-Honoré at Françoise's, although less crunchy. And, as I learned years later, loaded with rum! We sang carols (which I knew perfectly from school) with Mr. MacPherson wearing a tailored dark blue suit and red and blue-striped tie, at the piano. I worried that Mrs. MacPherson might bring up her religious questions again, but she didn't. They all spoke in lower tones than I was used to. Nobody gesticulated with their hands in the way that my family (or for that matter Françoise's family) did. I became self-conscious about this whenever I was at Lenore's house, and ever after as an adult in English Canada. At the end of the feast I received what seemed to me to be a truly grand gift from Lenore's family: a paint set with many bottles of different colored paints and long brushes as well as a table-top wood easel. This gift was a work of art to my eyes, as if it had been created by a great craftsman. I couldn't believe that I would be able to paint my beloved drawings using these luxurious paints, all the colors of the rainbow.

I always wondered how Santa Claus knew not to come to my home to deliver Christmas presents. I thought he probably wanted to include the Jewish kids, but if we celebrated Christmas then we wouldn't be Jews anymore. That was the sticking point. We got chocolate covered "coins" (candy money) on Hanukkah which was around the same time as Christmas but it didn't have anywhere near the same pizzazz. The celebration was quieter; we watched glowing candles burn on the Menorah, recited prayers in Hebrew and sang songs. It was much more private. I never heard anything about it on the radio or television. And there was never a menorah next to the Christmas tree in my school.

Hanukkah didn't have anything to do with Jesus. My father explained how the event took place many years before Jesus was alive and that it was about a miracle that saved the Jews from the

Assyrians who wanted to kill them. Judah Maccabee was the hero of the story. He led a little army against a much bigger one, yet the Jews won. There was a flame in the temple had burned for eight days which was a miracle because there was only oil for one day. The Maccabees could regroup during these nights and be ready for the enemy in the mornings. God had saved us.

I loved the *dreidls*. They were little tops that you spun and then they danced on the floor. Hebrew letters were painted on each side, *Nun, Gimel, Hay, Sheen. Ness Gadol Haya Sham:* "A Big Miracle Happened There." We must always remember God's lovingkindness was the message. But one thought nagged at me. If God was so kind and loving, why didn't He help his people, the Jews, in the war that had killed all my relatives? And why were there always people who hated Jews, and who wanted to hurt them, or make fun of them and put them down, even after the war had ended? I never thought about this at my French-Canadian friends' homes. There I could forget. And I never felt awkward there as I did at Lenore's. It seemed to me that Lenore's mother was always watching to make sure that I was minding my manners, as though I hadn't yet learned their rules. I was nervous each time I picked up the cutlery for fear of making a mistake. I figured out that, in and of itself, language was not enough. My English was just fine by the time I was in grade three. Indeed, my teachers always praised me for writing "such well organized and interesting" stories. I came to understand that there were many *other* ways of behaving that seemed just as important as knowing the language. That was the "culture" part. I realized that you had to be born into that way of life in order to understand it and feel comfortable, and be totally accepted.

18

HIGHWAY NUMBER 9

As far back as I can remember, I dreamt of getting away. To anywhere. I would hear the whistle of a train in the dark of night and start thinking about what clothes would be needed in order to get by, plus a hairbrush, toothpaste and a toothbrush. Most of all, I needed my diary where I kept my most important secrets. I would lie in bed organizing my strategy. *Just go. Get out. Leave this bleakness behind.* My suitcase was packed and ready, biding its time on the hallway floor of our house. In my mind I put on my shoes and coat. I took one last look around at what had been home. But it never really was home, was it? That's why it seemed so urgent to leave, because home was out there somewhere and I had to get started on the journey before I would lose my chance. Then I would fall back asleep and these thoughts would tuck themselves away for when the right moment arrived.

When my father bought his first used car in the late-1950s, some ten years after arriving in Montréal, he was transformed into a sporadic but avid traveler. He loved being behind the wheel where he could finally taste a bit of freedom. Our first road trip to New York City became my initiation on the path to other landscapes. My older brother sat in the front with the map showing Highway

Number 9, the route to New York City before the New York State Thruway had been completed and my father placed him in charge of helping to navigate. I was in the backseat with my mother and baby sister. My father gave me the task of keeping my eye on the signposts that marked Highway 9. "Keep looking for the little number 9 on the highway signs," he called back to me in Yiddish.

Suddenly, I had a purpose, a destination. That one digit became my compass. All those lovely villages and towns we passed: Plattsburg, Lake Champlain, Lake Placid, Schroon Lake, Lake George, Glens Falls, Saratoga Springs and onward. The green Hudson Valley and the farms with bright red barns and silver sloping roofs and tall trees against the Adirondack Mountains and the dazzling Hudson River. I took it all in as they whizzed by – a pastoral beauty that felt restorative.

We stopped at fruit stands and the taste of those cherries still sweetens my mouth in delicious memory. I was also struck (albeit unconsciously) by my father's decision to escape his brokenness – at least for a while – and to be present with what was right there in front of him.

Travel became nourishment filled with the life force. Mother Nature was summoned to feed my father's broken spirit with her beauty. This was one of the great lessons I learned from him: that we must choose to endure the suffering and make joy from it – even if for fleeting moments. If you are in the darkness, you must strive to move toward the light, no matter how distant it may be. Keep looking for the highway sign 9. Keep your eye on the road. Keep searching for everything that is missing: home, safety, adventure, love. Keep going.

Of course, it wasn't just about picturesque views. Canada had plenty of that. What was exciting was that we'd crossed the border into the United States for the first time. My father, mother and brother who arrived on that day at the border between the Province of Québec and New York State were newly minted citizens of Canada, "greenhorns" but Canadians nonetheless. My sister and I were the "real" Canadians, having been born in Montréal. The fact that I was born in Canada allowed me to hold my head high in front of my classmates whose families were "established" Canadians. When asked where I was born (with my unpronounceable Polish name) I could answer proudly "Right here in Montréal, Québec, Canada."

Like all Canadians, we couldn't help looking to our powerful neighbor to the south for comparison. Montréal was the only cosmopolitan city in Canada at that time, but New York City was where everything *really* happened, especially on the *Ed Sullivan Show*. We watched that TV program each Sunday evening with my aunt after dinner. My father was dazzled by this American confidence and vivaciousness which the show so richly exemplified – precisely what he lacked. As poor immigrants in Canada, we were always the "other" with noses pressed up against the windowpanes peering into the real party.

However, there was more than that. Even at that young age, I figured out that I would have been much more accepted and acceptable in New York City. There were so many Jews there. Even the non-Jews there seemed Jewish. Everything about the U.S., at least in the urban centers, was louder, more exuberant, more brash, more ambitious and more passionate. If nothing else my family was indeed loud at times, forlorn at others, then at other times hysterical and weepy – way too intense by English-Canadian standards. We resembled the French-Canadians, and the New Yorkers.

The closer we got to New York City, the more hopeful my father became about the possibility of being in the audience at the *Ed Sullivan Show* which had a live audience in those days. When we finally arrived at Times Square in Manhattan, the lineup for free tickets snaked around many streets. My heart sank. We would have to give up on that dream. As I turned to my father to console him, I was amazed at the defiance in his eyes. He took me by the hand and together we hiked the several blocks to the administrative office. Some people glared at us; others looked confused. Nobody criticized or stopped us. It was as if my father was wearing a bullet-proof vest.

He strode into the office and right up to the assistant and demanded to speak to the manager. It was as if my father had gone into a phone booth as Clark Kent and emerged as Superman. The assistant, a young woman, looked annoyed but got up and returned with a self-assured man who seemed unruffled by this situation. As the man was about to speak, probably to politely tell us that our request was impossible, my father's voice took command. In broken English, he explained that we were Canadian tourists who had come all the way to New York City to watch the *Ed Sullivan Show*. He told this man that this was our first trip to the United States and that there was no way he could disappoint his family. His determination was unshakeable. Who was this strong confident man holding my hand who would not take no for an answer? My pride swelled after I recovered from my surprise. Magically, the manager finally offered us five tickets and we sailed out of the office. My father winked at me and I learned right then that human beings are indeed complicated and contradictory beings. When we got back to our car my mother was delighted and said as my father walked towards the driver's door, "This is the man who saved my life in the concentration camp."

We were led to our seats that evening. The studio was packed to the rafters. All of us in the audience had this truth in common: we were winners. We watched the little mouse *Topo Gigio*, a puppet moved by invisible hands. But the star of the show was a young Ann-Margret who was soon to become a famous movie actress. She sang *Bye Bye Birdie* from her new Broadway musical. When it was all over, my father – God rest his soul – hurried us to the backstage door to get her autograph. He handed me the program with her signature. I couldn't believe I was standing right in front of her. She had hair the color of hazelnut ice cream piled high on her head and her big sea green eyes shone with girlish innocence in an oval face. She wore an emerald-colored sequined bodice fitted at the bust line and a long, flowing pleated chiffon skirt. Her shoulders were covered with a stole of the same material as her skirt. She actually bent down and gave me a kiss on the cheek. Her perfume was like a field of wildflowers on a breezy day. To me she seemed like a princess from a faraway kingdom. Her own father, tall and regal, in a black tuxedo and starched white shirt with a black bowtie, stood next to her, protective. He shook my father's hand and then he and his daughter were whisked away in a waiting limousine.

19

MADAME SIMON

My French teacher Madame Simon looked like a model in a fashion show every day. The first time I laid eyes on her, she was wearing a rose-red wool tweed jacket fitted close to the waist with sparkling pink buttons up to the small collar at her neck where a lacy white collar peeked out. She also wore a straight gray skirt that fell some inches below the knee, and black pumps on her feet with the most delicate looking ivory nylon stockings on her shapely legs. Hanging from her arm was a leather canary-yellow purse with a silvery clasp. Slender and tall, with cobalt eyes, her black hair was done up in a *chignon*. Her high heels made a clacking sound as she walked around the classroom dictating words for us to write into our *cahiers* during *Dictée*. Her soft voice, mingled with perfume, travelled through the air. I felt blessed to be in her regal presence.

This woman looked as alluring as my aunt, perhaps even more so because of her French accent. I worked as hard as possible to mimic that fancy accent of hers that came straight from Paris. I felt that if I could speak French like Madame Simon then I, too, would become elegant. I became her disciple, although I never told her so – for I was too much in awe. I always had the right answer to any question. Puzzled by my enthusiasm, she approached me early on in the year and asked whether I had a French-speaking mother. I had to tell her "no" wishing that I could have said "yes."

My daily French classes in school were lanterns of hope, and Madame Simon became my Fairy Godmother. Decades of time have not tarnished the glow of those lessons for me. For an hour a day in school I found myself immersed in some kind of French fairy tale, or should I say *conte de fée*. French was a compulsory subject of daily instruction from grade one onwards. French classes were like a magical garden and became my foster home. These classes coupled with my *imaginings* of belonging to the French-Canadian culture lit up my days. I felt safe at my desk in class writing stories describing the lives of French-Canadians because it opened an escape route from the ghosts who haunted my conscious as well as unconscious moments.

My mind often wanders back to those French classes because it was there that I first felt the joy of the verbal games and grammatical puzzles of learning a new language. I was building a structure, from the ground up, discovering new ways to look at the world, new ways to communicate. I was creating a new identity, a route of escape. *La langue française* said to me: "You will always find strength in your love for me. There will always be a home for you here. *Bienvenue*."

Young as I was, I could recognize a blessing when I saw one. I thought: *So this is what a French teacher looks and acts like* and I tucked that knowledge away for future reference. I sought out every opportunity to let French words pour out of me. And they poured from pencil to paper as well. I continued to watch television shows in English on Channel Six and in French on *Canal Deux*. There I caught my first glimpses at the possibility of peaceful coexistence within diversity. And I figured out a neat trick. I realized that certain English television programs would later appear on the French channel but dubbed in French. I would diligently watch the English language version first and then the French one, figuring out the new words. If I ran into any difficulties I asked Madame Simon about their meaning next day in class. She was surprised and also confused at my motivation as were my classmates, many of whom were also immigrant children, satisfied with the English language curriculum. They didn't see the value of French in their everyday lives. In fairness to them, it is they who were "normal" and I who was unusual.

In French, I became a person filled with purpose and desire. When I was in grade six I participated in a school project to be a "student teacher" for the pupils in the grade two French classes. I made sure I wore my whitest blouse and that my tunic was in perfect condition and that my shoes were shiny black. I wanted to make Madame Simon take notice. I had written out my lesson plan the night before and looked it over at breakfast. The lesson was to be about going to play at a friend's house after school. I had put together a little skit.

I arrived at school and went to the room where the "student teachers" were to meet. Madame Simon was to assign each of us to a class. There was never any doubt in my mind that I could pull it off. Madame Simon must have noticed the purposeful look on my face because she sent me to the "gifted" class. (It wasn't called "gifted" then but everyone knew this class was where the smart kids were.) I strode into the class as my heart fluttered in anticipation. With a big smile I introduced myself and explained what we would do. I felt as if my hair was piled up in a bun and I was in high heels and carrying a yellow purse with a silver clasp. Suddenly, I was grown-up and in charge. Not a whiff of uncertainty. I could tell I was on the right track when the children became excited about the skit and hands shot up to participate. In front of a class – and especially in front of a French class – I became the master of my own destiny. I was going to be just like Madame Simon. I was going to become a French teacher.

20

HIGH SCHOOL

How well I remember my homeroom teacher Miss Crumm. She always had a pinched look on her gaunt face. She was unattractively thin with long bony arms that protruded from a scratchy-looking dark wool jacket and stick-skinny legs peeping out of a long black skirt. Her beady little eyes made you feel like you were always being watched and judged, especially if you were from the wrong side of the tracks as I was. The CNR (Canadian National Railway) railway tracks were the boundary between my lower middle/working class side of the school district and the middle/upper middle class on the other side. I do not have the exact numbers but I recall that it felt like about a 25-75 percent divide in favor of the well-to-do kids.

Many boys and girls (especially boys) who came from the right side of the tracks were treated like royalty. Miss Crumm (and several other teachers) treated a particular boy, the one from the most prestigious family, like a prince. When Matthew's hand went up to answer a question he was never ignored. He hogged the show in class, hardly ever letting anybody get in a word edgewise. We girls kept our mouths shut but some of the other boys took him on. No teacher ever admonished Matthew for anything. In fact other boys were frequently blamed for wrongdoings that he had perpetrated. Miss Crumm would almost swoon in front of Matthew whenever he would utter some inane comment or other. One afternoon she had vehemently reprimanded another student, Robert, for being late to class. "How dare you take your schooling so lightly," she roared. "You will have to go to detention for the rest of the week and it will be marked in your file."

Robert came from my (wrong) side of the tracks and I knew that he had to make lunch for his three younger brothers because his mother was always in bed suffering from one "ailment" after another. He didn't live far from me and we would frequently walk to school together. One morning I entered his apartment with him when he had forgotten a notebook for class. A ferocious looking man with a hairy chest (no shirt on) pounced on us, "What are you doing here, at this hour? Shouldn't you be in school?" Robert shot me a look to stay silent and I suddenly noticed, through a tiny opening of the bedroom door, his mother lying disheveled on an unmade bed, wearing a ratty looking negligee, her bare arm hanging over the side, a bottle of liquor in her hand. The youngest of his siblings, a toddler who resembled Robert, ambled in our direction looking confused. He only had diapers on. He smelled as if he hadn't had a bath in a long time.

The man was not Robert's father. His father had taken off years ago. This guy, with tattoos all over his arms, was the latest of many boyfriends. I felt a chill creep over my body. If that man had had a gun or knife in his hand, we could have been history. The situation had to be kept secret – "Or," as Robert put it, "those social worker ladies will take us away from our mom if I tell." The neighbors kept quiet because they knew they could also be targeted for one offence or another.

In class I felt a heat rise inside me as Robert muttered an out-of-breath response to Miss Crumm's scolding about his lateness, "I ran all the way, Miss Crumm, really." He was ashamed to say that he had to feed his siblings. The teacher hurled a brutal glance at him and shouted, "Sit down. You'll never amount to anything anyway." Then Matthew the Prince sauntered in late. This was not the first time. When Miss Crumm asked where his homework was he retorted with a swing of his blond head and a smirk on his lips, "The dog ate it." All eyes were on Miss Crumm, hoping for some retribution. "Oh, Matthew, stop being such a comedian," she responded with revolting delight.

Streaming was the vogue then. We were placed in classes according to ability. The lowest level of classes was nicknamed the "Bobo" class by some nasty snotty kids. This group was considered doomed by the teachers in terms of an academic future, or perhaps in terms of any future at all. One afternoon I could not attend gym class, so I was sent to spend that particular class period in the Bobo class. The classroom epitomized chaos and indifference. As I was led to the desk I would occupy, my eyes fell upon kids napping at their desks, while others chatted loudly with one another and someone in the back was listening to pop music. The teacher, a tall young woman with mossy green eyes tried unsuccessfully to get them to pay attention. They ignored her and she looked terribly bored, perhaps wondering why she had been placed in this classroom of "losers." That's how everyone in school described them. She walked back to the front of the room and began dictating a passage in a monotonous voice. Several students seated in front of her were painfully trying to spell the words out loud. It was clear that nobody wanted to be there. I felt like I was on holiday in a strange universe. It didn't feel good. I had a library book. It was *Catcher in The Rye* by J.D. Salinger. I adored that book, and the protagonist, Holden Caulfield, who will always be a symbol for teenage angst and rebellion.

I looked up from the book and watched students switching seats while a new group began reading aloud from their reader to the teacher. From what I heard, the story was scripted and meaningless. They were trying to sound out the letters. It was agonizing. Holden Caulfield would have said something poignant about the Bobo scene, like; "What kind of lousy sham is going on here?" A flash of a question sparked through me. "Why are these students given such dreary stuff to read? There must be more interesting books for them even if they can't read well. Maybe books that would make them *want* to read!" I was ready to shout that out in the class but kept my tongue. It wasn't my place. I felt grateful I hadn't been relegated to this fate. That was because of my father who, in spite of his life circumstances, loved reading, loved languages and so did I.

In my own classes I was regularly ignored by the "in-group," I wasn't stylish or confident enough for them. Thankfully it was mandatory to wear a uniform: a black or navy-blue box-pleated tunic and a plain white long-sleeved blouse and black or navy oxford shoes with black or navy socks. I can't imagine how intolerable life would have been if the "rich girls" could have worn their latest fashions to school. Still I was in the scraggly out-group. This lack of status brought forth deep-seated feelings of inadequacy and loneliness that had originated at home. When I got 97 percent on an exam I wanted to tear myself up that I didn't get 98 or 99 or 100 percent. And if I did get 100 percent how long could I maintain that?

Although my report cards were stellar, I remained empty and agitated inside. I would come home to a mother who could not see me for who I was. Something about my ambition continued to irk her deeply. Her habitual remark was to compare me to her friends' children, to always find me come up short. This one was prettier; that one was more outgoing, the other one was more obedient. In turn I kept trying desperately to get the highest grades in all my subjects to the point of obsession.

The litany continued. My mother complained that I studied too hard, that I didn't have enough friends, that I didn't help her clean or cook enough, that I did a terrible job of making my bed, that I slept in too late on weekends. She would purposely vacuum the carpet in my room early on Saturday mornings to get that message across. On and on it went. I kept bringing home star-studded report cards and she kept mentioning how lovely her friend's child, the girl across the street, was becoming. "For a girl, beauty will get you much farther in life than smarts. That's how you get a good husband," she explained with a twisted smile one afternoon when I brought home a commendation for an essay written about the importance of poetry. I looked down at this shiny gold medal.

Suddenly, it became worthless. I held back my tears and entered the sanctuary of my bedroom. My sister was often at a friend's place in the afternoons, so I would have the bedroom to myself until suppertime. As usual, my mother got on the phone and bragged about my achievement to her friends as if it was her own and had nothing to do with me. I felt as if I had been robbed – again.

One day something inside me snapped. I walked in the door of our house after school, dropped my schoolbag on the vestibule table and entered the kitchen to get a cookie. My mother, eating a hunk of chocolate cake, sat at the table lying in wait. "Alyssa, Mrs. Wryba's daughter was complimented today by her teacher that her grades have improved," she announced as if Alyssa had just received a Nobel Prize. (Alyssa was a shy and rather dull girl who lived on our street, no malice intended.)

When I heard these words coming out of the mouth of a woman who always ignored my substantial accomplishments, something rose to a boiling point. Hot anger locked up for so many years, fueled by puberty and the rage of hormones, started to flow upward and out. I rushed into the living room and began pulling the curtains off the rods. I wanted to demolish the place. My mother galloped after me, mouth gaping open and crumbs from the cake sliding onto the carpet.

My father was not yet home from work. My brother was at university and my sister was visiting a friend. My mother, red in the face, looked like she was ready to slap me hard but I just kept pulling at the curtains with one hand and shielding my face with the other. A look of fear spread over her face. It was the first time I witnessed that. She stumbled out of the living room like a wounded animal and I strode into my bedroom with newfound energy and slammed the door shut. I could have lifted a building.

When my father came home that night I could hear her weeping about what a crazy daughter she had. My exhausted father tried to be the peacemaker. He kept racing back and forth from their bedroom to mine, like a messenger boy. I felt an odd mixture of embarrassment and pity for him. I almost apologized. Yet something inside me said, "No, you have done nothing wrong." It would have been much easier to simply apologize and get it over with as I had done countless other times for lesser transgressions but this time I was intent on holding my ground. My father shot me a look of sheer defeat. I finally ended up writing the perfunctory note of apology and slipped it under their bedroom door and then went to bed. Nobody discussed the matter the following day.

One week later, after my father got home from work, I announced that I was leaving school to become a waitress. My parents were wide-eyed, stricken with panic. What would their friends think? I didn't relent about quitting school for days until finally it became a matter of truancy. When the principal was informed of this situation, he decided to come to our house in order to explain to me how important high school was as a "steppingstone" to university. He was a tall dignified man with silver hair and a kind face. His name was Mr. Stewart. He had a pained look in his soft gray eyes as he shook my parents' hands. They looked bewildered. He must have felt sorry for me, watching this bright girl trapped in this weird family. In any case, I will always thank him for offering me the idea of a "steppingstone" to university. It sounded magical and I wondered whether he was an angel in disguise. How many principals come over to a young student's home to invite them back to school? It seemed extraordinary and so I agreed to return to school. Mr. Stewart winked at me and I knew I could make it through the next four years.

Then something unexpected happened. I became interested in boys and they in me. I began to notice that they thought I was pretty. I went out on double and triple dates and would still feel awkward but the more I saw the expression on the boys' faces and heard their compliments the more I gained confidence. Nothing ever went beyond kissing. I was petrified of getting pregnant. I knew next to nothing. Maybe if a boy pushed his body too close to mine I could become pregnant. Veronica, a petite, quiet girl who lived around the corner from me had been "knocked up," and the guy took off. She was about to turn 16. She had to disappear to some place for unwed mothers and then put the baby up for adoption. Abortion wasn't even discussed as a possibility. She was Catholic. Not to mention that having an abortion was illegal then anyway.

Another neighbor, Josephine, who lived several blocks away and had quite a resemblance to the movie star and then princess of Monaco, Grace Kelly, had tried to use a coat hanger (a common but very dangerous method in those days) to induce a miscarriage and she almost bled to death. It was just a stroke of luck that a friend of hers had decided to come over to study with her for an exam and found her on the bathroom floor unconscious in a sea of red. She raced down to a neighbor who called the emergency room at a nearby hospital. An ambulance came roaring down the street to Josephine's apartment. Her mother (I remember her as a woman who looked washed out from fatigue) was carrying a bag of groceries after a long day's work at a factory and watched, horrified, as the paramedics carried her daughter down the steps on a stretcher into the van. I heard all about it at school the following day. Thankfully Josephine lived.

I joined two after-school activities: *Le Cercle Français* and *Magnum Opus* and spent a lot of time at these meetings so I could arrive home late, have a quick supper, go to my room and do my homework. Languages and cultures, in particular French and Latin, remained oases throughout my high school years. There was no change in my home situation. But the scowl on my mother's face was becoming a little less ominous. However, she could still worry me to death about some possible illness or another. When I had a minor case of acne, she shrieked that I would lose any looks that I had. Why hadn't I been more careful? Or when I colored my hair auburn, she screamed that I looked like a prostitute and would end up in the gutter. "How could you do such a stupid thing?" her face contorted in rage.

My feet dragged me to school as if I were Atlas carrying the load of the world on my back. One of my classmates who lived upstairs usually walked with me and we struck up a friendship. She too was considered an outcast at school. I shall never forget her mother. Sometimes, after a vicious verbal attack by my mother I would rush out of the kitchen through the back door exit and perch on the fire escape to recover. Often my friend's mother would quietly creep down the stairs and pat me on the shoulder and whisper, "Don't worry. You're so smart. I'm sure you're going to go a long way in your life." I'd feel grateful and lonely at the same time.

The last few weeks offered the final punch. My mother admonished me for not getting the top marks in the province on the matriculation exams. "You always did so well, then when it came to the end of school, when it really matters, you let your grades slip," she hurled at me. True, by that point I was running around with boys, nevertheless that wasn't the reason. I think I deliberately messed up because this time I knew it would bother her that she wouldn't be able to brag to her friends. I did achieve grades in the highest percentile in all my subjects and would have no problem getting into McGill University. I was awarded the highest marks in the Province of Québec in Latin, and was truly elated. My mother couldn't have cared less about Latin.

Even so, I was becoming more hopeful about the future. A boy I had been dating on and off invited me to the prom and this time I bought a dress by myself. I didn't want to hear my mother tell me how skinny I looked. I had my own money because I worked part-time at Eaton's department store downtown, the largest one in Montréal. Being bilingual was a real asset in terms of securing jobs. As an employee, I got 25% off. I bought a canary yellow lace A-line dress with light brown suede pumps and ankle straps and a purse to match. I was also able to afford a spectacular pair of gold plated dangling earrings in the shape of butterflies and a bright yellow velvet bow which held my long hair all piled up on my head.

My date, Keith, showed up at my house with a wrist corsage of pale pink roses and sprigs of baby's breath. He was a classmate who came from the "right" side of the tracks, well-mannered and well meaning, and I knew that he adored me, but to tell the truth I couldn't adore any boy at that point in my life. I pretended to be his girlfriend, in order to attend the prom. I am not proud of that. When he asked me to "go steady" at the end of the evening I simply said, "No, thank-you." "Why not?" he asked incredulous. "I thought we had such a good time and that you wanted to be my girlfriend."

Keith knew I was from the "wrong" side of the tracks, and so, if anything, "going steady" would be a step up for me. That somehow wasn't important to me. The problem was that he was not a terribly bright student and had little confidence in himself. The few times I met his parents at school events, I sensed that his father bullied him. Meanwhile his mother was the proverbial "dishrag" who seemed to have to agree with everything her husband demanded. An imposing man, his father, very tall and impeccably dressed, was some sort of investment broker and I felt that he thought he owned the world, especially his son. I was turned off by this and wanted no part of that stifling scene.

All I could say to my prom companion was, "I'm sorry, I'm entering the Honors French Literature Program at McGill, so I won't have any time for dates because I'll have to study non-stop." Keith's mouth dropped open. He hadn't expected a girl of my social-economic background to get into McGill. (I was one of the few who did make the grade.) He looked as if I had knocked the wind out of him. (I found out later that he hadn't been accepted to McGill but rather to a run-of-the-mill college in town. His father must have been furious.) I didn't know what to say and retreated behind a "thank you very much for the corsage and for such a beautiful evening." I closed the front door behind me and slouched against the vestibule wall, tears rolling down my face and onto my exquisite lace dress.

21

HOME FOR THE AGED

In preparation for the expenses I would incur at McGill, I searched for part-time work in my fourth year of high school and was overjoyed when I was offered a well-paying job at a Home for the Aged (that's what it was called then) located near my house. I was interviewed in April by the supervisor of Dietary Service, a nutritionist who looked like she ran a tight ship. Mrs. Ferguson, tall and buxom with flaming red hair, exuded a no-nonsense attitude but she was not unkind. I answered her questions honestly and told her how much I needed this job in order to be able to afford being at McGill. She must have been in her late thirties or early forties while I hadn't even turned 18 yet. Sitting behind her office desk she fixed her sea green eyes on me and said matter-of-factly, "You have the job but it is difficult physical work. Are you up to it?" I replied with a breathless "Yes." Mrs. Ferguson (I never, ever called her by her first name Margaret) led me down to a locker in the basement and gave me my key. The workers were all climbing into their uniforms. The pink uniform, which also included a white starched apron and a pink cap (into which I crammed in all my hair) was waiting for me inside the locker. We shook hands and I began a part-time shift the following day – and then full-time in mid-May once my high school matriculation exams were over.

On that first day I made the mistake of wearing sandals. What was I thinking? Mrs. Ferguson looked down at my feet disparagingly. I didn't understand why until later. I discovered what it means to be on one's feet all day, sprinting back and forth, in and out of the kitchen, and into the dining room carrying trays full of food and drink, as well as running up and down flights of stairs. By the time I got home that first day I felt like I was ready to be admitted to the same institution. My feet were swollen to what seemed like twice their normal size and I could hardly get them out of the sandals. I soaked them in a pail of hot water and Epsom salts and wore sturdy oxford shoes thereafter. The learning curve was steep in terms of keeping on top of all of the duties necessary for proper food preparation. As time went on, I learned the routine and became more at ease. I even became friendly with many of the regular staff, most of whom were Black women from the Caribbean. At first they had ignored me as a young "college girl" who was there only because she needed money for school and could fly in and out of that job at any time she wished. They, however, were providing not only for themselves but were also sending remittances back to families in their home countries. Most of them were from Jamaica. I adored their accents and told them so. They seemed utterly shocked by this. I remember the day, several weeks later, when they first included me wholeheartedly in their conversations during breaks and lunchtimes. In hushed tones, they passed around pictures of their children back home – many of whom were born out of wedlock and living with grandparents or aunts. I felt flattered to have been included in their "secret" conversations at break time.

There were six or seven floors in the building and nearly 30 residents in all. Each floor constituted a world unto its own. One of the two industrial-sized kitchens was on the fourth floor, and the other was on the fifth. Dining rooms were attached to each of the two kitchens. I was assigned to the fifth floor where many of the residents suffered from dementia or Alzheimer's (although this term had not yet been coined at the time). The entire place was immaculately clean with cheerful pictures on the corridor walls and in the dining rooms. Large windows allowed ample streams of light to flow in. And each round table – set for four or five people – was always covered with a sparkling white tablecloth and a fresh floral centerpiece.

One day, as I was pouring hot coffee for a crotchety old man, he threw the steaming cup at my face. "This coffee is too cold!" he shouted. Luckily, I had ducked just in time. Upon hearing the commotion, Mrs. Ferguson rushed out of the kitchen and put an arm around me as the man was hurriedly wheeled away by a nurse. I was grateful that nothing worse had happened. Mrs. Ferguson looked chagrined, and whispering, she confided to me that this man's behavior was becoming more and more angry and paranoid. It upset me that this old man should have taken such a dislike toward me, but the supervisor's words soothed me. I can still see him furiously shaking his almost translucent arm at me. Today we know more about the symptoms of dementia and Alzheimer's disease. Perhaps I reminded him of a family member who never came to visit him. That was also the case for many of the residents, many of whom had children who lived far away. There were few visitors.

Mrs. Kaye

One morning, two days after I had begun work, Mrs. Ferguson asked me to deliver a book to a certain resident on my floor. It was to a room at the end of a hallway and as I knocked on its open door, an elderly woman sitting in a wheelchair glanced up at me with such a mournful expression in her gray-blue eyes. Somehow, I immediately felt drawn to her. Was it the color of her eyes which reminded me of my father's, or was it her mournful expression? Or both. As I handed Mrs. Kaye the book she asked whether I had a moment to sit down and have a chat. I did. And within about a half-hour, we had both "adopted" each other. Had Mrs. Ferguson planned for this to happen? I'll never know. But from that moment on, I would visit Mrs. Kaye in her room in that alcove every chance I got – and usually after my day's work. Each time I entered I felt as if I had stepped into another world. Her room exuded privacy and elegance and smelled of a fresh meadow. A cherry wood dresser and matching chest of drawers stood proudly near a large window adorned by lace curtains. A blue and pink oriental rug decorated the floor. A glass vase with fresh cut flowers always sat atop her bed table (also made of cherry wood). I remember orange roses, yellow lilies, pink tulips and stunning sunflowers.

A large sepia-colored gold-framed picture graced one end of the dresser: a handsome young man with thick black hair all dressed up in a black tuxedo, wearing a white ruffled shirt and black bowtie holding the hand of a blond woman (she looked so young). She wore a shimmering wedding dress with beautiful lace swirls and floral designs which were embroidered over a cream-looking lace background. Her delicate face was covered in a white lace veil and her dress was designed with a v-neckline in the front, lace trim, and pleated ruffles on the cuffs of her elbow length sleeves. The gown flowed on the ground around her as she was holding a bouquet of assorted flowers. She looked like the princess in a fairy tale. I asked her when had this wedding picture been taken? In June 1903. She was 23 years old and had just completed her degree at McGill – which meant she was born in 1880. Oh, how I wish I had taken a photo of Mrs. Kaye and of that wedding picture. Today that would have been so easy to do with my iPhone.

At the other end of the dresser was a second picture – also in black and white – of a baby propped up in an old-fashioned English pram. The child was wearing a frilled bonnet as well as shirt and pants. Finally, a picture of a handsome man in a formal suit and tie, with a briefcase in hand, took center stage on Mrs. Kaye's dresser. White doilies had been positioned underneath each of the three pictures. The bride and groom were Mrs. Kaye and her husband of 55 years; Mr. Kaye had died ten years earlier in his eighties. He had been a lawyer – a partner in a law firm in Montréal. The little baby was their son who "now lives far away" although I never found out exactly where. "He is a busy successful person, also a lawyer, so he doesn't have much time to come and visit," Mrs. Kaye explained in a small voice.

I visited Mrs. Kaye during breaks at least two or three times a week to share tea and cookies. The corridor to her room, brightly painted in a deep yellow, had several landscape paintings on its walls. Her striking blue eyes lit up whenever I walked in. I enjoyed how the light would play on the design of hand painted pink roses and blue bows on the porcelain of her tea set. (At the time I could not know that it was Limoges bone china.) It was like enjoying a tea party in a magnificent garden. Mrs. Kaye was frail, all skin and bones. She remained in her room most of the time and her meals were brought in to her. I don't know whether that was her personal choice or whether it was a medical decision. I did get a sense though that she did not want to mingle with most of the others there. She seemed to prefer staying in her room and reading.

A pile of books stood on the side table near her bed. I glanced at some of the authors: Ernest Hemingway, James Joyce, Hannah Arendt, Winston Churchill, Aldous Huxley, Vladimir Nabokov, Henry James, among others. We did eventually have many deep discussions about literature, particularly when I visited after my shift was over in the afternoon. Although we had come from such different cultures, there was so much we shared in common. As she sat in her wheelchair next to her bed, I sensed her melancholy. Her neck, although wrinkled and bony, looked like a ballerina's. Some weeks into my visits a nurse took me aside to confide that Mrs. Kaye insisted on having her (this nurse) help her put on her best outfits, comb her snow-white hair into a bun and complete the look with pearl earrings and necklace before my visits.

I sat in a velvet green-and brown-striped armchair (it looked as if it had come from her dining room). All the furniture in her room had obviously come from her former home, in an upscale neighborhood in Outremont not far from where the late Prime Minister Pierre Elliot Trudeau's family had lived. She regaled me with stories about the Trudeau household and how close Grace – Pierre's mother – was to him, the middle and the most precocious of her three children. "I always knew that Pierre, that whippersnapper, would end up doing something important in his life." She clasped her arthritic hands in mine and told me that she adored the name Grace and how it suited me. She made me feel special. "Where did you get such thick golden hair?" she would marvel. At the time I had colored my naturally medium-brown hair to strawberry blond – a contrast with my dark brown eyes.

Mrs. Kaye didn't tell me much about her life except that she missed her husband terribly and that she couldn't wait to join him in heaven. She asked me about my future plans. "What are your aspirations, dear? Remember, it's important to have a profession." She was delighted to hear that I was about to begin my undergraduate program at McGill. "Women think all they need to do is find a man, get married and have babies. They need more than that to feel good about themselves. I was lucky that my parents encouraged me," she said.

Her father, originally from England, became a surgeon at the Royal Victoria Hospital near McGill and her mother met him, as a nurse at the same hospital. Mrs. Kaye was their only child and they had doted on her. She received a degree from McGill at a time when few women students were admitted. Even so, she was not on the regular campus. She attended McGill's Teachers' College in suburban Ste-Anne de Bellevue, some 20 miles from Montreal. She ended up teaching English at Baron Byng High School, a school in a predominantly Jewish immigrant neighborhood on St. Urbain Street which became famous because of who had attended it. Many students from that school grew up to become noteworthy Canadians, such as the author Mordechai Richler, songwriter Leonard Cohen, poets A.M. Klein and Irving Layton, and medical researcher Philip Seeman, to name a few.

I brought little party sandwiches, chocolates, pastries or other goodies to Mrs. Kaye (all approved by Mrs. Ferguson, of course) and the two of us would enjoy them in a leisurely manner as we chatted in the afternoon hours. It felt like such a reward after a hard day of work for me. (I had the breakfast-lunch shift, so I began work at 6 a.m. and ended at 2 p.m.) What a pleasure to watch Mrs. Kaye's appetite increase whenever we ate together – so much so, that I was encouraged by the nurses to spend time with her whenever I was able. She finished everything on her plate whenever I was there.

As for my part, Mrs. Kaye gave me a taste of the loving attention that a grandmother could give. The nurses chimed in every time they saw me: "You can come visit your granny any time." *Granny!* The word filled my heart with warmth. However, I was intimidated by Mrs. Kaye's background of high English-Canadian privilege and was very surprised by her interest in me. I hesitated to tell her about my Holocaust background and of my parents' emotional damage, worrying that it might turn her away from me. When it finally slipped out one afternoon, she took my young smooth hands into her old gnarled ones.

Her eyes turned into oceans of cloudy blue. "What can I say except that such evil is beyond what our Lord should allow. I am so terribly sorry for what happened to your family and to you. You must fight hard to allow yourself to have a good life." I could hardly take in her kindness towards me. I even told her about the incident that had occurred years earlier when that woman in another nursing home hurled antisemitic epithets at me as I hurried past her every morning on my way to school.

"Oh yes, I know such people," Mrs. Kaye responded with a shake of her head. "That sinful behavior is all around us. What a world we live in. Don't let it destroy you, my dear. That is what they want. Rise above it." I burst into tears and Mrs. Kaye bent over from her wheelchair and gathered me into her delicate arms.

In mid-August Mrs. Kaye died, three months after I met her. I missed her terribly. I would walk by her empty room where a piece of my heart remained. Two weeks later my first year at McGill University began.

PART II

22

FIRST YEAR AT MCGILL

On that first morning of my first semester at McGill University the world was transformed into technicolor. It was the late 60s with the counterculture in full swing. Still living at home, I climbed onto the bus at the end of my street and sat down in a seat, sensing myself moving farther and farther away from the stifling atmosphere of my home life. The money I had made from my job at the Home for the Aged was used for books and for the latest styles in clothes. (I had also received a bursary to cover tuition). I arrived on campus wearing a knitted mini dress way above the knee in bold-colored plaids and stripes, together with printed tights (that was the rage then). None of us students knew where anyone else had come from. I breathed in a refreshing sense of hope in this anonymity. I could start over again.

Most of my courses were housed in a stone building with an impressive entrance near the Student Union. Peterson Hall, then the center for modern languages, still stands on McTavish Street in Montréal. A three-story stone building, the first floor sported a comprehensive library and administrative offices, classrooms on the second, and professors' offices on the third. I cavorted with French and French-Canadian playwrights and authors – Corneille,

Racine, Molière, Sartre, Claudel, Mauriac, Flaubert, Blais, Roy, and many others. I devoured all the readings like a starved wolf.

Almost immediately I became friends with a girl named Natalie in my Honors French class who came from Nova Scotia. She lived in a dorm on campus – her father was a chemist and so she could afford the cost. I also had a crush on my French professor. He was the proverbial "tall, dark and handsome" man, in his thirties or early forties. Natalie and I would visit him in his office after class and discuss, in French, the existential woes of *la condition humaine* and *le péché originel*. We wore short dresses, flimsy blouses, mini-skirts. Le Professeur Thériault told me that he thought that I "ran the risk of being too intelligent for my own good." These visits stopped as Natalie and I became less and less comfortable over time with the way Monsieur Thériault was looking at us. We were innocents and we didn't yet understand the power of our physical youth.

Also, I began to spend more time at the Student Union with other students. This was the place where one could fritter away many hours in socializing, card playing, and in all sorts of other non-academic activities. I fell in with a group that came from an English suburb of Montréal and I was beginning to feel a sense of camaraderie with them. Then one afternoon, as I was sitting at a card table with some of the girls, watching the boys playing cards and drinking beer, I heard these words coming out of the mouth of the guy who was considered the most popular. (He looked like a mix of James Dean and Robert Redford.) "Did you notice how many Jews they are letting in now? They're always trying to take over everything. And don't those Jewish girls look fat?" I felt as if I had been hit by a MAC truck. I realized they had no idea that I was Jewish. My surname was Polish and I guess I didn't fit the stereotype. I was rail thin.

I quickly got up from my seat and said, "I'm not fat and I'm Jewish, so you don't know what you're talking about." It was the best I could do in that unexpected moment. They all paled and I heard the guy saying as I walked away, "It was only a joke!"

From then on, I avoided the Student Union. No great loss. It was filled with kids who were doing poorly in their classes and I was focused on getting good grades. I started to spend many hours every day seated at a carrel in the oak-paneled Redpath Library, studying. Such peace I felt in that place. I stayed as late as possible and rarely went home for dinner. I ate in the restaurants around McGill with classmates and budding friends. Ben's Smoked Meat, a diner just a couple of blocks from campus was my favorite. This place – with short-order cooks working their magic in the kitchen and with pictures on the walls of the many movie stars who had eaten there – was a mecca. The brisket that had been smoked in pickling spices for hours came to the table piping hot and piled high in strips on rye bread, together with a cup of coleslaw and another of mustard and a side of French fries, golden and tart. I have never tasted better French fries anywhere in the world than these *patates frites* from Ben's (except maybe those made by my friend Françoise's mother back when I was a child).

The smoked meat tasted as soft as butter. I usually ended with "Dad's Oatmeal Cookies." On evenings when I had studied particularly hard, I permitted myself a slice of hot apple pie topped with a scoop of vanilla ice cream. The flaky crust and cinnamon spice caressed my taste buds. Then I would return to the library with renewed vigor. This minimized my time at my home much to the displeasure of my mother. But she said little because I was studying – and how could she criticize that?

I was flying high in that first year deeply immersed in all the books in my courses. Even the less interesting professors fascinated me. What mattered was they cared and shared their love of literature with us. Most of them read out passages as if on stage. They discussed the assigned readings in excited voices with their hands moving everywhere. The classes seemed like an interactive play. No student fell asleep there. And for "mood music" while I studied for exams in the basement at my home I listened to Charles Aznavour – the popular French singer – on my record player. My other courses were Classics (mainly Latin literature), English literature in the Age of Chaucer, Interpreting Shakespeare,

Introductory Modern Russian literature, and Modern German literature.

One evening, at a gathering in Natalie's dorm sitting room reserved for "gentlemen callers," I met a guy who was in third year, well on his way towards an engineering degree. Tom struck me as being a solid and amiable fellow with an intense sense of purpose. He was very tall with dark wavy hair and built like a football player. There was a twinkle in his sky-blue eyes that made me feel safe. We had fun dates together; we started to go out regularly, to movies, plays, parties. Big and strong, Tom had a gregarious way about him and a protective tone in his voice. I enjoyed how sheltered I felt in his company. The only problem turned out to be that he indicated an interest in having an exclusive relationship with me. I told him I couldn't commit, nevertheless he kept going out with me anyway, probably hoping for a change in my attitude. We often had heavy petting sessions in his car but I was too afraid to go "all the way." He respected that.

Tom invited me to a fraternity party. I had never before been to a frat house and felt like I was moving up in the world. One Saturday evening, Tom picked me up at my friend's dorm and off we went. He looked very handsome in a dark formal suit and striped silk blue tie that matched his eyes. I had dressed to the nines feeling sexy in a maroon velvet mini-dress embroidered with tiny red roses and a soft brown leather belt that cinched my narrow waist. The high heels I wore accentuated my long legs. I flung a lacy black shawl around my shoulders. We arrived at the frat house, located in a stately old stone mansion with an imposing turret on a hilly street off the main thoroughfare, Sherbrooke Street, near McGill. The guy stationed at the door was dressed in a tuxedo and held a list of names. He asked for Tom's surname and Tom gave it to him. "I'm sorry, we don't allow Jews into our frat house," the door-guy said matter-of-factly. Tom was actually Catholic but had a Jewish sounding name.

"I'm not Jewish," he replied. "I'm Roman Catholic." We were whisked in immediately. I couldn't help feeling guilty that I hadn't said anything about my being Jewish to the frat boy and I had a hard time enjoying myself that evening. The outsider once again. I told Tom about it during one of the dances and we left and had a long conversation at Ben's Diner over smoked meat. Tom was very sympathetic but I felt he couldn't really understand how raw my heart was.

In all fairness, Tom was a caring person and said that he would go back to that fraternity and chew them out. I told him to leave it alone but he did go back to tell them how their antisemitic comment had hurt me. He said to me that he should have called them on their behavior right at the moment it happened. I appreciated the gesture even though at that time I was much too wounded to know how to accept his care. I just wanted to flee the scene, so-to-speak. Tom, however, wanted very much to protect me. I realize now how much he must have loved me. But I couldn't fall in love with him at the time. It did feel good to be with him but it was either bad timing, or more likely, I just couldn't see him (or anybody else) as becoming my life partner. Tom was a real "doer" whereas I was looking for a real "thinker." I broke it off at the end of the academic year and felt fragile and forlorn about the whole thing.

A great consolation was that my studies were going extremely well. In that first year, along with French, I passed English, Russian, German and Latin with flying colors. I won Highest Marks in German in that first year. All of which combined into a heady beginning for my entry into a new world.

23

JET-LAG IN PARIS

In my second year at McGill, I decided to study Italian literature. It had been a toss-up between Spanish and Italian. I had recalled the Sunday mornings of my childhood when I would watch local Italian-Canadian singers perform on television. Their songs reached out to me as if I were personally being serenaded. I was smitten. Not only did I choose Italian; it chose me. To this day, when I am amongst Italians, the sun always cuts through the clouds. Many people have commented that when I speak Italian, my voice, my mannerisms and even my spirit seem to change.

That year I entered a competition sponsored by the Italian Department and won. I was awarded a scholarship by the Italian government to study at the *Università Per Stranieri* in Perugia from April to October, all expenses (airfare and accommodations and even some spending money) were covered. I was never to be the same again. Just as for Cinderella, my Fairy Godmother showed up right on time. When I read and re-read the letter informing me of my scholarship to Perugia six months earlier on its embossed paper and its elegant letterhead of the Government of Italy, it occurred to me that the landscape of my life might be transformed forever. I was completely unprepared for this and yet I had always longed for it.

My parents were terribly over-protective and too emotionally impoverished to have been able to see this gift for what it was: a step toward a bright and fulfilling professional future. It required a visit from my Italian professor, Michelangelo Picone, to convince them that I would be safe and well taken care of. They did finally give in, but I was left with a distinct ambivalence about this great opportunity. I moved as if with lead boots on my feet while I packed my suitcase, laden with the fears of my parents. Guilt took hold of me and it required all the energy I had to say goodbye to them at the airport. My mother wept at the departure gate as if I was going off to war, never to return. People turned and stared, wondering what incredible misfortune had befallen us.

Paris was to be my first stop during that study trip. I had bought a student ticket in downtown Montréal months earlier. My friend Natalie and I planned to first visit Paris as a stopover and then to spend a month in my ancestral homeland, Israel. She would return to Montréal while I was to continue onwards to begin my program in Perugia. The flight path was to be Montréal-Paris-Tel Aviv-Rome. Unfortunately, Natalie became ill and was unable to make the trip. Suddenly, I was on my own at age 18. I was going to Paris, solo. All alone! I had to pay homage to the city which Madame Simon had so passionately described in our French classes.

I still see myself in a seat over the wing on that Air France flight peering out the window dazed by the bright sunshine above the clouds before we made our final early morning descent. I uttered a silent statement to myself that *this* is what I wanted in my life. "*Madame Simon, je suis arrivée!*" were the words that swept through my mind as the airplane touched down. I moved through the immigration line as in a dream, lugged my suitcase onto the metro and then dragged it to a hotel off Boulevard St-Michel. I checked in at the desk and then jammed the valise into the tiny elevator. Finally, I opened the door of my matchbox size room. The bed took up most of the space and opposite was a wall with a small dresser and a closet that could hold at most three or four items. Ahhh, but there was a window. I rushed straight to it and looked out over the silver rooftops of the city. I never asked what any of it meant. I just stared out in awe and wonder at the gift that had been offered.

The second thing I did was to place a holy picture of Mother Mary on the dresser. I had also brought my small elegant 14-karat gold medallion of Mary. I had found it several years earlier in a jewelry shop in Montréal. I didn't allow the fact that it was expensive deter me. I had money thanks to my part-time jobs and so I could afford it. As a teenager, I had begun to wear it daily around my neck though I would take it off when I got home. (Even though I was Jewish, I had "adopted" Mother Mary as my protector way back when I was five years old. She was my special secret and helped me through many anxiety-laden episodes as I was growing up.) One morning my mother had been rummaging through my purse (without permission) and found the medallion. She railed at me: "How dare you wear that thing when all your relatives died in concentration camps?" Her coal-black eyes burned and I felt like a traitor sentenced to life imprisonment.

My mind was in a jet-lag fog as I washed my face, brushed my teeth, re-applied make-up, put on a fresh blouse, changed from jeans to a skirt and left the hotel room. I sauntered down the narrow staircase to go outdoors. Then my heart skipped a beat when I passed the telephone booth on the landing. My mother had ordered me to call immediately after I checked into the hotel. I hurried past the booth feeling as if I had just robbed a bank. I left my key at the hotel desk and strode out into the shining light of the bustling Paris morning.

People were already sitting at cafés reading newspapers or chatting while they sipped steaming espressos and savored *confiture* on their baguettes. It looked like those pictures of Paris in my French textbooks at school. Interesting, sophisticated French people. I had always desperately wished I could jump into those scenes and leave my life behind. I sat down at one of the cafés and ordered a *croque* and a cup of rich espresso. In an instant I became one of the characters in my French textbooks. I couldn't help sweeping my long hair up into a chignon using a barrette. And poof – I suddenly began to *feel* Parisian! I ordered a second cup of coffee because the jet-lag was strong but I refused to give in to it. I was intent on exploring *le quartier*.

I began to wander about, stunned by the architecture and tree-lined *grands boulevards* which invariably spilled into still more picturesque smaller streets. Every corner looked like an impressionistic painting. I became lost in a haze of artistic doorways, métro stops and parks, churches, newspaper and flower kiosks. On that mild day with cerulean blue skies, it hit me: this was *Springtime in Paris,* in fact *April in Paris.* I kept walking alone surrounded by *les Parisiens* going about their daily routines, overwhelmed by the acrid smells coming from the sewers and *pissoirs.* I delighted in the sounds of the French language that surrounded me, sounds that had given me so much solace and hope when I was a child. I became a pilgrim, a sojourner, a lost soul searching for her heart just three months before her 19th birthday.

I stopped walking for a moment, stood still and looked up at the skies and did what anyone who first arrives in Paris should do: offer a prayer of thanks. The prayer was laced with a tinge of confusion and a lot of guilt as I stood standing at the intersection of my private and public world, with roots that reached back to my earliest childhood. My shabby existence had been swept up by some great current of the Universe. This was the first time I knew for sure that life was really worth living.

I passed *une boulangerie* whose *pâtisseries* looked inviting. I strolled inside and asked the server whether I should order the *millefeuille* or the *éclair,* both of which I knew well from Montréal. He was surprised that I spoke French so fluently. "Vous êtes americaine?" he asked.

"Non, je suis canadienne, de Montréal," I replied. "Ah maintenant je comprends," he moved his arm with a flourish as he suggested the *millefeuille.* I stood at a counter table and my mouth slithered into the creamy texture made up of three layers of puff pastry, and two layers of fresh *crème pâtissière.* My tongue skated across the topping glazed with alternating white icing and chocolate strips.

Outdoors again, I came upon a lingerie boutique. The lacy

undergarments in the window were so glamourous that I couldn't resist. Très chic! I walked in and began chatting with the saleswoman. Upon hearing that I hailed from Montréal, she told me that she had a cousin who lived there and that she was planning to visit her. I ended up walking out with several silky camisoles and underwear that made me feel unbelievably sexy and alive. I was reinventing myself. The saleswoman had told me that I looked French. Madame Simon would have been proud. I walked to the Seine which was gleaming in the sunshine and spotted a *bateau-mouche* tethered to the sidewall. Stalls with the paintings of artists were strewn all along the embankment just as they are today. The more I walked the more I felt that I was becoming liberated. I thought then (and I still do now) that if beauty can heal, then having an opportunity to be in this city could rid one of many ills.

The author Adinarayana of India wrote that "walking is a prayer with feet." I loved the rhythm of walking from larger areas to smaller more intimate ones, tiny enclaves discovered unexpectedly. I popped in and out of all sorts of bookstores and antique shops on winding streets and alleyways. I visited *Shakespeare and Company*, the famous English language bookstore and literary shrine. On these eloquent streets, and in these shops conversing with people, I delighted in hearing my voice. Yet, every time I passed a phone box I felt like I was being chased (I had still not called home) and I quickened my step. I became afraid to stop walking. Then without warning I broke out in a sweat of panic.

Suddenly, I remembered the girl in the fairy tale, *The Red Shoes,* where the red ballet slippers were given to her by a demonic shoemaker in order to control her and force her to keep dancing until her death. I should have gone back to my hotel room but I was too agitated and kept walking, walking, walking. By sunset I ended up in Montparnasse and my feet had turned into lead. Every muscle in my body ached. As I searched for a café where I could find a seat and refresh myself, I could not divert my eyes from the burnt orange of the sky, colors that were wild and yet gentle at the same time. It turned out that it was not hard to find a café. Montparnasse after all had been the epicenter of the "Roaring

Twenties" or *Les Années Folles* [The Crazy Years], that manic interwar period where many American ex-pats, artists, writers, intellectuals and political exiles daily and nightly congregated in cafés.

In front of me stood Le Sélect, one of the historic cafés with its open *terrasse* and interwoven green and beige seats. The ghosts of those decadent years intermingled with the ghosts of World War II which had arrived not that long afterward. I tried to picture this place in its heyday of collective insanity, a harbinger of the horrors of World War II that was to come. Again, I was reduced to feeling like a traitor and ingrate. My parents never had the opportunity of enjoying life in the moment. What the hell did I think I was doing? And they were probably panicking because I still hadn't phoned them. I actually thought I might faint. I quickly sat down at a table and ordered a glass of sweet Muscadet. And then another one. My overwrought brain was finally beginning to chill. I sat for a while people-watching (of course) and also imagining all the famous conversations, the laughter, the sketching, the writing that took place in Montparnasse. I imagined Ernest Hemingway, Pablo Picasso, James Joyce and Gertrude Stein sitting in that very café. Eventually it grew dark and in a kind of stupor I hailed a taxi and made it back to my hotel. I fell into a deep sleep.

The music that permeated all the cafés and bistros seemed bittersweet to me. I could disappear into the songs of pop singer Françoise Hardy. Her soft melodious voice could be heard on the radio and in so many restaurants and it stirred something within me. And, wonder of wonders, I looked a lot like her, with long chestnut brown hair (I had returned to my natural color after several years of strawberry blond), big eyes (although hers were deep blue and mine dark brown), slim body and a heart-shaped face. English pop singer and songwriter Jane Birkin and her new partner Serge Gainsbourg were also wildly popular. Their song *"Je t'aime... Moi non plus"* was so erotic that it ended up being banned in some countries. Even in France one could only hear it late in the evenings.

And then there was the great Charles Aznavour and his *La*

Bohème. In Montréal I had fallen hopelessly in love with the nostalgia of *La Bohème*, a song about lost youth. When I first heard it in Montréal bitter tears fell from my eyes. The song brought out feelings of being a jilted lover. And in a profound way, that is exactly what I was. My father had "left" me (emotionally) for a younger girl, my baby sister, years ago. Suddenly in Paris, when I listened to the great Aznavour I wasn't alone. (Also, at that time I had no idea then that Aznavour was a child of Armenian genocide survivors.) I was a young woman, determined to enter a new life story. I had managed to escape to an exquisite royal ball as Cinderella had – at least for the time being.

24

SOJOURN IN ISRAEL

After my visit in Paris and before beginning my language studies in Perugia, my plan had been to spend four weeks in Israel, a longtime dream. I flew from Paris to Tel Aviv. I was young enough to feel that time was endless and that no decisions about my future were necessary. When the land of Israel came into view from the air, passengers started clapping and began singing the national anthem *Hatikvah* [The Hope]. I stepped off the airplane onto the tarmac and the sweet, warm air hugged me. Some passengers bent down and kissed the ground. I was so far away from the place where I had been born and raised, and yet here everything seemed as if I had already lived it.

I stayed with a distant relative of my father's, Mendel (Meniek), who had survived the war. Mendel was older than my father and a tailor by trade. I remember him as a slight and gentle man with soft blue eyes and a receding hairline. His wife, Sura, was a stout, vivacious woman who cooked mouthwatering meals. The more I ate, the more she cooked. It was a relationship that blossomed quickly. Mendel would awaken me each morning with a ceremonial knock at my bedroom door and a cloth napkin wrapped over his forearm pretending to be an elegant waiter in the finest of restaurants. We joked and laughed but I noticed the tattoo of digits on his wrist. We communicated in Yiddish: "*Gut morgen. Wie hast du geschlofen? Bitte, kum arayn fur den fruhshtuck.*" [Good morning. How did you sleep? Please come in for breakfast.] Mendel loved to play-act and I was enchanted by his broad smile.

Their only son, Shlomo, was older than me. I never got to meet him because he had left Israel after his military service for a teaching post in Europe. I knew that he had been born in 1946 in a DP camp. I had been told by my parents that he had been a "difficult" child and had to be moved around among various schools. It is hard to fathom the challenges of being an only child of Holocaust survivors. Several years after my trip, he did return to Israel with a European woman who became his wife. They settled in Haifa where he taught in a college and she became a physical therapist.

I was to stay with Meniek and his wife Sura for a week at the beginning of the trip and several more days at the end. They lived in a modest flat on the third floor of a six-story apartment building in Tel Aviv. Each morning I would open the window shutters, stare out at the cloudless sky, and listen to the chattering of birds and to the mélange of Hebrew and Arabic songs coming from radios in other apartments. I started catching Hebrew words as though they were butterflies. I rolled Hebrew names along my tongue and began to enjoy my given Hebrew name *Zehavah* [the Golden One]. Arabic words sounded even more exotic. Radio stations came in from nearby Jordan and many Israeli stations also carried Arabic. I felt that I was where I was meant to be. It surprised me that I could feel this way, so quickly. When I finally made the long-distance call to my parents, it was from the safety of Mendel and Sura's hospitality. When my mother asked why I hadn't called from Paris ("I almost lost my mind wondering what happened to you") I simply passed the phone to Mendel and Sura.

Bursts of anemone flowers, red, purple, yellow, white, ubiquitous in Israel, and irises, lilies, roses bloomed everywhere and I felt as if I too was unfolding as their petals welcomed me. Birdsong filled my heart with dreams. I learned that Israel's location on their migration route from Europe and Western Asia to Africa is responsible for the large number of bird species in the country. The words from the biblical "Song of Solomon": *"The flowers appear on the earth; the time of the singing of birds is come"* … *"I am the rose of Sharon, and the lily of the valleys"* rang in my ears.

The skyscapes of golden orange, deep apricot, wild plum and glowing cherry-red, were magnificent. Families would often eat dinner on picnic tables in the nearby park. Large pots of food as well as tablecloths, napkins, plates, glasses and cutlery were laid out carefully on the tables. Everybody sampled each other's cooking. It reminded me of the French-Canadian neighbors of my childhood. That same down-to-earth vitality.

Each day I awoke in anticipation of a fresh adventure. In fact, I did become a tourist for while. I left Meniek and Sura a bit sadly. They had become like doting grandparents. However, I knew I would see them at the end of my trip. I took tours: to the Dead Sea, to Masada, to the Galilee, to a kibbutz, to the tomb of the Patriarchs and to the tomb of the Matriarch Rachel. All of the stories from the Old and New Testaments came alive. My anxieties were now officially on hold. My first glimpse of the Dead Sea startled me, in its arid melancholy and harsh, petrified beauty. I likened it to a moonscape, to a mystery unsolved. When I floated in the sea (it is impossible not to float in it because of its high salt content) all the tension in my muscles traveled toward the Judean mountains in the distance.

The tour to the Galilee offered radiant displays of streams and waterfalls, vast fields of greenery and colorful wildflowers, olive trees, Jewish holy sites, such as the graves of the sages and ancient synagogues in Safed [*Tsfat* in Hebrew] and Tiberias; farming communities and nature reserves. So fertile and verdant. Our tour group had dinner at one of these collective farms [*moshavim*] called Moshav Kinneret and stayed overnight. The view of the indigo blue of the Lake Kinneret (or Sea of Galilee) sparkled in the shimmering sun. The tour also offered many Christian sites. I was with tourists from many parts of the world who were tremendously excited to follow the places where Jesus had lived and preached. One stop was at a small church with a white stone facade where it was told in the Gospels that Jesus had turned water into wine by the request of his mother at the wedding in Cana. It was a charming little place and I sat down on a ledge nearby.

There we had a 10-minute break at a rest stop with a take-out eating place. It was hot and I ordered a falafel and vegetables and a large bottle of mineral water when a child came up to me and began to speak in English, asking where I was from. I told her I came from Canada and I asked her how she had learned English. It turned out she was an Arab child from this village, Kafr Cana, and she told me how she loved seeing the tourists and slowly learned more and more words with each tour that passed through. She wanted to become an English teacher. I told her I loved languages too and that I was on my way to Italy to continue my Italian studies. Her dark eyes framed by long lashes looked so eager. It was a sweet encounter and I shall always remember her hopeful face. I hope she became an English teacher.

After more than a week of touring, I spent several days at a convent near Jerusalem. My childhood which had been so enlivened by French-Canadians allowed me to become not only familiar with but also comforted by aspects of the Catholic faith – and especially my special connection to Mother Mary. Several nuns in Montréal were older sisters or aunts of my friends. So when I learned that the convent of the Sisters of Our Lady of the Ark of the Covenant [*Les Soeurs de Notre Dame de L'Arche de L'Alliance*] a French Order of St-Joseph in a hilltop village near Jerusalem rented guest rooms, I jumped at the chance. The entrance of the convent made of pale pink stone had an imposing white statue of Mary and Child on its roof. My room was on the second floor – simple, with a cot, a black crucifix on a white-washed wall, a desk, a wash basin and a simple rug on the mosaic tiled floor (mosaics that were the remains of the Byzantine era). Light streamed in through the window every morning as church bells chimed. The bathroom was outside in the hallway, always sparkling clean.

I was the only guest at the time, so it turned out to be a particularly intimate visit. The Sisters took care of me as though I was a baby chick and they the mother hens. I shared meals with them at a long rectangular table. I also helped with kitchen work. A sense of peace permeated my being as I scrubbed the pots and pans after meals. These meals were mainly vegetarian, middle Eastern in terms of spices. What stands out is *za'atar*, a richly scented and flavorful seasoning that blends the flavors of thyme, oregano, and a lemony citrus summer taste. It goes well on fresh doughy bread. I have found *za'atar* in Middle Eastern grocery stores in Toronto and that sharp tangy taste in my mouth recaptures the memory of that time.

I loved the chapel, a modest room at the edge of the cloister with wooden chairs facing a simple black cross on a white wall. The ceiling was decorated with frescoes of angels on a blue background framed in dark wood. A spacious courtyard adjoined the cloister. I sat and wrote on a stone bench there for hours surrounded by palm trees and fir trees and flowers.

What I cherished most were the conversations with Mother Superior, an efficient woman who was in her late seventies then, still tall and slim but with arthritic hands. Nonetheless she appeared strong and in control. We took an immediate liking to each other. Mother Superior and I spent hours discussing Judaism, Christianity and the Holocaust.

"I want you to know that I am Jewish, a child of Holocaust survivors," I told her. A kindly woman, she shared with me her deep regret that theology took a tragic turn in the Gospel of John with its message that the Jews had killed Jesus. "They were all Jews, including Jesus," she said in misery, "so that made no sense. And look at all the harm and destruction it has caused." Her hands wove a rosary around her gnarled fingers as she spoke.

I had not expected to find such an understanding of the roots of Christian theology. Her compassion soothed me. This was many years before Pope John Paul II officially apologized to the Jewish people for the antisemitism that is so deeply embedded in Christian theology. She held out her hands that were enveloped in the red beads of the rosary and reached out for mine. A clear image of the hands of dear Mrs. Kaye from the Home for the Aged in Montréal holding mine popped into my mind. We both wept and I lowered my head as Mother Superior prayed.

As planned, I returned to Meniek and Sura in Tel Aviv ten days later and then would take the regular bus into Jerusalem to wander around. One afternoon at a café near the Bezalel Institute of Art in Jerusalem, I met a young man, Yossef, who was working on his PhD program at the Technion, one of the world's leading scientific institutions. We began to go out together, to restaurants, movies, museums, and day trips. He was an up-beat, ambitious young man who had been born in Tunisia and immigrated to Israel as a ten-year-old with his parents and sisters in the early-1950s. I was invited several times to his parents' home in a suburb of Tel Aviv. It was comforting to be a part of a big, bustling family with Yossef's married sisters' children running about. And I enjoyed listening to his mother's lyrical Judeo-Arabic. I also noticed that they lived in an area that was considered lower middle-class, if that. Their apartment block exuded an overcrowded and drab feeling. The windows looked like they hadn't been cleaned in a long time, the balconies and doors and hallways were dark, paint peeling away. Even Meniek and Sura, my hosts, who were not at all affluent, lived in a building that was in better condition.

Yossef had dark thick hair and stormy charcoal eyes. He was also deeply reflective and I fell for him. We spent a week at kibbutz *Ein Shemer* where one of his sisters and her husband and their two-year-old child lived. The kibbutz is located in the Haifa district of Northern Israel a few miles from the town of Hadera on the Israeli Mediterranean coastal plain some 30 miles north of Tel Aviv. We stayed with Yossef's sister and her husband, in their tiny but comfortable house. There were few luxuries but they did have an indoor bathroom and hot water. I slept on the couch in their living room, while Yossef slept in a sleeping bag on the porch. To be honest, we ended up on the porch in his sleeping bag most nights making love (but not to the point of "going all the way," I just wasn't ready). I can't imagine that his sister and brother-in-law didn't hear us.

I helped out in the orange groves – grueling work in the hot sun – proud of how I was able to do tough outdoor physical work for the first time in my life. I picked oranges which glowed crimson in the fierce sun and climbed on ladders afraid that I might fall and break my neck. Nevertheless, I knew deep down that I wouldn't fall. Not there. I enjoyed helping out in the children's houses and the school. I watched toddlers who sat squirming in a circle listening to their teacher read stories. But what affected me most was the love with which the children were tucked in at nighttime by their caretakers. In those years children in the kibbutzim lived in group houses and not with their parents. Everyone ate in the dining hall. I was enthralled by the communal aspect of kibbutz life, so different from how I had grown up. Here was a new way of living and I grew tanned and fit on the kibbutz. In this organic, natural world of purpose and its common goals of restoration and recovery, I had felt it might be possible to carry my burdens in a more meaningful way.

As I write this, I realize that I had entered a fantasy while I was there. It all seemed so perfect because I was hungry for a more robust sense of being Jewish. The truth is that as a visitor I could ignore any interpersonal problems that invariably happen in communal living spaces. I found out years later that a friend of mine who had grown up in a kibbutz such as this one had mixed feelings about living in the children's group houses because she had only seen her parents one hour a day. She felt abandoned and frightened, nevertheless she knew that she was part of a group that did things that mattered in the world.

For me, at that time in my life, the kibbutz seemed to offer a sense of safety and community and I decided that I wanted to live on that kibbutz as a volunteer sometime in the future. I, who could still hear the screams of the children at Auschwitz over and over like an endless satanic tape, was being offered a new model. In Israel, instead of bleakness and despair, I could see energy and color and life for Jewish people. For the first time I felt that being

Jewish did not solely entail suffering and marginality. I knew that growing up with parents who were Holocaust survivors would not have been easy anywhere, but perhaps if I had been raised in Israel I would not have felt quite so alone or so out-of-place in mainstream society. In the days of my childhood no one in Canada spoke publicly about what had happened to the Jews of Europe; some were indifferent and looked away; for others it was too shocking in its magnitude, and they felt flooded with guilt and fear. The underlying message was that the victims should forget and move on. If only it could have been that easy. It is a tragedy that good and affordable psychological help was not available in those days in Canada. And certainly not for poor survivors such as my parents. Nobody wanted to be around victims. (The notion of PTSD did not enter the lexicon until the 1980s.) The established Jewish community felt guilty that they hadn't been able to do anything to help the European Jews. They endured their own unspoken feelings of remorse for their powerlessness in a Canadian society whose bureaucratic doors had shut its doors to Jewish immigration before, during and even immediately after the war.

Israel seduced me with the possibility of what seemed at the time to be "normalcy" for Jewish cultural identity. In the back of my mind, I began to formulate a plan to pursue a Masters Program in Comparative Literature at the Hebrew University in Jerusalem after graduation from McGill University, two years hence. I imagined that my nomadic existence, my existential wandering could finally come to an end. Yossef and I even discussed marriage and names for our future children!

Life would have different plans for me.

I had reserved several days to wander through the streets of Jerusalem. I had been waiting a long time to witness this special feeling of homecoming. Knowing that I was stepping on the same ground that the biblical characters had trod was both exciting and humbling. Every tiny alleyway led to some new discovery. On a street in downtown Jerusalem I saw a plaque with the words: *Talitha Kumi* [Wake up, Talitha], the site where Jesus brought Jairus' young daughter back to good health as she lay dying in her bed. The white Jerusalem stone buildings glittered in the sun. So did the gold of the Dome of the Rock as I sat on a balcony in the Department of Education at the Hebrew University overlooking the Old City.

I walked through ultra-Orthodox neighborhoods wearing a long shawl which hid my hair and a blouse reaching down past my elbows as well as a long skirt which flowed down to my ankles. Men in black caftans and black hats with and sidelocks hurried by, careful not to make eye contact with me, a woman they did not know. All the women wore kerchiefs and long skirts and long-sleeved blouses. They chattered with neighbors and friends while carrying bags of groceries and pushing baby carriages. Throngs of children ran about, playing noisily. I struck up conversations with people in shops and on the narrow dusty streets, using Yiddish, their language of communication. Nary a word in Hebrew because for them Hebrew is the holy tongue, reserved for spiritual purposes. "How is it that you speak Yiddish so naturally?" One woman wheeling a chubby baby in a stroller with a mop of jet-black hair asked me as I came out of a shop. A crew of at least four or five children stared up at me. Her older children.

"My parents come from Poland and we spoke Yiddish at home. They came to Canada after the war. My father had a surviving sister in Montréal so that's why they ended up there," I told her. A bunch of people, men as well as women, had congregated on the sidewalk. To them I was a novelty. One woman with three children, a girl and a boy of around three or four years old and a baby on her hip invited me to her home. I was flattered and readily accepted. Their small apartment looked rather dilapidated but I noticed two polished silver candlesticks on a shelf ready to be lighted for Shabbat. It was indeed Friday afternoon and she was baking *hallah* [egg bread]. A huge pot of chicken soup with vegetables was simmering on the stove. I breathed in the healing aroma. This woman did not look much older than me and already had three children.

"Can you stay for Shabbos meal tonight?" At first I was going to refuse, but then I thought, "Why not?" I called my hosts. They didn't mind. And I was curious to be in an ultra-Orthodox home for Shabbos. The young woman told me her name was Miriam and I told her that my Yiddish name was *Goldele* [little Golda]. I asked if I could help. She gave me a broom and I swept the vinyl floor. The two older children poured in from the street and created mayhem. Ultra-Orthodox families are not known for disciplining their children. "Do you keep kosher?" Miriam asked. I said I did not.

She told me to wash my hands and I was thankful there was no judgmental look on her face. I helped her take off the "ordinary" tablecloth and place a special white linen cloth on the table. She took the two silver candlesticks from a shelf and lovingly positioned them in the center of the table. When the oldest child, the four-year-old boy, asked why my long hair was uncovered, Miriam said that I wasn't married yet and that in any case she would bring in a kerchief for me before saying the Shabbat prayer.

"Not married yet?" exclaimed the little boy. "Isn't she getting old?" We both burst into laughter. His mother replied, "She will get married when God brings the betrothed He has chosen for her." I liked that.

At sundown her husband, a tall, thin intense young man in a wide-brimmed black hat and long black silk coat arrived from synagogue. He averted his gaze. We all stood around the table as Miriam lit the two candles, and waved her arms in a circular motion above the candles three times, as if she were gathering the light to her face. She then covered her eyes with her hands and said the blessing followed by a silent prayer. When Miriam uncovered her eyes, the family all said *Gut Shabbos*. On the table covered with a velvet navy-blue cloth embroidered with golden Hebrew letters were two braided *hallahs*. Then the father recited the *Kiddush,* the blessing over wine which gives thanks for the Sabbath and recalls the importance and holiness of resting. It welcomes the Divine Presence of God, the *Shechina*. The father also blessed the hallahs with a prayer and we all received a piece of the holy offering. I popped the soft moist piece into my mouth and couldn't help thinking about Holy Communion in the Catholic Church. Of course, I didn't say anything about that.

The father and children sat down. I helped Miriam bring out the fish first and then the chicken soup, meat, potatoes and *cholent*, a hot potato pudding adorned with onions, pepper, barley and beans. Savory with a hint of honey in the broth. I felt comfortable with both Miriam and her husband and told them how I had come to be in Israel. Then I began to realize that they were leading up to something. The husband gave his wife a nod and as if on cue she asked if I had ever considered becoming religious [*baalat tshuva*, returning to the faith]. I wasn't caught off guard by the question. Most ultra-Orthodox Jews try to bring secular Jews back to the fold when the opportunity arises. I gently told them that I do have faith but I was not ready for the gift of leading an ultra-Orthodox life. They were the ones who looked a bit startled. I think they were surprised at my use of the word "gift." To their credit, they did not press the matter further.

A visitor is always welcome at a Sabbath meal: it is a blessing to include at least one visitor to a Shabbat meal. It is just as important as welcoming in the Holy Spirit, the *Shechinah*. The candles flickered throughout the festive meal, and I let my mind wander. What would it be like to live in such a circumscribed but safe and secure world (or so it seemed to be from the outside). I realized later that I had the luxury (again) of skating over the interpersonal and intercommunal complications and just be "in the moment" and dream of what their lives were like. The candle flames shed light and embraced us in the darkness. (Using electricity is considered work, so lights were off except for a nightlight in the bathroom that had been turned on before sundown). Even the children calmed down. All was languid. I was thankful to be in communion with the *Shechinah* in this humble household of unwavering faith. The Divine Presence had brought stillness, gentleness. I let go as if in meditation. The father recited grace after the meal and we all said "Amen" and then it was time for bed. I stayed overnight in a sleeping bag on the living room floor. (One cannot drive on the Sabbath – that is considered work).

I woke up early to the sounds of boisterous children jumping about near me. Soon they and their father went to *shul* [synagogue] and Miriam and I had a chance to relax before the family would return for the midday meal. Again, she broached the subject of my being secular, this time in a more inquisitive way: "How does it feel to live in the world without protection? The secular world is so filled with temptation and iniquity. Why don't you allow God to bring you into full faith? It would be so much better for you."

I didn't want to start an argument but I had to say something that felt true to myself. "God is in my life in a way that is different from what you know. Perhaps it is more of a struggle for me and I do envy you your sense of security but I can't believe you don't have any problems in your life. God tests us all. I believe that God has not shut me out just because I don't follow the religion the same way you do. There has always been a tension between the secular and the religious in Judaism. That's what makes it so interesting." Her eyes grew wide and she slowly turned her head away and looked out the window with a puzzled expression. Perhaps she was taken aback at my form of devotion to the Almighty or maybe she thought I had blasphemed. I hoped I hadn't been unkind.

When the father and children returned home we sat down for the midday meal. We ate a meal of *laban* [yogurt cheese], smoked salmon, herring, tomatoes, cucumbers, olives, hummus, and that mouthwatering cholent (albeit cold because turning on a stove is considered work). This was all topped off with dried fruits and coffee cake. Everything had been prepared the day before. Everyone took a nap in the afternoon and later the husband went back to *shul*. I accompanied Miriam and her children to a neighbor's house for the afternoon reading of Bible stories to the children. The children listened carefully because there was always discussion afterward. Questions and answers were hurtled back and forth.

Finally, at dusk we celebrated *Havdalah* [separation]. This ceremony takes place after the appearance of at least three stars in the sky and it marks the symbolic end of the Sabbath and ushers in the beginning of the new week. The father lit a special *Havdalah* candle, a braided candle with several wicks, and said the appropriate blessing with a cup of wine. They passed their hands lightly over the intertwined flames.

"Do you know why we do this?" the father asked.

"No," I answered.

He sat like a prince on his chair presiding over the occasion. He had replaced his black hat with a black skullcap. I noticed for the first time that he had luminous dark eyes. His voice was soft and had an instructive tone, like that of a young rabbi in training. "It's so that we can feel the heat of having lived with the *Shechina* during the Sabbath." I told him that it had indeed felt warm and loving. A broad smile swept over his face. His wife was delighted. The children were playing with their hands moving over the flames and both parents turned their attention to cautioning them. Then the father passed around sweet-smelling spices housed in an artistically decorated pewter container. "The spices are meant to revive anyone who feels light-headed after having been so close to the *Shechina*," he explained. Then everyone rang out the words: *A Gut Voch* [Have a good week!]

Suddenly we were back in ordinary time. I thanked them for their hospitality and got ready to catch the bus. I hugged my host and she looked at me with what seemed like a hint of gratitude. Maybe we had reached some sort of understanding. And I had managed to accomplish what God had intended on that day: to rest and to refresh myself.

A few days later I visited the Western Wall in the Old City, the section of the supporting wall of the Temple Mount which has remained intact since the destruction by the Romans of the Second Temple in 70 C.E. The wall became a symbol rooted in the national consciousness and is considered to be the most sacred place of prayer for the Jewish people. According to Judaic tradition, even after the Second Temple was destroyed, the Divine Presence never left and shall always be there. The wall became a center of mourning over the destruction of the Temple and the exile of the Jewish people. It offers religious communion with the memory of the land of Israel's former glory and also fervent hope for its restoration. Hence its colloquial name: The Wailing Wall. It was not accessible between 1948 when the Jordanians seized it, until the second day of the Six Day War in 1967 when Israeli soldiers recaptured it. The Jordanians had deliberately turned it into a dung heap. The Israeli soldiers who saw it for the first time on that June day in 1967 wept. I saw it two years later.

There are always people praying at the wall. A popular custom is to write a supplication on a piece of paper and place it in one of the many cracks and crevices between the ancient stones. I felt as if the Divine Presence had been waiting for me all this time. My hands were trembling as I placed my own piece of paper into one of the cracks. I asked for forgiveness, I asked for mercy, and I gave thanks. In the heat of that afternoon, my head and arms were covered with a shawl which I wrapped even more fully around my face as my tears streamed. There were others around me, also praying. We were all of us together, all of us in front of the One Who Has No Name. It was a public scene yet also an intensely private moment.

With my piece of paper snugly in the crevice, I looked up for a moment and watched the light that was burning gold, shining as from a throne on high. I turned my face away for fear of being struck down. There was a tiny flutter of wind behind me. When I turned around, I saw women who were sitting and praying. The men's and women's sections are separated. All heads were covered. It was so quiet. Some women were standing at the wall next to me. They too prayed silently. Some murmured. Others wept. I looked over to the men's section, which was fully visible. They swayed back and forth in fervent prayer [davening] almost as if they were in a trance. We all knew that Our Father in His glory was there with us. I sensed that those there believed every word of the Hebrew Bible, the Old Testament. And I mused that it was not a one-way street. We pray for the Lord's lovingkindness but we, His children, must become His comforters. We save each other; we carry each other. We carry the memory of God. And prayer is a form of memory. Is prayer what many did to keep themselves alive as long as possible in the concentration camps?

I don't know how long I stood transfixed by the light as it transformed from white to gold to bronze and then to a strange violet color. The light kept changing and whirling and playing and calling. As I looked up again, I suddenly saw the light that I had seen in Montréal all those years ago coming through the frozen crystals on the windowpanes of my childhood. Yet this light in Jerusalem was even stronger and more insistent. A tidal wave of desolation hit me hard in the back of my head. I could hardly swallow. I could hardly breathe. I could hardly move. But it was not like the desolation familiar to me from the past. It was the solitary presence of the Divine, a Presence of sorrows beyond our ken. The tips of my fingers clung to the ancient stones of the Wall.

The light spoke to me as if from some shining grave of consolation. How I wished that I could embrace Our Father who had suffered with us. I placed my cheek against the cool stone and felt released from fear.

25

PERUGIA

After four idyllic weeks in Israel I arrived in Perugia with a head full of steam and a singing heart. South and east of Florence, in the province of Umbria, Perugia is built like a medieval fortress some 1600 feet above sea level. Steep hills abound and many of its streets consist of stone steps invariably leading up to the only level part of the city, the *centro storico* (historic center) with its ancient flowing fountain and Cathedral of San Lorenzo.

I walked the city's labyrinthine streets with their steep stairways, as if in reverie, surrounded by the lyrical language of Italian and by breezes perfumed with the flowers that were scattered everywhere. I learned that the Etruscans, of whom virtually nothing is known, settled in Umbria and Tuscany and were noted artisans and builders. They sculpted delicate stone figurines – little statues indented into the walls of buildings which had survived wars and earthquakes. They didn't use mortar, but instead carved stone to fit perfectly. When the Romans conquered the Etruscans, they didn't destroy what they had built; instead the Roman arches and walls were constructed above and around whatever was already there.

My *pensione* (run by a certain Signora Frizza) was situated on a narrow and steep street called Via Pinturicchio named after a famous local painter. She was a battle-axe of a woman who didn't let any nonsense escape her vision. All her boarders had to obey her rules. This resulted in a spotless place and exquisite meals. The taste of her pasta, and especially her *penne* with black truffles and her mouth-watering minestrone soup delighted my taste buds. The grilled vegetables were drenched in the local varieties of olive oil called "liquid gold." The chicken cooked in rich red wine or the roasted lamb served with lentils, farro and polenta could make my taste buds lose their bearings. It was hearty and simple, "*cucina povera*" and in some ways it reminded me of the French-Canadian meals I enjoyed in my childhood at my friend Françoise's home. I always asked for seconds and even thirds and Signora Frizza loved me for that.

As for my running around with local Italian boys (I call them boys because they really were as young or younger than I at age 18), Signora Frizza turned cold as stone. "*Tu sei disgraziata*" [you are disgraceful] she would say pointing an accusatory finger at me, quite unaware of my innocence. I would end up on motorcycles with boys racing around town and when they wanted to go further than a kiss or two, I fought them off. Why I even got myself in these situations shows my contradictory behavior. I was a frightened little girl who had no intention of letting myself be carried away. After I realized that all the boys "talked up" and exaggerated their dates with me, I stopped paying them any attention. In any case no one could have imagined that the "wild" attitude that I displayed there was nothing but a mask.

I shared my room and its sweeping views of rolling hills with a student from Capetown, South Africa. Theresa's father was a doctor who had been imprisoned on Robben Island because he had treated a black man at the scene of a terrible car accident. Theresa was a devout Catholic, and she placed pictures of Mother Mary on her side of our shared dresser. She also draped a rosary around the mirror. After we became closer, I confided to Theresa how important Mary was in my life. We started to roam around Perugia and to the neighboring villages checking out all the chapels as well as the larger churches. We did a lot of praying to Santa Maria and we also did a lot of eating of delicious Italian meals as well as much studying of Italian. She and I began to share conversations in Italian, shaping and reshaping words like children playing with plasticene. As we messed around with all those new-found words we sometimes surprised ourselves with the verbal treasures we were able to string together, forming sentences. We delighted in the spontaneity of these linguistic wanderings and usually ended up at one of the outdoor cafes on the Corso Vannucci.

I gave myself over to Italian studies at the Università Per Stranieri [The University for Foreigners] with enthusiasm. The main building, The Gallenga Stuart Palace, built in the 18th century looked so dignified and this encouraged me to take my studies seriously. Classes in the language began early in the morning and ran until midday. We students, a few hundred of us, would meet in a large hall for the introductory part of each lesson and then we were divided into groups of ten for the remainder of each class. On our arrival each of us was given a student card, and an account at the local bank. Each of us was assigned to a sort of mentor (usually a man who worked in the administration of the university) and it was comforting to know that he was there to help in case anything went wrong. I was enrolled in the Anglo-Saxon group at first, but I quickly transferred to the French group. No surprise there. When I wasn't speaking Italian I was speaking French. The Morlacchi Theater, where plays and operas were regularly performed, became the place where students congregated. Even though this theater was small, we all managed to cram in. There were excursions to nearby towns and villages. I enveloped myself in this atmosphere and almost never spoke English.

The cafés in the town square, frequented by local townspeople, were always abuzz with gossip and news. We students crowded in and threw our own thoughts and information into these conversations. Many of the town folk were interested in where we came from, what we thought of Italy, and in particular of Perugia. I remember telling one old man that I was bewitched by Perugia and Umbria, and that I wished I could have been born Italian. His eyes grew wide as did his smile. And he told me, *"Tu puoi essere un'Italiana onoraria"* [You can be an honorary Italian.] I shook his hand and gave him a hug. My sojourn in Perugia offered me an opportunity in which I could begin to dream, albeit tentatively, of personal and professional goals. For the first time I sensed a future filled with culture and language as I walked under the Italian sun, amidst wildflowers and the vineyards of the Umbrian countryside.

My trip to Israel had made me proud of my Jewish heritage. What was perhaps more surprising was the fact that my revived Jewish identity took root in the fertile ground of Perugia. It was in Perugia that I tried to reinvent myself and did manage to pull it off, at least within that pocket of time. I was able to enjoy the fragrant countryside, sit under ancient olive trees, and taste Italian poetry on my tongue. I shared my feelings with some of my classmates who became good friends, some of whom I am still very much in contact with today. I spoke freely and enthusiastically about my recent trip to Israel and one afternoon I met a guy who looked like he was of Middle Eastern descent. He had olive skin, dark, piercing eyes, Semitic looking. He told me that he was from Ramallah in the West Bank and was now studying political science at the University of Michigan, Ann Arbor. We had laid eyes on each other in class and he invited me for coffee. We clearly were attracted to each other and started going out on dates. Jabbar was smitten by me, or so it seemed. He would stare deeply into my eyes and I would feel a jolt of electricity pass through my body.

We became inseparable although there was a whiff of danger in the air around him. One evening after a heavy make-out session, we stumbled out of his room onto the balcony into the fragrant night air. The moon was full and so white that the ridges on it were fully visible. "Isn't it romantic?" I mused aloud feeling languid. "Yes, but I want to know why Israel is so important to you."

"What kind of question is that?" I couldn't understand where he was going with this. "I told you about my Holocaust background and that it only proves that Jews need a homeland just like other people. Antisemitism is no joke."

"Oh, it's not that big a deal," he retorted. "Jews are treated well, especially in North America. Why isn't that enough? Why do you need Israel?"

I was stunned. I tried to have a civilized discussion, but he kept going on and said that Israel was illegitimate and should not exist at all. He finally exclaimed that he was a member of a relatively new organization, The Palestine Liberation Organization (PLO) committed to the dissolution of the state of Israel through the use of armed force.

"I like you a lot," he said in a delicate voice which soon turned harsh, "but if you end up on the other side of me in the conflict, I won't hesitate to blow your head off." His face became contorted. His hands were clenched and his eyes twitched. The casualness with which he uttered these words made me shudder. What had happened to the affectionate, sexy guy I had known just moments earlier? The monster with the iron hook from my childhood smirked in the background of my mind. I hid my shock, walked purposefully back into his room, picked up my jacket and purse and said goodbye. There was no common ground possible. He had made up his mind that if I was for Israel then I was his enemy. Those words were like a knife in my heart. They carried a dark foreboding which I tried hard to suppress at the time.

During the three-week study break, three of my classmates from McGill University and I hitchhiked from Perugia all the way to Istanbul. Our route was via Brindisi where we took a boat to Croatia (still Yugoslavia then). From there we went to Bulgaria, and then to Greece and on to Turkey. In those days hitchhiking was still considered relatively safe. At the side of roads my two girlfriends and I would put out our thumbs and our male friend, Jacques, hid behind a tree or road sign. When a car stopped, he rushed out of his hiding place and jumped in along with us. The girls took turns sitting in the front with what turned out to be all male European drivers, except for one American couple. It was important to keep as politely distant as possible so as not to give any wrong impression to these men. It worked well, except with the last driver who was a Turkish businessman driving back from Germany to

Istanbul. He picked us up somewhere in Greece. It was my turn to sit up front.

Little did I know that Jacques had made a deal with this man that I would be the "girlfriend" while in Istanbul. I ended up in the man's hotel room at a specific time because Jacques had told me that his room was to be the meeting place for us all to go on a tour of the city. The door opened and the man was already in his shorts expecting me to undress. He grabbed me and pulled me into the room. My heart started pounding. I tried to squirm out of his grip. He was terribly strong. I began screaming. He let go immediately, looking surprised and surly.

"What is your problem?" he shouted. "This was all arranged."

"I'm going to the police!" I yelled as I ran out the door.

When I told the girls what had happened, we all shrieked at Jacques and he apologized, not realizing that the man had been serious. "What were you thinking?" we asked him. We couldn't believe his stupidity. He felt contrite and started telling us about his life, as if to explain his behavior. It was then that we discovered the aching loneliness that haunted him. His father was a high government official in Québec but his parents had divorced when Jacques was eight years old. His mother had been too lenient and spoiled him endlessly whereas his father had been strict and distant. Jacques had acted out as a child and became a "behavioral problem" and was then sent to a boarding school. All this came out as we lunged at him verbally.

Still we did silly things. We, the girls, ran around the Grand Bazaar in mini-skirts. We were shouted at by the stall keepers and quickly realized the error of our ways. We changed into jeans and lived to tell the tale. We saw the world as only teenagers can. Our energy was limitless. We enjoyed a boat ride on the Bosphorus Sea and Jacques was so excited that he almost fell off the boat into the water which glistened like one of the emerald gems at the Topkapi Museum. Then I noticed a child playing with a balloon at the edge of the boat. Suddenly the little boy with a head full of dark curls lost hold of it and it floated far up into the sky and he cried, broken-hearted. His parents tried to calm him down. All it took was that little incident to make me feel as forlorn as that child. My friends seemed to be enjoying themselves so effortlessly. I, on the other hand, was watching my doppelganger having fun while I felt a knot in my stomach. It was as if my own parents were standing right next to me, anxious that something would go wrong with the trip and we would all be injured or killed in some devastating accident.

After the holiday, the three of us returned to Perugia ready to dive right back into our studies. I ended up receiving one of the highest marks in the course – no small feat, as it had been attended by several hundred students. Signora Frizza (who by that time had forgotten all about my earlier perceived indiscretions) baked a celebratory three-tiered chocolate cake with scrumptious vanilla cream icing in my honor. Perugia is famous for its chocolate, *Baci Perugini* [Kisses from Perugia] made with ground hazelnuts and dark chocolate. She also fashioned a tinsel crown to plant on my head.

Nevertheless, there was a darker and more hidden side to my sojourn in Perugia. I tried hard to escape the demons. I really did. I slipped out of their grip whenever I could. But they lurked in the background, waving the chains that would rebind me. After I returned home, I began to sense something disturbing: my parents were not really interested in hearing about the trip. It was almost as if it shouldn't have happened. When I returned to my third year at McGill I was congratulated for my excellent grades at the Università per Stranieri by my professors, but their words seemed to arrive from far away and I could hardly hear them.

The implicit psychological deal was that I always had to pay a price for the fruits of my ambitions. This I usually accomplished by messing things up so that I would not be able to enjoy any such experience again. The easiest way to mess things up would be to forget a deadline for the re-application process as a follow-up to the original scholarship, and this is exactly what I did. It would have been granted automatically, however by the time my professors realized what had happened, the Awards Office in central administration had given the prize to another student. So I had denied myself the opportunity to return the following summer, which would have greatly helped my academic progress and preparations for graduate school. I did not see that I was re-enacting the *Alice in Wonderland* fiasco all over again.

Instead of going to Perugia a second time I helped my father in a clothing store which he had opened in a low-income neighborhood. The store was not doing well and he himself did not look healthy. He started snapping at me for putting an item on the wrong shelf or taking too long a break and I felt terribly uncomfortable. A dark mood grabbed me and brought me low. A nagging thought crawled around my brain: "You could have been in Perugia instead of here. How could you have been so stupid? What about graduate school?" I felt that all the color had been drained from my life.

When I remember that first time in Perugia it feels as if I'm dusting off a piece of jewelry which has been lying in a closed box for a long, long time. It took decades to unearth this artifact of my personal history. It had to remain buried – as did so much of my past. We, the children of survivor parents, had been too close to the fire even if we didn't know it, tattooed by the traumas of our parents. I was not like my classmates, who didn't have to carry the Holocaust everywhere they went.

Finally, more than 30 years later as a university professor, I was invited to give lectures at the University of Siena. I enjoyed the experience immensely and after the two weeks of my stay there ended, I knew that I was finally ready to return to Perugia. I boarded a train from Siena and arrived in Perugia a few hours later. It was all just as I had remembered it. The pastel colors of the buildings, especially those with that apricot hue. The stone archways. The *Corso Vanucci* where I had devoured open-air meals with fellow students and shopped in its markets. Those steep stairs. The views of the Umbrian countryside so high up: on top of the world. In my mind's eye I could see my classmates sitting on the steps of the Cattedrale San Lorenzo near the Fontana Maggiore in the Piazza IV Novembre studying for exams, as students still do today.

On the second day of my stay I sat at a table covered with a crisp tablecloth on the patio of a trattoria eating pasta with vegetables and pecorino cheese cooked in white wine blanketed with olive oil which tasted so pure. Fork in one hand and pen in the other, I wrote in my journal. Bittersweet tears began to flow from my eyes. I had found my way back into the arms of Perugia. Yes, I had won the lottery many years ago, but only decades later could I come and claim the prize.

26

CHANGING DIRECTION: TEACHER

Andrey and I returned to Canada from Berkeley after he received his PhD degree. Our destination was Edmonton, Alberta in Western Canada where he took up his first faculty position at the University of Alberta and I entered a teacher-training program. I had applied to the PhD Program in the Italian Department at the University of Toronto and at the University of British Columbia because Andrey had applied to these two places. I got scholarships to both graduate programs. Our first choice had been Toronto, but Andrey was offered only a one-year appointment there. He was adamant about a tenure-track position so he declined that offer. Unexpectedly, the University of Alberta offered him a great position and it was impossible not to accept it. It was too late for me to enter the Comparative Literature department for graduate work with any sort of remuneration, so that's how I ended up – once again – at a university where I hadn't applied to graduate school.

I walked out of the building that housed the Comparative Literature Department feeling despondent about what seemed to be a continual run of bad luck in terms of having to decline graduate fellowships. As I continued on the path deep in thought, suddenly in front of me stood the Education building. I stopped abruptly as memories of my elementary school experiences and my summer language playschool both flowed through my mind like refreshing rivers. And, of course, the encouraging words of Professor Ruddell at Berkeley popped into my head: "You're a natural [teacher] and it sounds like you could do a lot for bilingual education in Canada. Why don't you try the classroom for a while? Your students would be so lucky!" I walked into the building and entered the Professional Diploma after Degree (PDAD) program. The graduate fellowships which I had to decline still gnawed at me, and I tried to stave off those regrets with the conviction that teaching was to be a temporary stop on a journey toward something I could not yet define.

The pre-service PDAD program, however, turned out to be a remarkable experience. Students were divided into groups of five and each group was assigned to a mentor who would observe our teaching stints. The mentor for my group was a professor who was already retired and simply working for the sheer love of it. An exceptionally kind-hearted man, Roly Ward, always saw the good in people. He had been a superintendent of schools in Edmonton and eventually an adjunct professor in Educational Administration at the University of Alberta. Of all our professors, this man possessed the most hands-on experience in the schools and had created an extensive network of people and resources in school boards across all of Alberta. He was well known as a teacher and an administrator in both rural and urban areas, and also on an Aboriginal reserve.

My chosen specialty was bilingual education and my mentor found the perfect school for me in which to student teach: a bilingual school in a small Franco-Albertan town called Vimy situated some forty miles north of Edmonton. In the morning, subjects were taught in French, and in the afternoon in English. Hailing from Québec, I was viewed as a bit of a celebrity – as someone who had come to them from the "home country." What mattered was how genuinely enthusiastic I was about French-Canadian culture and, even though I myself was not Catholic, how much I knew about their religion. They accepted me to such a degree that I was even allowed to teach religion classes there – surely a first for a non-Catholic.

I told them that I was Jewish and they respected my wish to teach from the Old Testament. The children in my grade four class came to love Moses as much as they loved Jesus and they were also intrigued by my personal connections to their Virgin Mary. This was an exercise in inter-faith dialogue. For many of the people in Vimy, I was the first Jew they had ever met and I felt like an emissary. How strange it was that after having yearned for such an experience in my childhood, there I was, finally, in a French Catholic school – although not as a student this time, but as a teacher.

Our stay in Alberta was very hospitable and we enjoyed its frontier character. Everybody wore cowboy hats and boots. It was a small city, easy to get around. We would constantly be invited to supper (nobody called it dinner) at people's homes, "come as you are." In restaurants mouth-watering prime rib steaks could be had for a song. This was beef country after all. The huge Western sky offered a sense of luminous possibility. It seemed as if a mysterious artist would use that sky as a palette and swirl ever-changing colors on its canvas myriad times a day. And the great big fluffy clouds would carry us all. Winters were incredibly cold. It was in Edmonton that we learned that the Fahrenheit and Celsius scales merge at -40 degrees. And it was often -40 degrees. The air was so dry that the snow was almost brittle and the sun shone brightly. You had to be careful not to get frostbite if you stayed out without covering up fingers, toes, ears, nose. Once we stood in line for a movie and when I got inside the theater I realized that I couldn't feel my toes. (They did finally thaw out not long afterward but the pain was nasty.) The winter days were terribly short. I got up to go to school in the dark and came home in the dark.

The Northern Lights, however, offered an especially spectacular show in the winter, truly the work of a divine artist. Sheets of green and pink and yellow and purple would flow behind the stars. We would stand and watch this display feeling humble and grateful to have the chance to witness such splendor. In the summer, daylight lasted until after midnight and so everyone ate supper late and went to drive-in movies well into the night. Country western music events and ad hoc dances abounded. We all felt like teenagers on dates. And I will always remember the cookouts of corn and marshmallow roasts over bonfires hosted by friends who lived on farms outside of Edmonton.

The mosquitoes were horrific. I remember we were out in a field taking a walk one late afternoon and I looked up and saw a black cloud overhead. "It looks like it's about to rain," I said to Andrey. Then we looked up again and realized that the cloud was a swarm of mosquitoes. We broke into a run to our car and every inch of it was covered with those insects. You could hardly see its bright yellow color. It was a frightening sight and we had to unlock the doors as quickly as possible and rush in. Some mosquitoes shot into the car with us and I swatted them with my purse as we quickly drove off. We were bitten up by these little beasts and had learned our lesson not to venture out of town without repellant.

Yearning to return east, it was not difficult for Andrey to accept the offer of a tenure-track position at the University of Toronto two years later. In our hearts we had always known that Edmonton was a temporary way station. We arrived in Toronto on a warm afternoon in mid-July and stayed in temporary university housing until we found an apartment. Hoping to find a teaching position, I had placed an ad in the Toronto *Globe and Mail* newspaper from Edmonton several months before our moving date. This was a time of teacher surplus so it was not easy for a new teacher. What I had going for me was my specialty in teaching French. It was rather unusual to place an ad for a classroom position in a newspaper. The usual approach was to fill out application forms at local school boards. I did that too, but I knew that many applications would be piling in and probably many would never be read. So I thought I'd increase my chances with that ad in the *Globe and Mail*. One principal responded. I was elated. A week after we arrived in Toronto, he interviewed me at his school in an inner-city neighborhood.

The janitor greeted me at the door with a wide smile. It was the summer holidays: desks and chairs were piled up in the hallways. He brought me to the office and I shook hands with the principal. A good handshake, I noted to myself. He was a pleasant looking man and we both looked each other over. We chatted for more than an hour. He was impressed with my teaching evaluations and letters of reference, but warned me: "This is a tough inner-city neighborhood." He talked about subsidized housing, unruly kids, a culturally diverse school and low-socio-economic status. It was the mid-1970s and Toronto already had an interesting mix of cultures and races although it was nowhere near as large and diverse as it is today. I nodded with some enthusiasm and replied, "I would like a chance to teach these children." He obviously liked my response (or just as likely, he was desperate to fill that teaching slot) and offered me the position on the spot.

I am an arctophile, an avid teddy bear collector. On the Labor Day weekend before the first day of school, I brought in several of my bears as well as a number of colorful posters to decorate my grade five classroom. The classroom was dusty as classrooms always are at the end of summer and there seemed to be an expectant air. It was as if the room was waiting for me. The walls were bare. I had brought along three bears who seemed eager to visit this new classroom of mine. One was Paddington Bear who wore a blue raincoat and large red boots. The other was a little Japanese bear named Naoko, in a sunshine yellow silk kimono. And the third was Little Rascal with curly brown fur who wore green and blue plaid overalls and was always getting into mischief. As I was arranging my posters on the wall a large, older woman poked her head through the doorway. "I'm Ann. I teach next door," she announced. "You've got the class with Calvin and Armando and Rita in it. It's the worst class in the school – I doubt if you'll make it to Christmas." And then she disappeared. Her demeanor said: I've got experience and you don't.

Suddenly my posters didn't look quite so colorful and even the bears on my desk looked frightened. I sat down at my desk and suddenly felt very alone. I was still adjusting to life in a new city. That morning I had been so excited to be coming to my very own classroom yet in an instant a pin had burst my balloon. I became filled with anxiety and dread. I sat down and suddenly a powerful thought came over me: If my parents were able to survive the Holocaust then I surely should be able to survive my first day here as a teacher, even if my students turn out to be a pack of hellions. With renewed vigor I got up and finished taping my posters onto the walls. At the end of the day I went home and tried to enjoy what was left of the Labor Day weekend.

Sometimes, they say, the first week of teaching predicts the future. While heading toward my classroom at 8 am that Tuesday morning I met the teacher who was across the hall from my room. We both walked to the staff room and chatted over tea. His face beamed with smiles and it turned out that this too was his first day at the school. Mine was a grade five class and his a grade six. Ann was nowhere to be seen. I was starting to feel more comfortable and then the bell rang. Everyone made their way back to their classrooms weaving through the lines of the chattering and pushy children in the hallways. I stood by my door with a sense of adventure, waiting for my students to arrive.

I watched their faces as each child shuffled in – faces marked by neglect, by poverty, by not knowing that their lives had meaning. They were fascinating, as children always are. I had been told that in my class no fewer than ten cultural groups were represented. I felt in awe of the possibilities inherent in this new classroom full of new faces. They reminded me of the places where I had grown up in the working-class east end of Montréal. I felt that I had an important role within this classroom and I wanted to respect the complexities of these children's lives. It soon became apparent to me that I was both an "insider" and an "outsider." An "insider" because I had grown up in circumstances not so dissimilar to their own – a child of trauma and poverty. However, I was also an "outsider" because I was not their peer but rather their teacher – an adult, an authority figure.

No sooner had the children settled into their seats that they started jumping out of them. Paper airplanes began to fly through the air. I somehow got through roll call – names, names from all over the world. I tried hard to pronounce all of them properly. I became alarmed when I found myself yelling for attention. This was not my vision of the teacher I wanted to become. And it wasn't even an hour into my new career. "It's a tough school... You'll never make it to Christmas." Ann's words echoed in my ears...

I had prepared a reading lesson. It was based on a standardized basal reader series. I remember feeling apprehensive while planning that lesson. The stories in those readers seemed stilted, inauthentic. Basal readers were meant to develop specific reading skills, taught in a pre-determined sequence. There is no doubt that what they offered were the most basic skills; meaning did not seem to count for anything. How would any child relate to such contrived and uninteresting material with stories that had no meaning for them?

At that moment, as total chaos was about to break out, my eyes turned to the shelf that housed those dreadful readers. I made a decision which I knew would make or break my status as teacher in the minds of these children. I marched over to the shelf and gathered up as many of these books as I could hold. Fortunately, my classroom was located on the ground floor and also fortunately it was not raining outside. I strode over to the window, opened it wide, and then I proceeded to throw out the books. I literally threw them out the window. It was a moment in time when everything stands still and waits to be born. The children stopped their running about, returned to their seats, and sat down. All of their disbelieving eyes were upon me as one could have heard a proverbial pin drop.

This is what I said to my students: "I don't blame you for not being interested in these books. They look pretty dull to me too. I wouldn't want to waste my time with them and I won't waste your time either." Their eyes grew larger. They looked bewildered, and I was starting to relax. "Books should be full of stories that catch your attention," I went on. "Those are the kind of stories I want to read with you in this class. Have any of you ever heard of Greek myths? They are stories about ancient gods and goddesses and all their adventures." I saw the wonder that began to envelop the children. I don't know whether theirs was wonder at the anticipation of reading Greek myths or at the prospect of spending a year with such a strange new teacher! Whatever the reason, this became a sacred moment.

There were white faces, brown faces, black faces, yellow faces and red faces staring at me and they all seemed transfixed by the exciting invitation that had just been offered: "We will read *interesting* stories and they will have *meaning* for all of us." Nobody in school had ever made such a promise to them before. Suddenly "the thing with feathers," that intangible sense of hope pervaded our classroom. I had found children's versions of the Greek myths in a bookstore and I brought those treasures to the class with me the following day. These children were all well below their reading grade level and some of them had no reading skills at all.

So I read to them. I made a pact with my students because they all knew instinctively that we were embarking on a subversive adventure. Greek myths were not part of the school curriculum and so we were entering uncharted territory. I told my students that it might happen that the principal or the school district superintendent would visit our classroom one day to watch me teach and that if we were ever in the middle of one of our Greek myth reading times, and that if by chance my back was turned, they (my pupils) must motion to let me know that either the principal or the school superintendent (or both) had entered. I would then be able to quickly put my books away and go on to teach something considered more acceptable. In this my students were willing accomplices.

Thus began a year of sharing stories during Language Arts classes: the Greek myths, fairy tales, and yes, stories about my own childhood. If there was one lesson I wanted to share with them, it was this: that in spite of everything, there will still be love in all sorts of hiding places. The trick is to find it. They listened and soon began telling their own stories. It was an organic process: building, story by story, a bridge to understanding one another a little better. Certainly, there were more than a few tough moments, as well as some trying discipline problems. There were days when I came home exhausted, feeling like I wasn't getting anywhere with these children. But through it all, I always felt affection for them and I respected their struggles.

One mid-October morning I was reading aloud the story of *Ceres and Proserpina* to my class, the Roman version of the original Greek myth of *Demeter and Persephone*. There are many themes in this story that related directly to the realities of my students' lives: loss, violence, abuse, a mother's sorrow, a child's being torn away from home. There was an air of reverie in our classroom that morning as we were all commiserating with the mother and the daughter in this story. Suddenly children's hands began flailing about! There was intense anxiety on their faces. In an instant, I sensed the presence of a human being standing right behind me. I turned around and there he was – the SUPERINTENDENT of the school district! My heart sank. I was not following the curriculum and I had been caught red-handed. Somehow my students seemed to understand what this meant and they too were terrified.

The superintendent asked what I was doing and I told him the truth: that the basal readers were uninteresting, that it wasn't fair to foist such meaningless text onto students; I told him how stories need to fire up the reader's imagination, how my students were beginning to enjoy reading because these Greek myths really spoke to them. My students' heads were all nodding in agreement. I had said my piece and was now prepared for the proverbial axe to fall. A smile began to spread across the superintendent's face. "Well," he answered, "this is irregular, but I have seen these students before and this is the first time that I see them involved in their work. You are clearly doing something right. I will mention this to your principal." He shook my hand and at that moment my students all began to clap their hands. From that moment on there was no doubt that teaching was to become my safe place in the world.

Many years later, on a summer Sunday afternoon, I happened to be taking a friend's four-year-old daughter for an outing. My friend's little girl and I had been at a park and we decided to go to McDonald's, her favorite place, for a snack. The young woman on the other side of the counter had big hazel eyes in an olive-skinned face and curly dark hair up in a ponytail. She asked: "Are you Mrs. Feuerverger?"

"Yes, I am," I said, surprised. "And who are you?"

"I'm Rita from your grade five class at Laurelea School. I never forgot those Greek myths you taught us. I really began to enjoy reading after that."

She was standing at the cash register wearing a crisp uniform and around her graceful neck was a shining silver heart pendant. "I took all my younger brothers and sisters to the library over the years and I read those same stories to them," she said. Then a smile exploded across her face. "I'm now studying to be an early childhood educator. It's all because of you."

I was stunned. Rita had been the eldest of five children. Her mother had been on welfare and her father in prison. Rita had to become a surrogate mother to her younger siblings. In class she had always looked tired and older than her years. Now I was facing a bright young woman who was augmenting her finances with a summer job on her way toward an interesting career. What had become of the other students who had been in that class, I wondered? What had happened to Dominic, who stole a table lamp from a restaurant in order to be able to bring me a present for Christmas. Or to Calvin, whose father frightened me when he told me: "I love Calvin to death. If he acts up, just tell me and I'll beat the s--t out of him."

Mandy

There is one student who will forever hold a very special place in my heart. Her name was Mandy. She had the largest dark eyes one can imagine and flowing raven-black hair. Her skin was pale and her laughter a gift to the world. When she walked into my classroom on the first day of that school year she looked like an Aboriginal princess. She had the face of a young warrior, proud and majestic. Indeed, her mother was Aboriginal and her stepfather came from a mixed Aboriginal and European background. I somehow sensed that Mandy was meant to teach me something important.

Laurelea School was located near a Children's Aid Society home and over the years several of the students that I taught lived there. In their cases, the abuses they had suffered in their family homes were so severe that they had to be removed. Usually, the abuses had been discovered by someone and these children then became the ones lucky enough to have been taken away, if one can call that lucky. However, instead of being comforted by living in their new quarters, these children were stigmatized by their non-institutionalized peers who viewed them as the dregs of society. I quickly learned that there were three unspoken strata of child society in the school. The lowest were those in "Children's Aid." Then there were the foster kids – they, at least, were in a family. And at the top were those who lived with their biological parent or parents. This, of course, did not necessarily mean that all was well for them, but they could at least pretend.

Mandy had been placed in Children's Aid after having been shuffled about for several years from one foster family to another. Her parents had succumbed to alcoholism and drugs. She once told me that if only she had behaved a little better, her parents would have surely kept her. That was her version of reality to which she clung. After some weeks I looked at her file that was housed in the school office.

"Ten-year-old child, very cooperative. Brutally beaten by stepfather at age eight. Concussion, ribs broken, lacerations, serious bruising. Hospitalized for six weeks. Unsuccessful stays in foster homes. Placed in care." This was at the end of a school day and I was alone in the classroom as tears trickled down my face. I closed the folder and stared out at the maple trees in the schoolyard which were starting to flame in the colors of fall – burnt orange, golden yellow and fiery red. I felt my heart burning as brightly as those leaves.

Mandy tried so hard to do well in school and was a leader in some of the games on the playground. Her hand often went up to answer questions in class. At other times she sat sullenly in her seat, immobile and impossible to reach. Along with our discussions about Christmas and Hanukkah, we learned from her the story of Mighty Gitchee Manitou who had created the Universe. And Mandy played the most believable Virgin Mary in the Christmas pageant that I have ever seen. I shall never forget the look of wonder in her eyes as she knelt before Gabriel the angel when he announced that she was chosen to give birth to Jesus. She showed such maternal protectiveness and awe toward the Holy Child in the manger scene.

One winter day, after having been on yard duty during a bitterly cold recess period, I returned to my classroom and discovered that my desk had been ransacked. My purse was gone. I was stunned. Who could have done this? I discussed it with my students. Every one of them was perplexed. Days went by and the puzzle remained unsolved. I decided to give it time. I assumed this had been an act of desperation by one of the children. Later the thought occurred to me that perhaps somebody had broken into the school during recess – a different matter altogether. I began to wonder whether I shouldn't report this matter to the principal. In the late afternoon of the following day as I was preparing a lesson plan I heard a gentle knock on the door. I opened it and there was Mandy, eyes drowning in tears. She was clutching my purse in her little hands. I brought her into the classroom and closed the door. I dried her tears and put my arms around her. "Why did you do it?" I asked her quietly. "Because I wanted to be like you," she sobbed.

All I told her that afternoon was that, although I had lived with my parents when I was a child, I had felt alone because they had not been able to take care of me in the way that I had needed. In the way that all children need to be taken care of. Mandy looked at me, searching my face for any hint of a lie. When she realized that I was telling the truth she began to put everything neatly back into my drawer. Mandy never took anything from me again.

Mandy's stepfather, the adult who should have cared for her, had almost killed her during an alcoholic rage. Her mother was too high on drugs to take any proper notice. In this sense Mandy was twice assaulted. Even so, after being released from hospital, she longed to be reunited with her parents. The foster homes into which she had been placed could never live up to Mandy's needs and she had behaved badly there. *"If only I had tried harder, my parents would have wanted me."* This fatal survival mechanism: to believe one's parents as being good, no matter what. For how else can a child explain such brutality, such injustice?

Mandy sometimes reached out to others in unexpected ways. She helped those who needed attention in the reading circles. Her presence cast a large spell. From where did she receive the strength and will to do her good deeds in the classroom? Then one day, she offered me an enormous gift. Here is what happened. A racial slur had been hurled by one of the teachers toward a student in a classroom next to mine and I had overheard it. I was beside myself in anger. Schools are not necessarily safe places. We have to fight to make them so. At that moment I was afraid. It would have been my word against hers, and I did not yet have my permanent teaching certificate.

Then something even more abominable happened. This same teacher decided to bar a child from the end-of-year track meet because of some minor offence. This struck me as cruel and unusual punishment and it seemed to me that it had to do with the color of his skin. Some of the other teachers were equally distressed. The principal who had originally interviewed me had been a caring, decisive man, but he had been promoted to another position at the last moment. The principal who replaced him was a weak man who was under the thumb of this teacher. Instead of dealing with the situation, he barricaded himself in his office and did nothing. The students who belonged to this boy's team were upset because he was one of their star players. Mandy was also on that team. I decided to open a discussion with my class about this injustice because the details had leaked out anyway. The safest thing to do would have been to ignore the episode, but I found myself talking with my class about tolerance and respect for diversity in a multicultural society. This was long before it had become generally fashionable to do so. As the children heard me speaking, I could see that a sense of relief swept over them like a fresh breeze in a heat storm.

Suddenly Mandy spoke up in a determined voice: *"Express yourself, Mrs. Feuerverger. You are a teacher. You have a right to."* She might as well have been coming down from Mount Sinai with the Ten Commandments. There was silence in the classroom. Then all of the children began to nod their heads in agreement. The clarity of Mandy's defiance astonished me. We had been living on the inside of a local tyranny and she had blown the whistle. I knew in an instant that I had to live up to Mandy's words. I walked through the small corridor of light which she had opened and I kept on plowing through it until the decision was reversed and that boy was allowed to participate in the track meet. Mandy's voice liberated me that day, and all of the other children in my classroom witnessed it. I have been trying to live up to her words ever since.

27

MIRACLE IN TORONTO

Toronto offered me the joy of stepping into my own classroom and to vicariously enjoy the beauty of childhood in my position as an elementary school teacher. But it offered me much, much more than that: one of the greatest miracles of my life in the guise of a man named Dr. Ernest Michaels. He was a psychiatrist – and not just any psychiatrist, a healer. The son of a rabbi, originally from England, he had moved to Canada in the early-1950s with his wife and two young children. When I met him in the late-1970s he was close to retirement. Dr. Michaels was gray-haired with a stubbly beard, wild dark eyebrows, a high forehead and gentle eyes the color of cocoa. The sort of eyes that are reserved for a rabbinical sage or a shaman or a lama – or for any wise guide. Interestingly, the literal translation from the Greek of "psychiatrist" is "physician of souls."

It happened this way. In my second year of elementary school teaching I became friendly with one of the teachers in my school, Alanna, who was five years older than me and a more experienced teacher. A good-natured and kind person, she had become a kind of mentor and we began to meet for dinner on a regular basis. I loved her pixie haircut and the creative way in which she tied scarves around her slender neck. Her blue-green eyes against her blonde hair had a violet cast to them which reminded me of a clear and unclouded skyscape. I sensed I could trust her. We both shared many confidences about our lives.

One December I invited Alanna to join my husband and me for the Christmas holidays in Montréal. She stayed with us at my parents' place and also met my in-laws and some of our friends. I didn't know it then, but nothing escaped those eyes of hers during that two-week stay. She hardly blinked one afternoon when she and I sat having tea with my mother who began to complain loudly: "When will Grace ever give me a grandchild? She has already been married for several years! Our neighbor's daughter who is even younger already has two children. It's enough with all the teaching. A woman needs to have a baby. That's what counts."

I remember feeling something akin to a sharp slap on my face as I tried to shrug off my mother's comment with a joke: "I already have 26 children – in my classroom." Alanna's eyes turned from my mother toward me and delivered some eye contact comfort.

On a snowy evening in Toronto about a month later Alanna and I were having dinner at a Chinese restaurant near our school and she brought up the "grandchild" incident.

"Does your mother always talk like that about your having a child? She hardly knew me, and I wondered why she would do that in front of me."

"Oh, that's just the way she is," I responded. "She suffered so much during the war and lost all her family. I really should consider having a child."

"Do you want to have a child? Do you want to be a mother now?" asked Alanna.

I was 25 years old at the time. At first I bristled at Alanna's questions, but then suddenly my eyes welled up with tears and I heard myself admitting to her: "To tell you the truth, when I think about becoming a mother all I can imagine is entering a prison and never getting out. I guess I'm just not ready for such a life-altering change, but it does hurt each time my mother tells me that 'so-and-so' just got pregnant."

Alanna's green-violet eyes gazed upon my tear-stained face and uttered words that would eventually transform my life: "I'm seeing a truly special psychiatrist. Throw out any preconceptions you may have of what that might mean. This man is beyond anything you could ever imagine. He is a true healer. He is one-of-a-kind." As she picked up an egg roll I put my chopsticks down and asked: "A healer, what do you mean?" Some kind of weird cult leader with mad, darting eyes and disheveled long hair sprang to mind.

She replied with a smile, "He doesn't work according to any one prescribed manual. He's real and he's compassionate and incredibly insightful. It's not just a profession for him; this is his calling – straight from the heart. He's easy to talk to and he really listens and tells you stuff. He is not afraid of telling the truth. You have to see for yourself."

"Well, I'm not sure I need this. I think I can work things out for myself."

"There's no rush. Just think about it," Alanna responded wisely. I put it out of mind, or so I thought. My friend had piqued my curiosity because I knew she was not one for hyperbole, and I wondered what she meant by this man's not being afraid of telling the truth.

About six months later I finally walked into Dr. Michaels' office. I had no idea what I was in for. It was the end of the school year, late June. The children had given me much, but they had also taken much out of me. I was looking forward to the summer break as I sat down in a comfy armchair opposite Dr. Michaels. His office was located on the fifth floor of a professional building in downtown Toronto. He sat in a black leather chair and his large oak desk was adorned with framed pictures of two adorable little girls who were, I later found out, his granddaughters. He asked if I wanted a cup of tea and cookies. A kitchenette adjoined his office, complete with a fridge, a counter with a small stovetop, a pantry and a couch. I nodded and he went to put the kettle on and brought out an assortment of butter cookies which were from a European bakery located not far from his building.

As he set the tea and cookies down in front of me he asked: "What brings you here?" I told him about my friend's suggestion to see him. I immediately sensed a compassionate inquisitiveness about him. Something about his caring eyes made me feel as if a window was about to be opened that would bring in fresh, clean air. I told him about my family background and heard myself saying: "Of course I have some hang-ups, given what my parents went through." I talked for a while about how I had let go a scholarship to the Hebrew University to be with "a guy I met in Berkeley," and how I had sensed that "together we would become each other's salvation." I also told him about the other scholarships I gave up. "But I *adore* teaching elementary school," I said with perhaps too much conviction. As I drank tea and munched on my fifth cookie, I felt more and more at ease. Then something spilled out of my mouth that I hadn't anticipated: "I don't want to end up an embittered, old teacher at the end of my career." I was startled by what I had uttered. I stopped and waited for him to speak. I sensed he was not going to beat around the bush, but I didn't expect the shock that was to follow. This is what he said, plain as day: "I'm sorry to have to tell you this: you grew up in a poisoned environment and it isn't only because of the Holocaust. It's more than that. Your parents probably had severe emotional problems even before the war. And then their concentration camp experiences intensified everything." Dr. Michaels placed his hand delicately on his chin and continued: "It sounds to me like you were the child who threatened your mother the most. You were the one who wanted to be out there and make it in the world. That must have felt like a betrayal to her. It wasn't deliberate, but she has unfortunately done you a lot of harm. And so has your father in a different, more subtle way. At least he gave you a hint of a professional life. Your mother was a tyrant who was jealous that you would outshine her. I can feel pity for her, but right now you don't have the luxury to do that."

I sat there feeling like a gun went off in the room – almost sick to my stomach. I told him that I thought he was exaggerating. *What the heck is he talking about?* I was flummoxed. "That poor woman went through such hell during the war. Yes, maybe she transferred some of her anxieties onto me. What do you expect?" Then a line from a Dylan Thomas poem popped into my head: "Though I sang in my chains like the sea." I finally got up and thanked Dr. Michaels politely and explained that I had summer plans and would make an appointment for a second session in the fall.

I was to spend a couple of weeks with a friend, Marie-Soleil, whom I had met at McGill and who now lived in the picturesque Beauce region near Quebec City. My husband had to stay in Toronto finishing up a project and would join me toward the end of my stay. I arrived and my friend and I hugged each other. It had been many years since we had seen each other. We had kept in touch by phone and letters. Toward the end of my stay, Marie-Soleil told me that she had organized a trip to Ile d'Orléans, a lovely little island in the St. Lawrence River nearby. The morning we were to leave I awoke with some sort of 'bug' and we had to cancel that trip. I felt guilty that I had messed up such a great outing.

What was strange was that this incident unearthed deeply hidden memories of a summer visit to a classmate's cottage in the Laurentian Mountains north of Montréal when I was 13 years old. I had been so excited about this invitation. Marlene's parents were visual artists, eccentric, bohemian. I wouldn't have been able to describe them in those words at the time, but I knew they didn't fit into the world I came from. They were *interesting!* As it is, they lived in a little cottage behind a more conventional house on a small street right at the edge of our neighborhood that dead-ended onto a forest. Their house was filled with fascinating paintings (their own) all over the walls. Bold colors, abstract art, original and unusual. They welcomed me heartily into their home and told me how much Marlene admired my talent in English, French and Latin. Admired *me!* How could that be possible? It was all a mistake. As for Marlene, she possessed a quiet confidence that astonished me and what she could draw on paper was extraordinary. So mature, so beyond her years.

When the day came and I piled into her parents' car, a sinking feeling overcame me. A few days into the visit I came down with some sort of stomach ailment and became distraught. It was a panic attack. I had no idea that I had been suffering from an anxiety disorder throughout my childhood. All I knew was that I had to get out of there. I didn't know why. Marlene's parents were alarmed that it might be appendicitis and drove me back to Montréal. It turned out to be nothing and I felt terribly let down. I avoided Marlene from then on. She didn't understand – and neither did I – that shame had ambushed me. And fear. Fear of stepping out into a bigger world as if I would fall off a cliff if I went there. What stunned me was that this exact same feeling reappeared during my visit to the Beauce so many years later. Another anxiety attack which I still couldn't recognize for what it was. I felt embarrassed and uncomfortable. My friend looked perturbed. I couldn't wait to get away. The mix of shame and distress lingered for a time.

I called Andrey feeling very fragile and told him what had happened. He dropped everything and met me at the train station in Quebec City the following day. I fell into his arms as if into a warm and comforting shelter. He stroked my hair and whispered that it would be okay. It was as if he had arrived on a majestic white horse and whisked me off to a little holiday in Montréal where we visited our favorite haunts. My knight in shining armor. That may sound so cliché, but that's exactly what I felt. I remember every muscle relaxing as I began to breathe deeply. We ran around like teenagers and I regained my emotional balance. My darling Andrey, what would I have done without him?

A new school year began in September. A new Grade Five class where I felt safe and busy with my new class of children. I kept postponing the second appointment with Dr. Michaels. Then something impossible happened. One November morning, two months into the school year, I woke up with a jolt – sweating, extremely agitated. I had had a strange dream. An old woman, a teacher, was sitting hunched over her desk tears streaming down her wrinkled face. I heard her wail: "My life is over, I should have done much more with it. I shouldn't have given up those scholarships!"

I jumped out of bed and picked up the telephone and shakily dialed the number on the sheet of paper. "I need to see Dr. Michaels as soon as possible!" I muttered urgently to his secretary. She answered that he was booked solid for six weeks. I didn't think I could wait that long. I called Alanna, in a panic. It turned out that she had an appointment booked for that Thursday afternoon and offered it to me. When I returned to Dr. Michaels the first thing he uttered, sighing with relief, was: "I am glad you have come back. I was afraid that I might have said too much too soon. I realized it was 50/50 whether you would return. Now, let's roll up our sleeves and get to work." I was twenty-seven years old.

I began to see Dr. Michaels and continued to see him for at least once a week for several years. Through the therapy sessions, I began to unravel my emotional confusion and discovered how much I really wanted to regain the thread of my graduate work. It had never occurred to me that I wasn't supposed to sacrifice my life for my parents, especially my mother. That all my desires were normal, necessary. That I deserved to be out there in the sunshine. Believe it or not, it was excruciating to take this in. Almost every morning I would wake up with an anguished sense of doom. It was as if I were on a trapeze trying desperately to hold onto the past knowing that if I didn't let go I'd be hurtled into the abyss. I kept on teaching elementary school, but I began to feel like I was losing the balance in my feet, in my mind, in my thoughts. Sometimes I'd have to sit down and take a deep breath and collect myself. Sometimes sweat would break out on my hands and my face would feel like it was on fire and I would notice the confused looks on my students' faces. They kept eerily quiet in those moments, afraid of what might happen next.

Week by week Dr. Michaels helped me to find my way back to the moment when I gave up my scholarships to various graduate schools. I couldn't escape the feeling that a huge change needed to happen in my life, no matter how much I loved teaching and how precious my students were to me. He also encouraged me to tell Andrey about my therapy sessions. I had kept it a secret from him for fear that he would think I was crazy and leave me. What I hadn't counted on was that he had picked up a vibe that I was hiding something important. It finally came to a head one afternoon, when Andrey literally sat me down at the kitchen table and asked point blank: "What is going on? I have a right to know." I broke down and confessed that I was seeing a psychiatrist.

"Is that all it is?" he answered. "He sounds like a really fabulous man. I'd like to meet him sometime." He looked incredibly relieved that what I had to say was no more than that. (He had thought that perhaps I was seeing another man romantically!) My weekly sessions continued and they were as illuminating as a lightning storm. I finally tumbled down from that emotional trapeze and began to realize that there was no way out, but to discover what could be recovered from the foggy past. I realized that I had to resign from school teaching and to apply to graduate school at the University of Toronto. I couldn't ignore any longer what had been buried in my heart since those Berkeley days. For the first time I understood how much I was grieving over those lost scholarships.

My principal begged me to stay. The parents of my students pleaded with me. Stern voices in my head shouted: "How can you leave a well-paying job for which so many others are standing in line? And where will all this lead anyway? To an MA degree? To a PhD? It is your brother who was supposed to get a PhD, not you! You will surely be punished for it." Such were the demons blocking my way. Yet, I had become stubborn and more confident in spite of those moments of anxiety. A quiet, insistent voice whispered that this would be a chance for freedom. That if I didn't take this risk, I would indeed end up that embittered woman without any of the passion that had brought me to the teaching profession in the first place. "Have faith," this voice said. "Take the chance. You can't afford not to."

I remember how alive and renewed I felt after I had received my acceptance letter from the University of Toronto coupled with a graduate fellowship. Proof positive that I was headed back to recoup my losses. When I entered the University's Robarts library on the first day of the Fall semester to pick up my student library card, a bout of dizziness almost crumpled me. I rushed to find a chair at a table nearby, heart pounding, my hands drenched with sweat as I clutched my card. Slowly I gathered myself together and looked around. Students were searching through card catalogue drawers (this was before the internet). Their sense of purpose and the quietude of the library were soothing.

My mind turned back to the phone call with my parents in Montréal some months earlier when I had triumphantly announced that I was leaving my teaching position and applying to graduate school. There was silence on the other end of the line. I heard static. "Are you there? Did you hear me?" I asked. "Yes, we heard you," my mother roared. "What do you think you are doing? You'll never finish the program. You're not strong enough. You're throwing away a good job. Have you lost your mind?" My father was on the extension phone and he weakly added: "Well, maybe, if you want to do this, maybe..." His voice trailed off. It was as if someone had punched me in the face, hard. Then my head began to throb. Pools of tears gathered in my eyes. The call ended somehow. I put down the phone and told Andrey that perhaps my idea of returning to graduate school was unwise. "What are you talking about?" he asked in disbelief. "What did your parents say?" I told him what had happened. "That's your mother trying to stand in your way – again. You can't allow it. I know you really want to go back to graduate school, go for it."

Andrey had recognized the tyrannical ways of my mother early on in our marriage when she had visited us back in Edmonton. She had altercations with us over the color of our bedspread, the type of sofa or dishes or towel sets we should buy. And she had not expected to gain a son-in-law who was not willing to succumb to her absolute control. She probably never imagined that such a son-in-law existed on this planet. During that first visit to our new home my mother rushed around our apartment like a whirling dervish trying to "clean up" (I didn't ask her to do so, but she thought it wasn't clean enough.) In her mania she tripped over the television cord and the TV went toppling to the floor, the screen shattering into a million pieces. She never apologized, never offered to pay for a new TV set and complained endlessly about the pain in her knee as a result of the fall. I rushed to get her ice and bought a new television set the following day hoping to erase the whole incident.

In honor of her visit, we had purchased orchestra tickets for us to see the Royal Winnipeg Ballet that was performing at the concert hall. After the performance, my mother cooed how I would have made such a fine ballerina and that it was I who should have been up there on that stage. A memory of her having finally sent me to ballet class in a secondhand leotard, its zipper broken, held together with a safety pin, invaded my mind. I shoved the shrouded anger back down into my gut. When we saw her off at the airport she caught me in a vise-like grip and sobbed frantically. "You are so far away from the family. I miss you so much. You must find a way to move closer to us." A wave of guilt almost choked my throat. "I miss you too," I had said. "We will try."

Not long after my mother's visit I scratched my eye and had to wear a patch for a week and fell into a dark place of despair. Would my eye recover? How could I wash my face so that I wouldn't make the situation worse? Was this the beginning of blindness? I missed several classes in my teacher training program and stayed home in a haze of agitated isolation, fearing the worst. Andrey would return each day from his work on campus and try to comfort me. When they removed the patch, my eye had healed, yet I was afraid to wear eye makeup. When we arrived in Montréal from Edmonton that December for the holidays, my mother asked why I wasn't wearing makeup. I told her about the eye scratch. "Oh, Grace is in a mess again," she responded rather cheerily in a sing-song voice.

Two years later we moved to Toronto. During our first few years there, life consisted of visits back and forth to our parents in Montréal, each visit leaving me feeling more and more depleted because of the tension hidden just below the surface. My hypochondriacal worries escalated and I kept spraining and re-spraining my ankles in Toronto, falling off sidewalks, and once, when dizziness overcame me, I tripped on streetcar tracks. I ended up using a cane for a while and began to feel old (in my mid-twenties).

That is when Divine Intervention happened in the form of Dr. Michaels. During those years of therapy I began to realize that the word "poisonous" which he had used to describe my family situation was not an exaggeration. I began to see my mother – really *see* her. Suddenly, the monster with the iron hook and the attendant demons were not just about the Holocaust. It was a much more complicated image than I had ever imagined it to be. I began to understand Dr. Michaels' supposition that there might have been some kind of serious abuse in my mother's family in Poland before the war and that such trauma would have been intensified in her by the Holocaust.

I had dutifully called my parents in Montréal every Sunday afternoon since the Berkeley days. My mother demanded it. When Dr. Michaels told me that I had to stop making those calls every week I became extremely jittery, believing that this was impossible. My mother would never stand for that. How could I survive without my birth family? It would be like losing a limb, losing my footing in life. "I can't do that," I whimpered. He replied: "There is no other way if you want to have a life of your own." Thick darkness overwhelmed me like noxious smoke. I called him a few days later out of sheer panic. "Maybe I need to go to a hospital for a while?" I was pleading. "If you do that," he said, "then unfortunately I won't be in charge anymore. Other doctors will take over." I thought to myself: *Who knows what those other doctors might do to me? They might pump me with all sorts of medication.* Suddenly I visualized myself surrounded by patients who were chronically ill; and a horrifying thought assailed me: I would never get better.

Then a sudden memory emerged from deep within. At the age of about eight or nine, I began crying in class in a great state of anxiety, and a caring teacher called my parents and suggested that I see a therapist. My mother brought me to a hospital psychiatric clinic (we could not afford a doctor in private practice). I remember sitting in the waiting room staring at the bombed-out eyes of some of the other children. They didn't even look at me. They were absorbed in some nightmarish mind space that had swallowed them up. One boy had a tremor. A girl sat with a vacant expression, almost lifeless. Another girl clung desperately to her mother, a woman who looked like she could be a sergeant major in the military. Blood-red lipstick was smeared like a crooked line on her thin lips. The thought crossed my mind that she might have never smiled in her life. And another thought: maybe these children were on meds already.

I caught a glimpse of my mother and what I saw made me shudder. She seemed much too comfortable in that waiting room, not worried at all. She actually looked like she was glowing with satisfaction. As if that clinic would take me off her hands in some way. In that ghoulish moment I sensed that I was hanging between life and some sort of death.

I chose life. I resolutely decided that I would put a smile on my face and try to act like the "normal" kids in my class. I tugged at my mother's sleeve and told her I wanted out of that waiting room immediately. Her eyebrows shot up in displeasure and in a booming voice she retorted that we should at least keep our appointment. When we walked into the doctor's office, my mother took up the entire session weeping about all her suffering and losses during the Holocaust. The doctor never acknowledged me and instead looked like he was overtaken with pity for my mother. I never wanted to go back.

That memory awakened me to the torment still lodged in my heart. So when Dr. Michaels explained that other doctors would take over if I were admitted to hospital I knew I had no choice. I trusted him as my doctor – and him only. And I had Andrey at home as my rock, always there for me. My rock of Gibraltar. I don't think I could have gone through all that emotional uncovering, recovering, re-suffering, re-membering without Andrey by my side. I stumbled on in the weeks and months that followed as if I were at the edge of the abyss afraid to look down for fear of hurtling right into it. Images from my unconscious were beginning to surface, things I had locked away in the deep recesses of my mind as any abused child must do in order to survive. The anxiety attacks became more frequent. I ruminated about my predicament. And once again what popped up like a frightening jack-in-the-box was my fear of going blind. But I trusted Dr. Michaels. We had created a deep bond. I sensed how much he cared for me in a fatherly sort of way. He was so certain that I had the strength to overcome, and I began to believe him. "You are afraid of going blind because you are afraid to see what your parents did to you; how unfairly you were treated in your family. It will pass," he promised. "*The truth shall make you strong and it shall make you free,*" he would proclaim in the midst of a particularly difficult session. "No slouch was he who said that," he would add.

Dr. Michaels could always turn around even the most difficult moments with his deep insights and his incisive sense of humor. For example: "That woman must have gone to the same school as Attila the Hun. And she could probably have eaten him for breakfast." (I ended up dubbing her "Mrs. Attila the Hun" for that reason.)

How I laughed and cried in that oasis of an office. After each session I'd walk outside for a while and then find a quiet table in a restaurant or café nearby and write notes in my journal about what had transpired. On the day when Dr. Michaels pointed out that my mother must have had severe emotional problems way before the war (the evidence for this was that there were many Holocaust survivors who treated their children with much more care and love), a weight of enormous proportion lifted off my shoulders. Then, finally, up spurted the anger from deep within me like boiling, red blood.

I finally mustered the courage to stop calling my parents every single Sunday and this action threw my mother into a tailspin. It was as if I had been a soldier checking in with my superior each week and suddenly refused to do so. The strategy she chose was to give me the cold shoulder. Her voice turned to ice when we spoke over the phone. I could feel those ice pellets flying straight from the telephone into my ear. I guess she thought that approach would bring me back in line. Truth to tell I was petrified and guilt-ridden. "After all, she's the only mother you'll ever have," whispered some little ogre in my ear.

After several weeks of a hiatus, I called them one Sunday afternoon trying hard to be in an upbeat mood. I told my parents I was filling out the application forms for graduate school. I also mentioned what positive responses I had received from the professors who were writing letters of recommendation on my behalf. (My professor from Berkeley was one of them. Another professor from my Italian undergraduate program at McGill was another.) I guess I had expected that my parents might have come around and would show some enthusiasm for this next step in my life. Instead, my mother shouted, "How can you do something so stupid! I thought you would have come to your senses by now."

This time there were no tears in my eyes. Suddenly a wind gust of rage gathered me up and carried this message from my mouth over the telephone lines: "What kind of a mother are you? To not wish your daughter to succeed? You have done me so much damage. Because of you I have had to see a psychiatrist." She interrupted me and shrieked, "You're seeing a psychiatrist?? I always knew you were crazy!" That ended the conversation.

In my next session, I told Dr. Michaels about this incident and he looked a bit dismayed that I had mentioned I was seeing a psychiatrist. It probably was not the best thing for me to have said then, however he understood that I was at the end of my rope and was finally expressing myself. Then he added with a glint in his eye, "I hope you didn't give your mother my name or address!" We both laughed and out came those delicious cookies he always had tucked away in the adjoining little kitchen pantry.

My husband and I visited my parents in Montréal not long after. It was turning out to be a better than average trip and I was relieved. My mother seemed to have forgotten all about my outburst on the telephone. And then one afternoon she asked me in a nonchalant manner when she and I were alone in the kitchen: "Are you still seeing that psychiatrist?" She was casually leaning on the counter next to the sink. The light had been dwindling in the late fall afternoon. My whole body immediately tensed up. "Yes, I am. He is such a sensitive and kind man and I'm learning a lot from him."

"What do you talk about? Does he tell you that I hate you?" Surprised, I answered: "No, he doesn't say that at all."

The subject was dropped, but I noted what a truly odd question that had been. At that moment I remembered how as a young child I would ask my mother over and over again whether she loved me. I can't remember whether she ever answered me.

28

THE BOMBSHELL

This particular time it was my parents who telephoned me. My mother announced in a saccharin sweet voice over the phone: "Guess what? We're moving to Toronto!!"

"What!?" was all I could manage to utter. My father almost inaudibly added that they weren't 100 percent sure about the move. His voice was wobbly with a hint of resentment. My mother shot back: "We're definitely selling our house and we'll come to Toronto as soon as it's sold. I want my daughter back." Those last five words almost annihilated me. Mrs. Attila the Hun was about to enter my territory like an invading army.

I staggered away from the phone almost incapable of telling Andrey what had happened. When I did, he thought that perhaps she was just trying to intimidate me. After all, her home had always been her claim to fame. She had put all her energy into decorating that house over the years. She had always stated emphatically: "This house means the world to me." How could she give that up? Even Dr. Michaels looked shocked when I told him the situation and exclaimed she surely couldn't be that ferocious, not even her. That she must be bluffing.

Ferocity knew no bounds with Mrs. Attila the Hun. She had decided to "get her daughter back." She didn't care at all about uprooting my father. He had clung desperately to all his routines. His visits to the library and meet-ups with his reading buddies had become even more frequent, especially because he had just sold a business that had done poorly.

A terrible sadness had always seized me whenever I was confronted with the rage-filled disappointment my father harbored about his life. He always distanced himself from any of my own ambitions and this confusing behavior made me feel ambivalent about my achievements, as if all my hard-earned grades could dissolve in a puff of wind. The more I excelled in my studies the more he disappeared into his tough shell. When my mother came up with the idea of moving to Toronto, he didn't stand up to her – in spite of how much he loved being in Montréal. Dr. Michaels was mortified. "I knew she was poison for you – but to come after you like this? It's unheard of."

She called again the following week and demanded that we allow them (including my sister who was still living at home) to move into our tiny place while they would look for a condo to purchase. That was a line in the sand for my husband. I couldn't say no to my mother and yet I told Andrey that I didn't think I could survive this aggression. He wrote a polite, respectful letter explaining to them that we needed our space and privacy and therefore it would not be possible for them to stay with us, but that we would pay their hotel expenses for a little while. I showed Dr. Michaels the letter. He agreed that the situation was serious enough to warrant sending it.

A feeling of doom seized me by the throat. I didn't have to wait long. The phone rang shrilly a few days after the letter was sent. My mother went ballistic. "What daughter would not allow her parents and sister to stay with her while they are looking for a place to buy? How can you allow your husband to control you like that?" *She* was talking about control? If I wasn't sure before, I was sure then that sending that letter was my ticket to maintaining sanity. They stayed in a hotel when they came to Toronto and purchased a condo surprisingly quickly.

The onslaught continued even after they had settled into their condo. My mother began to complain that we didn't come to dinner often enough. Or that I didn't call enough times a week. Or that I didn't take my sister out often enough. Or that I didn't invite them over to our place as much as she thought I should have. This went on month after month. One evening as we were having a Friday night dinner at their place, I was trying to share what my week had been like discussing the ups and downs of my return to university as a graduate student after a hiatus of seven years. I remember trying really hard to keep the conversation light and breezy in order to avoid any altercations. I wore a pretty black knit pullover with red lace piping over a red pleated wool skirt. Andrey was with me. I never went there without him. Tension always seemed to crackle in the air when we came to visit. One could never predict when a skirmish might erupt over any stray comment. The familiar mixture of exhaustion and foreboding was already beginning to attack my body and mind.

The room was becoming too silent, too strained. My mother was hanging onto a large pot of steaming potato pudding (always a favorite dish of mine). It's a dense affair of potatoes mixed with eggs, onions, garlic baked in the oven for about an hour and a half until golden brown. This old-fashioned grated potato pudding is called *kugelis* in Russia or *kartoflak* in Poland. My mouth would water when I would be served this treat as a child. It was real comfort food and I always praised my mother for it. I also enjoyed her cabbage rolls [*golubki*] and I spied them that night on a large round yellow plate overflowing with rich hot tomato sauce on the table waiting to be served. I was about to say how much I was also looking forward to the *golubki* when my mother glared at me and flung a chunk of the *kartoflak* onto my plate as she shouted: "You have turned into a polite stranger; you would be able to get along better with the Queen than you are able to get along with your own flesh and blood!" Her coal-black eyes looked as if they could fire bullets. I stared at her and then at my father whose face had been contorted into one of a trapped animal, and then at my sister whose jagged frown made me wonder whether she had become a clone of my mother. My mother's mouth was still open, a gaping hole in the wildness of her dark face.

Without warning my father jerkily picked up what was the closest thing to him on the table. It turned out to be a frozen *babka*, another delightful Polish concoction: a rich buttery round vanilla cake swirled with chocolate. I became motionless as I watched him literally throw it at me. The cake, still thawing out, could have hit me hard. I was well aware that my mother had strong-armed my father into agreeing to move to Toronto. A bitter taste spread over my tongue as I saw that all he could do was to take his rage out on me. I ducked just in time. It didn't matter that the *babka* did not hit me. The ache in my heart was far greater than the damage the cake would have done if it had struck me physically. The cake went sailing across the dining room into the living room, landed on the sofa and sat there awkwardly like an unexpected guest. It would have actually been funny if it hadn't been so sad.

I rose abruptly from my seat at the table, glanced down at the *kartoflak* which at this point looked discarded and said quietly to my husband, "We are not welcome here. Let's leave." He got up, took my hand and firmly placed it in his and we walked slowly toward the hallway closet. My mother screeched behind us: "Where are you going? Come back here!"

As I put on my coat I remember these words leaping into my mind: "This is the beginning of the end." We opened the door, walked out, closed the door softly and then raced to the elevator. I didn't want to give my mother the chance to yell at me in the hallway. Thankfully, the elevator arrived almost immediately. When we walked outside into the coolness of the night my darling soulmate scooped me up into his arms as I broke down and sobbed.

In spite of everything, I still tried to keep up some semblance of a relationship with my family, but it became increasingly difficult. Their hostility toward me proved to grow more and more out of control. As soon as I stepped into their orbit it was as if I had entered a cabal of witches. The criticisms, the veiled rage was just as harrowing as the outright screaming – perhaps greater. And yet, I wanted so much to be the good daughter that I might have hung on forever, no matter the intensity of the insults. It is a known fact that abused children hold on to their abusers in spite of the ongoing pain and they simply blame themselves. With Dr. Michaels I had been on a heavy, laborious journey toward rediscovering that little neglected child who had been hungering for love. I finally understood clearly and fully what Dr. Michaels had tried to explain to me in one of our sessions: "You were a nightingale among the crows and they couldn't deal with it. And now that you are claiming your birthright they are livid. Their subconscious response is: "How dare you upset the whole family structure? You were the convenient scapegoat."

"What will I do now?" I mumbled.

That question hung like a thick fog each time I saw my parents or thought about them. I was wrung out and I mused: "If only they hadn't moved to Toronto. If they had stayed in Montréal I could have had a buffer zone and at least some sort of relationship. That would have been far better than this all-out war." Now there was no choice. They were in Toronto and there they would remain. A formidable thought crossed my mind more than once: "Perhaps we should consider moving somewhere else?" However, both my husband's and my professional lives were by then fully established and we appreciated the stable safe space that we had built together. And Toronto was becoming a more and more interesting city with immigrants pouring in from all parts of the globe, creating an atmosphere filled with diverse cultural activities in theater, in literature, in art – as well as a cornucopia of fascinating new restaurants. I was determined not to surrender to Mrs. Attila the Hun.

I plodded on. But I began to feel haunted and hunted as if by some secret service operatives. A kind of local paranoia set in. Whenever I'd enter a restaurant or go to the cinema I'd worry about whether my mother might be there. In fact, several years after they had moved to Toronto, my husband and I entered a restaurant one afternoon after shopping in a mall nearby. After we were seated, I spied my mother and sister from the corner of my eye in a booth. They didn't notice me. I gave my husband a look of utter panic and motioned that we had to get out immediately. I snatched my purse and coat and walked quickly to the exit. What a close call!

Often I began to feel shaky even as I walked on the street. I would hang onto Andrey for dear life. If not for him and for Dr. Michaels, I might have gone out of my mind. Although my graduate work kept me busy and offered solace and hope for the future, I was always on edge waiting for the house of cards to collapse. I even worried that my mother might show up at the university and berate me. It wasn't out of the question. This was hand-to-hand combat.

Thankfully, due to Dr. Michaels' guidance and care, and due to the abiding love and protection of my husband and my own dogged determination, I had a unified force against the enemy.

The days and months rolled on. Then the news came that my father was not well. It began with pains in his legs and ended with several heart surgeries over the following years. When he was in hospital, my mother expected me to be at his side constantly. She considered me a terrible daughter because my visits to the hospital were never enough in her eyes. When I would go to my father's bedside, my mother and sister shrieked: "Why do you even bother to show up? You don't love him or us." Patients and nurses would stop what they were doing and look in the direction where this weird drama was playing out. My father did come home from the hospital and started feeling stronger. The triple bypass operation resuscitated him.

I managed to defend my PhD dissertation and complete my program in the midst of all this family tumult. I invited my parents to the Convocation, an event meant to be joyous for the families of the graduates. My mother's response was: "We'll try to come, but your brother is flying in from London that night so we're not sure. I want to be right at home when he arrives." They did finally show up – reluctantly. I looked out into the sea of radiant faces in the audience of Convocation Hall and found my parents; my mother looked bored and impatient, my father dazed and confused. They rushed away as soon as the ceremony ended. They never came up to congratulate me. They never asked to see the bound copy of the dissertation – ever. Dr. Michaels also came to the Convocation. He stayed for the reception and the loving pride that shone on his face warmed me like a blazing fire on a freezing winter night. He was like the parent that I had always longed for. *In loco parentis.*

In the years that followed, my parents took several winter trips to Florida. During one of them my father had to be air-ambulanced back to Toronto. This time his condition seemed beyond repair. I would look at my father in the hospital bed as he slipped away. When I tried to speak to him, his eyes opened slightly and a frightened expression spread over his shriveled face. He was mute, like a forgotten child in an orphanage. My eyes fell upon his slippers on the floor next to the bed and I sobbed silently. As a child I would bring him his slippers when he got home from work. They made me feel useful and I loved watching when he took off his shoes and placed those slippers on his tired feet. They were dark brown leather with a white fleece lining, open at the back of the foot. I would run and get him his favorite book of the week and he'd sit down at his chair in the living room and begin to read and I'd bring my book over and read alongside him. He looked so snug in those slippers. I used to sneak my feet into his slippers whenever I could steal into my parents' bedroom after school while my mother was busy in the kitchen. The fleece was soft and cuddly and I flopped around in those way-too-big shoes. They caressed my feet so lovingly making me hope that my father could find a way to show me his affection more often. And now his slippers lay exhausted on the hospital room floor, the leather cracked and dry.

In spite of his many failings as a father, he had been, of the two, the gentler one and I had always hung onto him for whatever small comforts I could receive when I was a child. And in his way he did offer me a fascinating view of the world. I shall never forget how he shared his love of language and culture – and learning in general – with me. The excitement of that first visit to Gatineau Library with my father when I was a little girl, just beginning to read, will live in my memory forever. A few weeks later, he died. I couldn't stop crying at the funeral. People commented on this. My mother looked annoyed by what she thought was a fake display of emotion.

She couldn't have been more wrong. He was the only whiff of a parent I had ever known and now he was gone. I felt bereft.

The *shiva*, the Jewish seven-day ritual of mourning where friends and acquaintances come to pray and console the mourners and bring food, was held at my sister's house and it left me feeling like what I had always been in that family: the outsider, the unwanted one, the unloved one. My mother glowered at me, my siblings totally under her thumb. When my friends came to pay their respects my sister shouted: "Your friends have been here long enough. Tell them to leave." She blamed me for everything. I knew that she was just carrying out orders and there was nothing I could do. She had refused to see Dr. Michaels when I had suggested this to her years earlier. My brother on the other hand was fragile and huddled in a corner, trying to deal with what for him had been a terribly stormy relationship with our father. Only his wife, my sister-in-law, took me aside and said, "I'm sorry you are being treated so badly. You don't deserve this – and at your father's *shiva*! How shocking." I thanked my sister-in-law for her kindness. My mother and sister were like jackals trying to attack me. It seemed to me like they had forgotten to grieve my father's passing.

One morning during those seven days, I woke up and everything became illuminated. I knew that a Divine Presence had taken charge and I heard a voice within me say: "Your father is gone. Now you must walk away and live your life. You must free yourself. You have no choice. This is your father's gift to you. Take it." There is a commentary in the Talmud that a father's death opens a door for his child. Excruciating as it was, I took the gift and did what I never thought was possible: I had to walk away. My mother began leaving messages on my telephone answering machine. If there had been even a trace of softness in her voice I would have returned the calls. Instead, she blasted me with: "What kind of daughter are you? What have I done to you? How dare you treat me like this? I want you to call me immediately!" On and on these messages blared: not a shred of understanding, just naked demands for control.

I saw my mother briefly at the unveiling of my father's

headstone at the cemetery a year later. That was the last time I ever saw her. When she died almost 20 years later, I was not informed of her passing. I had been out-of-town with my husband at the time and a friend phoned to tell me what had happened. A cousin of hers had been reading the obituaries in a Toronto newspaper and had chanced upon my mother's name. I never received a message from my siblings. I never saw the will, never received any inheritance. Some friends suggested that I should contest this treatment, however I knew that in order to maintain the life that I had worked so hard to create, it was necessary for me to stay away from my sister and brother who had either followed my mother's "instructions" not to inform me of the funeral, or decided to do this on their own. I placed the matter in the hands of the Universe.

All I do know is that Dr. Michaels released me from the dungeon of a *still life* by opening my eyes to the truth: that I was a motherless child who would mourn that loss forever. The miracle is that not only would this truth not destroy me it would set me free and bestow upon me a beautiful, if hard-won, *real life*. He was not only a healer; he must have also been an angel.

29

OPPY AND ROSSA

We didn't treat each other as in-laws. It was as if we were really good friends getting together for a soothing chat. They will always be Oppy and Rossa to me. A sense of warmth would envelop the three of us during our conversations as if we were sitting next to a roaring fireplace. We were simply on the same wavelength. They really liked me and I really liked them. It was a match made in heaven. I would often visit my in-laws in Montréal on my own just to have some time with them in their humble apartment located on top of their small gift shop. Of course, their son and I also visited them together on a regular basis but these visits – when I had them all to myself – were a great blessing. I would sit with them in their tiny, cozy kitchen/dining room munching on one of my mother-in-law's exquisite confections (Rossa was a terrific pastry maker as well as a great cook), and we spoke honestly and openly. It certainly didn't hurt our friendship that I showed how much I enjoyed her cooking and baking. Whenever she knew I was coming to visit, Rossa would ask what I'd like her to make for me to eat. And I didn't hold back. I told her how much I adored "this or that" and "this or that" always awaited me in a shining pot on the stove or in a glistening baking pan when I walked into the kitchen.

How can I even describe how her sour cherry soup awakened

my taste buds. Or the sour cream and bread with *töltött káposzta* [stuffed cabbage]. And the *turus gomboc*, cooked soft cheese balls with a dollop of sour cream. For dessert I adored the *gundel palacsinta* filled with walnuts and chocolate sauce or filled with apricot jam and confectionary sugar sprinkled on top. Not to mention the mouth-watering flourless chocolate torte layered with strawberry jam and fresh cream. Surely this was heaven – not only because of the delicacy of the food, but also because of the charming look of satisfaction which glowed on Rossa's face as she saw how much I took pleasure in her cooking.

They had many emotional issues, and had walled themselves off from the world after the war. It was as if they were religious members in a cloistered monastery. They had no social life except for the interactions they had with their many faithful customers and this was enough for them. They never went out for meals or to a movie or on outings. This was their survival mechanism after the extreme cruelty they had witnessed and experienced. (They had both been incarcerated in death camps.) This reclusiveness was evident the first time I visited their home as their son's fiancée. It was as if time had stopped there. I understood the sorrow that lay behind it. And for me, as an adult who had not grown up there, that secluded environment calmed and soothed me. I also recognized that there was love – no matter what. The house I grew up in may have appeared attractive and lively, but what happened to me within that chaotic, uncaring, thunderously erratic family life made me recognize how little that sort of superficial ornamentation really matters.

However, this kind of seclusion had a myriad of negative effects on my in-laws' two children. There is something painful for Andrey about digging into his inner feelings at times of conflict, whereas I want to get right to the matter and resolve it. What I find very difficult is to let go of it and give Andrey some breathing space to work it out. I'm like a dog with a bone. But we're getting better at it. We have always felt like we're in this relationship "for the long haul," that we are each other's family, so we have always been invested in making it work even during rough patches. A long-lived marriage is a great blessing – maybe the greatest! –and as with anything else that endures you have to work at it. You have to tend your garden regularly, or the weeds will take over pretty soon.

Oppy and Rossa were able to relax and be themselves with me. I was not their child and that made it easier for us all to be who we really were. There was no anxiety or judgment or resentment on either side. We accepted each other wholeheartedly. They respected my intellectual pursuits and always complimented me on a current piece of research I would discuss with them. I remember the sheer delight on their faces as I presented them with a bound copy of my dissertation. Due to the circumstances of poverty and then the war, they never had the chance to complete high school, let alone attend university. They didn't have to understand the academic language in my work. I explained it to them simply. I always hated jargon anyway. They often told me how lucky their son was to have such a loving, brilliant and pretty wife. I could confide in them without hesitation. With them, I was an orphan no longer. They listened to me. They believed in me unconditionally.

One Sunday afternoon in the twilight of a winter day on one of my solo visits, I watched large snowflakes cascade to the ground through their kitchen window adorned with its white lace curtains. I munched on a piece of *Dobos* torte, sponge cake layered with chocolate buttercream topped with crispy caramel. As always, my mother-in-law had asked me in advance what I would like her to make and her *Dobos* torte was high on my request list. As the caramelly taste rolled around my tongue I told them how they gave me the feeling of being a loved child. How they fed me, body and soul. And how much I appreciated this amazing gift.

This particular meeting took place after my father's death and my subsequent need to break away from my mother. I poured out my heart to them and added: "Without your son's love and support I could not have endured this," my voice cracking with emotion. I visualized the three of us hugging one another in one of those little glass globes that you shake and snowflakes inside swirl around a peaceful winter scene. "Unfortunately," I continued, "my father could not rein in my mother. He was too soft – maybe too weak – to stand up to her. And I saw how he kept all his frustration inside and it made him sick. I think he died of a broken heart."

Oppy nodded in sad agreement. As tears were running down my face I felt blessedly safe with them. A strong wind began to howl outside as an icy mix of rain and snow began to tap against the window. Rossa got up to put water on to boil for second cups of tea. I sensed that she may have wanted to busy herself because my emotional distress was palpable and she may have felt overwhelmed by it. She smoothed the strands of shimmering white hair which had escaped from her *chignon*. Her sturdy apron flapped as she strode into the kitchen.

Oppy who sat facing me at the table, put down his fork and quietly said to me in Yiddish, *"Du bist mayn kind"* [You are my child]. His sapphire-blue eyes sparkled in his gaunt face. I heard the clock ticking away in a corner of the room and felt comforted by this caring expression. All else was silent. Rossa returned a little while later holding a pot of strong black tea in one hand and a plate of lemon wedges in the other. The teapot was of fine English bone china with a design of violets and the plate matched it. These items clearly came from their gift shop. (I had received many lovely such gifts from their store over the years, including some delicate pieces of jewelry.) She put the steaming pot down on the table and then poured the tea into matching cups. With her competent fingers she used a tiny silver fork to distribute the lemon wedges into the teacups. As she handed me my tea her hazel eyes glistened with wetness. Her other hand reached for mine and squeezed it tenderly.

My father-in-law continued in Yiddish: *"Du mus lozn es gayn. Du bist nisht shuldik"* [You must let it go. You are not guilty]. "It's a wound."

He said *wound*. How did he know that word in English? I wondered to myself. His understanding amazed me. *"Vayn nisht dayn leben avek. Du bist noch jung. Du mus leben."* [Don't weep your life away. You are still young. You have to live.]

As I wept he added: *"Zorg sich nisht. Es wird gut zayn. Du bist befrayt geworen"* [Don't worry. It will be all right. You have been liberated].

You have been liberated. Those last words came from a deep and devastated place from within his own soul. He had survived Buchenwald and his wife had survived Auschwitz. They met after the war in their hometown while they were searching for survivors of their families. The solace I felt in their presence transcends words. That night, with the moon shining high in the dark sky, in the comfort of my husband's childhood featherbed, I slept like the child I had always known in my dreams. Oppy and Rossa died, in close succession, years ago and I miss them deeply, but the gift of their love is mine forever.

Along with Dr. Michaels, my in-laws may well have belonged to the group of the 36 hidden "saints" that the Talmud speaks of: ordinary human beings who at any moment in time are given the power to perform comforting and valuable good deeds for those in need. This mystical concept of the *Tzadikim Nistarim* [צַדִּיקִים נִסְתָּרִים, hidden saints or righteous ones] states that at all times there are 36 such blessed people in the world, and that were it not for them, for *all* of them – i.e. if even one of them was missing – the world would come to an end. "In every generation these "hidden righteous ones," the Talmud goes on to explain, "have been given the blessing of greeting the *Shekhinah*", the Divine Presence.

One must never underestimate the arrival of good fortune, nor underestimate its opposite. It will always remain a mystery as to who gets through the door and who does not. I know that Walter, the kind elderly man who sat with me at that bus stop in Oakland those many years ago, cannot be alive anymore. He himself may well have been one of the 36 hidden righteous ones at the moment when I was so lost in that dangerous place. I want to tell an angel to relay a message to him, up in heaven, that I did "hang on" as he had suggested, and that I was lucky.

30

DESTINATION: PROFESSOR

Several months after my father died, I was unexpectedly short-listed for a tenure-track faculty position at the University of Toronto and after the full and complicated hiring process I was selected for the position. I felt like I had won the lottery! But it almost didn't happen that way.

Several years earlier, after I had completed my PhD, I was awarded postdoctoral fellowships focusing on language learning and cultural identity. I began to feel isolated during that time. My postdoctoral research was basically just an elaboration of my dissertation, adding several more language groups as participants. I conducted a statistical sampling study involving hundreds of university students who were taking first year language courses (Italian, Spanish, Portuguese, Mandarin, Cantonese, Hebrew, Arabic, Japanese, Russian, and Polish) at two major Toronto universities. The students were asked to fill out the 50-minute-long questionnaire about how they felt about learning their home languages in a formal setting. Each of their professors had given me permission to take over one class for this purpose. I stayed in the classrooms as the students checked off their responses to my questions.

About ten minutes into the first such class that I visited, a hand went up. "I hope you don't mind," said an eager young man. "I've never really thought about any of this before. And it's interesting. But if you really want to know how I feel about my cultural background and my home language, you won't find that out by my checking off boxes on a scale from one to five. You need to interview us in person." Many of the other students nodded their heads in agreement. "That would be great," I replied, somewhat crestfallen. "But I only have 50 minutes, so please could you fill out the questionnaire?"

In almost every class in which I gave out my questionnaire, students handed them back to me with pieces of paper on which they had written their phone numbers. *"I really want to tell you my story. Forget about the questionnaire."* That was their message. Although this litany was repeated over and over, I tried not to hear it because I had invested so much effort in my carefully constructed questionnaire and I wasn't able to see beyond it. "Maybe in the future," I answered regretfully.

Time passed. One day, I happened to pass by a bulletin board at the University of Toronto advertising a seminar with the title: *"The Self I Dream: A Narrative Reconstruction of a Personal Mythology."* The topic intrigued me. I was surprised to learn that there existed a place in an academic environment sponsoring this type of work. When I walked into that seminar on the appointed day I had no idea that my life was about to change radically. I remember participating vigorously in the Q&A that followed, drawing from a deep well of my own lived experience. They were talking about the link between personal and professional lived experiences. It was as if a secret door had been opened wide allowing me to enter.

A sudden thought arose: Should I go ahead and collect the stories of the participants in my research study, as my participants had wanted me to? I had become stuck in the rigid dynamics of Likert scales and statistical procedures and couldn't seem to give myself permission to follow the straightforward requests made by my participants. I had never taken any *qualitative* methodology courses during my graduate work, although I had actually majored in comparative literature studies in my undergraduate years at

McGill and had also audited some graduate courses in comparative literature at Berkeley.

At the end of the seminar I went over to the doctoral candidate to thank her for having given such a fascinating presentation and to wish her well. I was heading for the exit when the student's thesis supervisor approached me and asked: "Who are you?" I looked at him and said, "I'm a postdoctoral student doing quantitative research so I shouldn't really be here. But I enjoyed this session. Thank you." As I started again toward the door he stopped me and with a determined look he suggested that I make an appointment to discuss my research work with him.

A few weeks later I found myself in this professor's office telling him all about my postdoctoral work and the dilemma in which I found myself with the data collection. By that time I had begun to take the step to (surreptitiously) conduct in-depth interviews with a few of my participants and to finally allow myself to listen to their *stories*. Each one of their stories vibrated with the vitality of a language and a culture. They described what it was like growing up in their particular cultures all the while trying to fit into mainstream Canadian society. One student spoke eloquently about his pre-school years, at home all day with his Sicilian grandmother while both his parents worked in factories. He told me how afraid his *nonna* was when the prospective kindergarten teacher came knocking at their door one afternoon. His *nonna* forbade him to open the door as if hoping to keep this strange new world at bay.

Yet, in collecting these stories, I felt as though I was robbing a bank. In the course of sharing all my doubts and confusions with this professor who didn't know me and who didn't have to care, I began to realize that I had gotten lost in my work and that I didn't know how to proceed.

What Professor Michael Connelly told me that afternoon in his office allowed me to realize that my work needed to find its expression in a new direction. Mick (I always called him by his nickname) was the co-founder of a new qualitative methodology called "narrative inquiry." The narrative mode had suggested itself to me, but I had been working too much and too long in isolation to fully recognize how important was the power of story. That afternoon Mick simply said, "Doing narrative is not a crime." "Really?!" I blurted out. And we both laughed. With those few words he opened the door into an entirely new professional world, and gave me the permission that I needed to embark on this unanticipated journey.

I finally began to wholeheartedly interview all of the students from my research project who had expressed an interest in sharing their stories with me. The creative juices began to flow within me as I listened to them and wrote up my field notes. At the same time, I began attending the seminars in Mick's center for narrative inquiry and began writing about my own experiences as a child whose language at home was neither English nor French. I wrote and wrote and wrote and Mick encouraged me to show him my work. The suggestions he offered kept moving me forward.

My postdoctoral fellowships came to an end a year later and I was lucky to receive a research position on campus. I was assigned to a project (in another center) dealing with school literacy development for immigrant children. My office turned out to be on the same floor as Mick's, but on the other side of the elevator. One afternoon about six months after I began my research position, I was at the elevator on my way to lunch when I noticed a job advertisement for a tenure-track faculty position in Mick's center. I didn't believe that I was qualified for this position, so I didn't even consider applying for it. About a week after that, he burst into my office and apologized for the fact that he must have mislaid my application because he couldn't find it in the pile. I looked at him dumbfounded and replied: "Actually, I didn't apply because I'm not really qualified for this position." He was startled by my response and exclaimed: "What are you talking about? Please send in your application as soon as possible!"

I did.

I was amazed when I later found out that I had been shortlisted for the position. The first requirement of the hiring process was for the applicant to create a full syllabus for four graduate courses that would focus on issues of multiculturalism in education from a narrative perspective. I remember being utterly surprised at how quickly these came together for me as I sat creating the course outlines over a single weekend. It was as if all of my undergraduate, graduate, and postdoctoral work, as well as my elementary school teaching years had been a dress rehearsal for this moment. The quilt woven from all my disjointed lived experiences came together and fashioned themselves into four graduate courses: 1) *Multicultural Perspectives in Teacher Development;* 2) *Language, Culture and Identity: Using the Literary Text in Education*; 3) *Children's Literature in a Multicultural Context*; and 4) *Exemplary International School Language Programs.*

As part of the process I was also required to give a two-hour seminar in the Department. At that point all the doubts about my qualifications for the position vanished. I decided to talk about how language, culture and education saved my life. I spoke from my heart about the importance of place, language, landscape, and serendipity – and particularly about its relevance to the historical moment of global political, social and economic upheavals as well as the unprecedented rising level of international migration to Toronto. I stated that I would appreciate the opportunity to help educators help students in their classrooms who had experienced war, deprivation, and oppression. (I had no idea at the time that this presentation would become the precursor to this memoir so many years later.) As I ended my talk, I noticed the astonishment on the faces of my future colleagues. I glanced over at Mick Connelly. He had recognized my potential way before I ever knew I had any. He was glowing with delight.

I got the job. I was hired into a tenure-track position as an Assistant Professor at the University of Toronto and stepped onto what was about to become one of the wildest rides of my life.

Reflections on University Teaching, Trauma and Compassion

It happened every semester. I would walk into class and survey the new crop of graduate students. They were sitting, waiting. Some hopeful. Some hesitant. Some excited. Some had smiles on their faces. Some didn't. I placed my briefcase on the desk and introduced myself, as well as the course title and number. I stood in front of these university students as I had stood in front of my first grade five class years ago when paper airplanes were flying through the air and children were running about wildly, knowing now – as I did know then – that this is the moment before everything begins. Knowing that I had these first precious introductory moments to explain why this course was going to be an adventure, one these students had never experienced before. Most of my students were teachers and arrived weary from a full day in the classroom. Some were Museum Studies educators. A few were school principals or superintendents. Others were full-time PhD students with the goal of eventually becoming university professors.

One of the first things I told them was that there would be no formal lecture format, but rather interactive discussions based on assigned readings – a week-by-week attempt to thrash out what really counts in classrooms. I watched some of their eyes widen. Others looked as though they were beginning to wonder if they had just landed on some different planet. I gave out copies of the course outline and told them that nothing was set in stone and that this was only a guide. I gave the students time to read it in class. Then there was a short break. Sometimes I saw the furrowed brows of a skeptic or two. Those students might not return after the break. When asked why my outline wasn't organized week by week down to the last detail, my answer was: "I like to leave room for serendipity."

I will never forget the very first time I taught my *"Multicultural Perspectives in Teacher Development"* course. I floated into that graduate class on a cloud of euphoria on a late afternoon in early September. It was sheer magic. The delight of walking back into a classroom after a hiatus of almost a decade was intoxicating. And this time I was to teach a class of *graduate* students! The central question for myself as an educator will always be the one that I posed to my students in that first graduate course: *Why does one go into the field of education in the first place? How is one called to the profession of teaching?* The night before that first class a close friend of mine (who is not an academic) said to me, "Just share yourself with them. Let there be joy in the class." And I replied to her: "Yes, that's exactly what I will try to do." The words of my young student Mandy, from my grade five classroom of many years ago, echoed in my ears. "*Express yourself, Mrs. Feuerverger. You are a teacher. You have a right to.*"

We shared our life stories of dislocation, survival, and triumph over adversity. Just as I had tried to do in my own elementary school classrooms, I dared to kindle in these students – teachers all – a passion for discovery of one's place as insider/outsider in the wider society. As those evenings of encounter multiplied week by week, my graduate students discussed the assigned readings on educational theory and practice, and began to pay finer attention to the intricacies of home and school for themselves as teachers as well as for their students. This is how we can start to promote cross-cultural understanding. In a city like Toronto the question "How do you teach children about freedom when they have lived inside of tyranny all their lives?" is not a hypothetical one.

We confronted the chaos and triumphs of our experiences as educators, or to use Samuel Beckett's term "to find a form that accommodates the mess." And messy it was, and messy it always will be, for that is the stuff of education and we are here to bear witness to it. We felt summoned to discuss, in Maxine Greene's words, "the tasks of knowledge and action." Some of my colleagues who held endless academic debates about objectivity versus subjectivity in educational research had never been back in a classroom after their high school graduation. My graduate students appreciated the fact that my academic research was solidly grounded in actual teaching practice. It didn't take long for them to figure out that my heart will always reside with the children who were in my classrooms when I was an elementary schoolteacher. This first graduate course began not only to take shape, but also to gain soul, an aesthetic of improvisation. We danced on "high wires" without any safety nets beneath us.

An incident occurred some weeks into that first semester and it hit me broadside. We were discussing the assigned readings and how the personal and the professional are so intertwined as to be almost inseparable. From the buzz in the class it became clear that my students and I became present – really present – to one another. Even the most skeptical students who had at first sat immobile, hands held tight against their chests, began to loosen up and join the weekly round. One afternoon I had a meeting in my office with one of the students about her upcoming oral presentation. It was based on some of the assigned readings about the importance of the social and historical context for making teaching and learning come alive. I happened to mention to her that my parents had been in concentration camps in Poland and told her how that affected my attitude toward teaching, toward my whole life. I had assumed that our conversation was a private one and left it at that. The following evening in our class we discussed books from around the world for children and young adults. The books dealt with various difficult emotional issues in age-appropriate ways so as to give readers an opportunity to face their emotions in non-threatening ways.

Suddenly, the young woman who had been in my office the day before put up her hand and asked in a rather off-hand manner (or so I had perceived it at the time): "You who are a child of Holocaust survivors, how did you handle those feelings?" In that instant I froze. I don't know how many seconds passed before I uttered some lame statement and quickly moved onto another topic. She was a caring, diligent student and certainly had meant no harm. It was a moment of shock for me and I was completely winded by it, knocked off course. And everyone in the class sensed it. The student looked alarmed, but we all managed to crawl our way toward the break.

I felt numb as I walked back to my office and sat down at my desk. Soon I heard a soft knock at the door. I opened the door and there stood that student in tears. "I'm so sorry for asking that question. I really am." I brought her in and closed the door and reassured her that she had done nothing wrong. "Believe it or not, I have never spoken about being a child of Holocaust survivors in any classroom before. Your question was on target; I just wasn't ready for it. It's an enormous wound and your question has shown me that I have lots of work to do in terms of finding my own voice about my childhood experiences, painful as that may be."

We hugged and both went back to class where I quietly told my students exactly what had just taken place in my office. A sense of relief flowed through the room. My students looked as if I had just offered them a gift. But it was that one student who had offered me the real gift. A path appeared before me and I slowly began the journey of opening my heart to what had been shut tight for so many years. In that extraordinary moment, I discovered what I had thought was irretrievable: that I had a voice and that I needed to speak and tell *my* story: that I didn't have to masquerade in a borrowed identity; that I could draw from the well of my own sorrow and there I would find the jewel. And I could bring it into the classroom.

What I didn't fully realize when I began my university teaching was that I teach and write from a sense of both urgency as well as gratitude. I have never had the luxury of feeling a sense of security, false or otherwise. As a child, I was not just voiceless; my soul had been abducted. I was not meant to be a professor or a graduate student or much of anything else. I should have been six feet under or in a mental hospital: that is what was meant to be my narrative – or lack of it. People with trauma live their lives on parallel tracks. You could be taking a break from writing an article for a scholarly journal while sitting on your porch, sipping tea on a tranquil summer afternoon. And then – suddenly from out of nowhere – an emaciated corpse flies at your face. And not just any corpse. She looks like you. The one your father always spoke about in whispered anguish. His favorite sister...

The sense of fragility that will forever be my legacy is a muted and terrifying way of knowing the world. When children hear the screams of their parents from nightmares and when nothing about this can be expressed in the daylight at breakfast then they know in the depths of their souls (often unconsciously) that there is a monster loose that has more power than anything or anyone else in the family. This monster can jump over any fence, no matter how well-guarded, and come straight into the child's space and suddenly that child is a prisoner of war, just as her parents were. This monster begins to tag along in every activity the child is involved in. It invades every corner of the apartment in which she lives. Often it may wake her up at night even if there is no screaming from her parents' bedroom. The monster smirks and the child knows that something really scary has taken control. Suddenly she becomes afraid of all sorts of things that many children can't even fathom. She worries endlessly whether her shoes are in the right position on the floor. Or whether her clothes are hung up properly? Or are the windows shut tight before bedtime? Because if something is not in its proper place the monster might be activated. Are her books neatly piled for school? Going to sleep was a horrendous ordeal.

As I grew older other "rescues" from unexpected people and places arrived in unanticipated ways, and I reached out to them as toward a life raft. How can I ever thank them enough? They offered me the chance of a lifetime: a means to recover my voice. With this voice I hope I can speak for the voiceless; for those who are too weak or too wounded, or too lost to know that they deserve better. Perhaps that's why I always loved teaching so much. It gave me the opportunity to create community – a second chance at feeling alive and being a part of the real world. Teaching was my way of sharing hope: the sense of safety in the classroom, the love of learning, the connection with all those bright-eyed as well as not so bright-eyed individuals, all looking at me for direction and understanding. I think my students enjoyed coming to my classes because I enjoyed teaching them about the way the world was showing itself to me: about the sanctity of literature, of language, of culture: about the pleasures of reading, of hearing a healing story, of learning about new cultures, and of observing different ways of experiencing life: about the salvation that lies within all those activities. Every soul is sacred and I always tried my best to convey this to my students. I wanted them to know that they had dignity no matter how shabby their original circumstances. I knew all about the meaning of "shabby" and I had decided long ago to try my best not to allow it to defeat me. This is what I wanted to share with them.

The classroom became my true home. Education became my second chance at a fulfilling life and I chose to reach out to my students because a long time ago when I was hovering between life and death of spirit, School reached out to me and offered me shelter. Some of my teachers became my witnesses. In quiet ways they acknowledged my suffering. I discovered then that inside a good classroom you are always allowed to think – and to feel – with dignity. This is what the philosopher Matthew Fox meant when he said that: "the job of a teacher is not only to be an intellectual guide, but a spiritual messenger." For me it will always be about trust and safety, love and gratitude, as well as about building knowledge. And if the gods smile upon us, it may even become a road to redemption and salvation.

Some evenings after a particularly moving class, I stayed behind for a while. I closed the lights and sat in the empty classroom gazing out at the dark sky, silently giving thanks to whatever cosmic forces allowed me to feel that I was doing something that might strengthen my students and give them a larger sense of purpose in their own classrooms – and perhaps even a sense of adventure and, yes, even joy. I tried to welcome all the voices in my classes just as I would have wished my voice to have been heard when I was a child at home. Naturally, there were also disagreements, misunderstandings, and differences of opinion in my classrooms. How could there not be? Through it all I encouraged respect and understanding. And I hope it has made a difference in the lives of my students and of their students in turn. I know it has in mine. They have given me so much more than I could ever have given them.

A Glimpse at Thesis Supervision and Research Work

I also served on many doctoral thesis committees, as a member or as supervisor, but one in particular dealt me a body blow. It happened about five years after I began my university position. The doctoral student, Anna Maria, had written a dissertation about immigrant children and literacy development. At the last such doctoral meeting, which is a preparation for the Final Oral Examination, I praised her for having come so far from her own English-as-a-Second-Language background and from her sense of inferiority as a child of illiterate immigrant parents – a central focus of her thesis. I told her and the others on the committee that, in fact, for every one of us who are the "success stories" there are so many who have fallen by the wayside and that is why I went into education. "We are the lucky ones," I said. Anna Maria spoke about one of her participants: a young Iraqi girl in an elementary classroom in Toronto wanting to talk about her new Canadian dress rather than about the war she had escaped. I heard myself saying that we need to be wary of labeling these kids as victims because they don't want that. I didn't either. "I'm the Jewish girl who dreamed of wearing her friend's Holy Communion dress and veil and of being in the church procession. Somehow, I knew that this 'borrowed' identity was my only way to survive at that time."

A week later, Anna Maria passed the Final Oral Examination. Her 20-minute presentation was inspiring and she answered all of the questions from the committee members (including the external examiner) with poise and self-assurance. The celebratory party took place in our department. Tables were bedecked with all manner of savory finger foods, delicious cakes and cookies along with an assortment of cheeses and wine. A huge bouquet of flowers sat in the middle of the table. Colorful helium-filled balloons swayed from the ceiling. Anna Maria's parents were there: Italian immigrants from a village in Calabria in the south of Italy, who had come to Toronto in the early 1960s, working-class, humble and awed by their daughter's achievement. Her father was a construction worker, tall, dark and handsome (literally!) with hands that reflected his manual labor. He wore a dark suit, a conservative blue tie and a shirt that was gleamingly white against his bronzed skin. He looked almost bewildered at what this celebration signified. Anna Maria's mother was a petite pretty woman with bright hazel eyes and light brown hair who still worked in the same ladies wear factory where she got her first job in Toronto. She wore a lovely outfit: a green silk blouse and pleated skirt which she had sewed herself. They were still rather young – in their late forties or at most early fifties at the time. Neither spoke much English.

Mick, the thesis supervisor, raised a glass in honor of our new Doctor of Philosophy and said that perhaps we need to find a way to explore education that focuses on the lived experiences of students. "Professional tools are important," he said, "but they need to be in the background. The foreground is about a different way of thinking about one's place in the world." Glasses of bubbly were held high, as everyone sang "For she's a jolly good *Doctor!*" The rainbow of balloons bobbed about on the ceiling adding to the festivity of the moment.

I stood there with my bright smile as I wept inside. I also had immigrant parents, but they could not partake in my PhD celebration some 15 years earlier. Nor were they emotionally able to rejoice in my accomplishment and chose not to attend my party. In that moment I allowed myself to be transported to an imaginary world where my father's eyes would have sparkled with pride while he told the crowd how he had started me off on a good footing with all those visits to the library when I was a child. And there too was my mother who would have joyfully hugged me, holding my bound dissertation as if it were a priceless treasure.

Then my mind snapped back to reality and the full force of the loss struck me. I continued to smile and took what joy I could from the happiness that shone from Anna Maria and her parents. Photos were taken as they hugged and floated off with congratulatory cards and gifts. I stayed behind with Mick and a couple of volunteers to help clean up. My thoughts began to wander and to worry about my current research project. I was thinking ahead to my tenure process which was looming in the near future. The academic slogan "Publish or Perish" was (and is to this day) threateningly real.

Several weeks earlier, in the privacy of Mick's office, I had shared my concerns about trying a very new methodology, autoethnography, for a large research project I was conducting. I had already written and published many other studies in scholarly journals and they followed a more traditional academic approach. I was thinking ahead to when I would go up for tenure and I was concerned that the autoethnographic narrative approach I wanted to use for this particular research study was still considered "on the edge" and therefore riskier in terms of being accepted. What if it didn't get published and therefore I would not get tenure? Not getting tenure in academia means literally getting kicked out. End of the line. Total failure.

That afternoon in his office Mick just looked at me with his steady gaze and said, "Grace, you have such profound insights and you speak with such humanity. You don't need to hide yourself in critical pedagogy or critical ethnography, or critical anything anymore. You just need to tell the story. Let your research reflect that. Share yourself with your participants. Then the research will come alive." He trusted my instincts. And in spite of my concern about how colleagues on my tenure committee might judge the work, I followed this brand-new methodology and let myself become involved in the study not only as a traditional kind of researcher, but fully immersed as a fellow human being who would share my own narrative along with those of my participants.

This research project ended up becoming a nine-year study that I carried out in an extraordinary co-operative village in Israel named *Neve Shalom/Wahat Al-Salam* [Oasis of Peace in Hebrew and Arabic] – about hope in the midst of deadly conflict. By chance I had found out about this village at a dinner party not long after I began my first semester of university teaching. I had been ecstatic when I had received ethical approval and funding from the University of Toronto for my proposal which would document what was happening in that village. That first fall semester turned out to be extremely busy – as I should have expected – and I had begun to question the soundness of my judgment to fly to Israel during the Christmas holidays instead of staying at home and resting. On the other hand, I had felt that I owed it to those villagers to bring to light their efforts which had heretofore been unrecognized in the academic world (or the rest of the world for that matter). Nobody knew about them! Also, it had seemed appropriate for this to be my first professional step forward. Time seemed too precious to "waste." I flew to Israel after classes ended that semester. I would return six more times in the nine years that followed.

How fortunate I was to have met some of the most remarkable educators on this planet on their everyday journey toward peaceful co-existence. This project began as a professional journey, but soon became a spiritual one. I interviewed the children, teachers and parents connected with the elementary school where Jewish and Arab children study together, and the "School for Peace" which is a conflict resolution outreach program for adolescents on both sides of the conflict. I listened to very painful accounts and shared my own stories of childhood suffering. Such blessed moments of true human connection. From my own perspective as a child of trauma, I returned every evening to my guest room and wrote about the anguish and sense of victimhood that both peoples – Jews and Arabs – feel in their very different ways in this troubled land.

This research study became a book called *Oasis of Dreams: Teaching and Learning Peace in a Jewish-Palestinian Village in Israel* and is filled with stories and reflections about a vibrant, courageous community who by their actions invite us to become fellow dreamers of peace. When the time came I handed in to the adjudicating committee peer-reviewed articles I wrote which were precursors to the final book chapters – along with a myriad of other journal publications. I was granted tenure with glowing reviews. Then my manuscript was accepted by a well-respected academic publisher (Routledge, New York). My gamble had paid off. I had listened to Mick's advice. How fortunate I am that this man hired me and became my *de facto* mentor. His message (that the personal and the professional are intertwined) opened a door for me those years ago and allowed me to teach – and write – from the heart.

31

SACHSENHAUSEN

I gave lectures in many parts of the world during my career, however one invitation was very difficult to accept: to give a series of seminars at the *Freie Universität* in Berlin. I had refused them many times, but it finally came to pass because a colleague from my university was spending a few months there as visiting scholar. He organized my visit, and he was French-Canadian, not German, so I felt "safe" – or at least safer. The Berlin Wall had fallen a decade earlier so I was to encounter a unified city. I was told how interesting Berlin was, how it was the center of the cultural scene in Germany and very Western in ideas. I knew all these things. But there was the small matter of ghosts, wounds, and memories. This was not going to be a "fun" trip. I also knew there have been times when I am able to stare my demons down. I felt this might be one of those times. My professional cover would offer me emotional detachment. Also, and perhaps most importantly, my experiences in the village of *Neve Shalom/Wahat Al-Salam* had strengthened me emotionally in ways that I'm still trying to unravel.

I began writing my lectures on issues of second language learning and cultural identity for the *Freie Universität*, and I decided to throw in some personal narrative about my Yiddish voice: lost, partially found – and forever broken. I decided that I would tell them about my parents' incarceration in concentration camps during World War II. While I was preparing my talks, a kind of defiance began to show itself on the pages. I had accepted the fact that I was going to feel anxiety but there was something else that was beginning to happen. Indignant sensations arose unexpectedly from the depths of my soul. This new source of energy propelled me forward and onto the Lufthansa flight. I tried to sleep on the overnight flight. Instead I sat in my seat wide awake, feeling edgy but also proud that I was actually making this trip.

I had to change planes in Hamburg. There I had to go through security again. In Toronto I had asked that they not put my camera through the x-ray machine for fear that it might dull the colors of my film. These were the good old days before digital cameras were ubiquitous. I had never encountered problems with this request in airports. So when I stood at security checkpoint in Hamburg airport I made the same request. I was told that this was forbidden: VERBOTEN! The young man who said this looked as if he could have been a poster boy for the perfect Aryan. I lost it. He looked at my name, smiled and said it was a fine German name. I replied in a higher decibel level than necessary that it DEFINITELY WAS NOT a German name. At this he remained silent as his blond brows went up and his blue eyes opened wide in surprise. Then using an imperious tone of voice, he said that I must pass my camera through the x-ray machine. That was not the wisest thing for him to have done. I told him that it was not possible for me to do this even if I had to stand there all day waiting for him to change his command. He began to look uncomfortable and people in the queue behind me grew impatient.

I am not a belligerent person. Frankly, I was startled as I heard myself tell him in a haughty manner that I wanted to see his superior immediately. The line of travelers behind me was now long, but they seemed transfixed by what was unfolding. Here was this pleasant-looking woman who had turned into some kind of virago in front of their eyes. The young man called over another official, to whom I repeated what I had said. This second man seemed to realize that this could become an embarrassing situation. He took me aside and politely checked my camera by hand. Thus mollified, I boarded the airplane.

There turned out to be a severe thunderstorm during that leg of the flight and I thought to myself, *Good! I'll go down in Germany. How fitting.* I felt no anxiety, just clarity. I made it to Berlin and at the arrival gate my colleague was waiting for me. We retrieved my valise and took a cab to the university guesthouse located in Dahlem, a pretty residential neighborhood. It was a comfortable old house with large bedrooms, many bathrooms and a big kitchen. I was told later that many Jews had lived in Dahlem before World War II. I unpacked and went out to have a bite to eat with my colleague, feeling wobbly but intact.

The next morning was gray and drizzly, the first of several such days during my brief stay in Berlin. My colleague took me to the Applied Linguistics Department where I was to give my first seminar. I was introduced to the group. They were friendly and courteous and I was at ease and felt my usual self. My talks over the next several days went well with lively discussions. Everyone skated around the topic of the Holocaust and the air was laden with apologetic conversation. I handled it all artfully. Was I an accomplished actress or Wonder Woman, or what? I watched the scene as if from the outside. I was sailing through what I had fully expected would be an upsetting experience.

As part of my visit, my colleague was to take me to a special art exhibition at the Nationalgalerie. It was a show of paintings by Max Liebermann, one of Germany's most renowned artistic figures before the war. I learned that he had been an assimilated German-Jewish painter who had gained a fine reputation. The rise of the Third Reich put an end to Liebermann's pride in his German identity. He died in 1935 at the age of 88. The artist's wife, Martha Liebermann, had been forced to sell their villa in 1940. On March 5, 1943, at the age of 85 and while bedridden from a stroke, she was notified to get ready for deportation to the Theresienstadt concentration camp near Prague. Instead, she decided to commit suicide at her home hours before police arrived to take her away.

As I walked into the hall with Liebermann's paintings hanging on all of the walls, I noticed that television crews were present and many people were in attendance. It turned out this was the first day of the exhibition, and it was to be a gala event. All of Berlin's cultural élite had showed up. Suddenly, an enormous weight settled painfully around my neck and back. I could hardly move. I had to sit down on a bench and I told my colleague to go in first and that I would join him. I thought that it was the jet-lag catching up with me. A formidable plume of lava-like anger began to flow through my body and rush up to my head. I was shaking. Overcome with a rage that could have moved a mountain, I felt as if I had turned into the Incredible Hulk. With this newfound source of strength, I got up and marched over to the place where my colleague was standing and in a loud and shrill voice I spoke out to the gathered crowd: "Now everyone is running to see this exhibition of Max Liebermann's work. But we all know what happened to such works of art and what they were called during the Nazi era: degenerate dirty Jewish art. And we certainly know what happened to the Jews as well. So I don't want to be here now celebrating this work, as if the Holocaust never happened. I am leaving. I'm sorry to be making such a scene, but I just can't help it."

All descended into slow motion. The guests placed their drinks on the tables that dotted the room and the servers stopped giving out hors d'oeuvres. Many people stared downwards at their elegant attire. From my vantage point it seemed to me as if they were bowing their heads, but that was probably my imagination. The mixture of surprise, discomfort, and disbelief had destroyed the atmosphere of this Haute *Kultur*. One TV technician laid down his camera, bewildered and disconcerted; the other two decided to catch the unfolding drama. (It never made it to television.) I felt as if I could no longer breathe. My colleague rushed over to me and he left the room with me. I remember that the last thing I heard was the awkwardness of the silence behind us. We sat down at a nearby café where I wept inconsolably. Not *Wonder Woman* after all.

Sachsenhausen Concentration Camp (KZ)

On our trip to the KZ camp Sachsenhausen I nearly fell apart, but my colleague was there to pick up the pieces. Another colleague, an American Jewish woman, who had for many years been a faculty member at the *Freie Universität*, accompanied us on that trip. It was she who drove us out to Sachsenhausen which is located in Oranienburg, some 35 kilometers north of Berlin. This concentration camp was used primarily for political prisoners from 1936 to the end of the Third Reich in May 1945. After World War II, when Oranienburg was in the Soviet Occupation Zone, the structure was used by the Stalinist Soviet forces to detain their own political prisoners until 1950. The remaining buildings and grounds are now open to the public.

Over the entrance gate to Sachsenhausen is the infamous slogan *Arbeit Macht Frei* (just as it is at Auschwitz and other concentration camps). When I think back to that moment, I see the three of us, like children holding hands, about to begin what we knew would be an unusual fieldtrip. Just like in a fairy tale. I didn't feel alone and knew I would be cared for by my colleagues. That was so comforting.

It struck me just how extensive the grounds were. It had been raining and the soil was muddy. We went to the museum first, a plain building with written information on posters as well as display items such as the prisoners' uniforms and instruments of torture. A small woman was quietly sitting at a non-descript desk. We read this: *"During the earlier stages of the camp's existence the executions were done in a trench, either by shooting or by hanging. A large task force of prisoners was used from the camp to work in nearby brickworks to meet Albert Speer's vision of rebuilding Berlin. Sachsenhausen was originally not intended as an extermination camp – instead, the systematic murder was conducted in camps to the east.*

In 1942 large numbers of Jewish inmates were relocated to Auschwitz. However, the construction of a gas chamber and ovens by camp Kommandant Anton Kaindl in March 1943 facilitated the means to kill larger numbers of prisoners. The chamber used liquid Zyklon B which was placed in small glass bottles in the ventilation system next to the door. The bottle was broken with a spike and the gas mixed with the air and was forced into the chamber.

One of the prison's inmates was Pastor Martin Niemöller, who famously remarked about not saying anything while they took away his neighbors. Nobody was left to say something when they came for him. (Niemöller survived both Sachsenhausen and Dachau, and later became a vocal pacifist.) The museum's literature included Niemöller's poem:

First they came for the communists, and I did not speak out – because I was not a communist;
Then they came for the socialists, and I did not speak out – because I was not a socialist;
Then they came for the trade unionists, and I did not speak out – because I was not a trade unionist;
Then they came for the Jews, and I did not speak out – because I was not a Jew;
Then they came for me – and there was no one left to speak out for me.

The prison regulations had extensively detailed the permissible modes of torture; however, quite a few segments of text in the exhibition seemed to be more concerned by the fact that the guards occasionally exceeded the rules of torture than by the fact that they were using torture in the first place. Official favorites included suspension from poles (resulting in bone dislocation and a slow, painful death), beating with iron truncheons, and whipping. The whipping was not allowed on bare buttocks until the regulations were amended in 1942 to allow it.

The weight of what we read followed us out the door as we began to walk through the muddy vastness. We walked in silence looking at the remains of what had been a place of unfathomable suffering. It was still raining as we trudged along those thick mud-filled paths. All was still, the barracks, the execution trenches, the infirmary where medical experiments were conducted, as well as the gas chamber. I felt myself losing balance, but I did have my colleagues to cling to. Fortunately, there were no tours (!) taking place on that day.

When we came to the gas chamber my colleagues knew that I needed to be alone to spend some time with the ghosts. I communed there with my dead relatives all of whom had come that day to visit me from their other concentration camps. There is no way to put this feeling into words. All I can say is I really *felt* their disembodied presences around me. I could almost hear the fluttering of wings as if they were spirits or angels. The sensation was one of being softly embraced. It was the first time that I knew them to be really near me in a loving way. This place of the murdered had, at that moment, become a home. I recited the *Kaddish*, the Hebrew prayer for the Dead. An act of remembrance, of respect, and of recovery, in a place where no recovery is possible. The spirits hovering about my head expected no less of me. I wished I had brought some bread to leave for them.

32

RETURN TO BERKELEY

Some years after I was hired at the University of Toronto, I was eligible for a half-year study leave and fortunately so was my husband. He suggested that we spend the time in Berkeley. Many years had passed since we had left that place, but it never let go of us. For Andrey, living in Berkeley as a graduate student had been his first taste of freedom. He had blossomed in the California sunshine socially and academically, far from the reclusive atmosphere of his childhood home. It must have been as exhilarating for him as Perugia and Israel had been for me. Unfortunately, Berkeley had not been that for me. At the time I felt as though I had barely escaped – much like a refugee fleeing from war.

During the first few years of our marriage, a nagging question that continually pursued us was: Should we have stayed in the U.S. instead of returning to Canada? This hung like a Damocles sword over our relationship and we stayed up nights arguing this question. I blamed myself for it at the time because I was used to blaming myself for everything. However, after many years away from Berkeley, I had become curious. I still felt wary but I knew I would not be returning as an aimless young drifter, but as a professor with a sense of stability and accomplishment from a highly respected research university. So we packed our bags and off we flew, back in time, and back in space.

We got out of the terminal at SFO and stood in line for the East Bay shuttle to Berkeley. I breathed in the cool sea breeze. My smaller carry-on valise with its veritable ton of books and the bigger checked-in valise stood at my side. Andrey had packed more lightly, but he too had brought a great many books. We called our heavy smaller valises our little "doggies" because they were the size of medium-sized dogs and each one had a fastened belt which one could pull. (Lifting those valises full of books for any length of time was out of the question.) The fastened belts looked exactly like leashes.

Our shuttle pulled up to the Berkeley City Club, the neo-Gothic masterpiece of architect Julia Morgan. A colleague had recommended this place to us. It was originally built as a women's social club in 1929 with vaulted ceilings, sepia-colored Greek columns and a Roman style swimming pool. Julia Morgan was the first female architect to study at the *École des Beaux Arts* in Paris and had also designed the Hearst Castle in San Simeon, as well as many stately homes in the Bay area under the tutelage of her mentor, Bernard Maybeck. At the moment I could hardly take in the awesome beauty of this building. After the tiring journey I just wanted to unpack and go to sleep. My head throbbed and my mouth was parched. I felt hot and only in the morning did I realize that I had come down with a bad cold or a flu.

Even though I felt out-of-sorts, I forced myself down to the buffet-style breakfast in the luxury of the dining room with its frescoed ceiling and the huge floral centerpiece that stood on a round table in the middle of the room. I didn't eat much. Andrey seemed to be in much better shape. He had planned to go onto campus, but worried about me. I told him I would be fine and that I would just stay in bed and try to sleep it off. I had been invited onto campus to meet several colleagues with whom I was to begin a literacy research project for vulnerable children. I had to decline on that first day and felt very badly about that. I kept my feelings to myself, took aspirin and hoped the fever would disappear.

Back in our room at the Berkeley City Club I fell into a deep and agitated sleep. I dreamt that I was a child again and the giant monster was after me again. This beast could leap over any fence, no matter how well-guarded, and come straight into my childhood bedroom at night. Then I was in my childhood classroom finally feel more secure. Suddenly my "Dick and Jane" textbook was missing! It was my prized possession. My heart began to beat so fast and my palms were so sweaty and I raced around frantic over this tremendous loss. I screamed but no sound emerged.

I woke up thoroughly drenched. I got out of bed and splashed cold water over my face and neck in the bathroom. Thank goodness, there was a large bottle of spring water on the counter. I gulped down the cool liquid, took off my soaked pajamas, showered and put on a fresh pajama. I climbed back into bed utterly exhausted. I didn't realize that I had slept for several more hours until I heard the door open. I awoke slowly as my husband tiptoed in. I sensed that my fever had broken.

"I'm starting to feel better," I managed to utter in a hoarse voice. He opened the drapes and a stream of brilliant California sunlight shone onto my face. "It's really incredible outside," he mentioned cheerfully. "Well, I'm not ready to go out," I retorted sullenly. Anger bubbled up from somewhere deep inside. Already Berkeley was leading me back to something raw, unfinished. "Maybe I need to just stay in tonight and you can bring back something for me to eat. I'm not that hungry anyway." I tried to sound less strident.

Andrey nodded and seemed perturbed. He made his way out of the room and I was left to collect my thoughts. I berated myself for behaving like such a spoilsport and yet I muttered adamantly to myself, "I don't have to like Berkeley. If worse comes to worst I can always return to Toronto." But the sunshine radiating through the large window of our room on the sixth floor soothed my head and shoulders.

I got up and drank some more water. I didn't feel quite so wobbly as before. In the hot shower the water washed over my aches and pains. When I got dressed I began to feel some hunger pangs. Good sign. When my husband came back a little while later

244

with a sandwich and a bowl of soup for me. I gobbled and slurped it all up.

The following day I still felt a little weak, but much better and so we took a spin around town in our rented car. We had decided to break our sabbatical into two-month tranches. Neither of us (and especially me) was sure that we could take more than that in any one stay. All the old familiar streets of Berkeley stared at us and we stared back. College Avenue where we had lived looked exactly as we had left it so many years earlier. It was eerie. I could feel tears begin to fill my eyes as memories of my shattered life there came charging at me. "Why the hell did I decide to return to a place with such memories?" I asked myself silently. My husband was probably wondering what I was thinking, but had the good sense not to ask.

Then we drove further down College Avenue for several miles and a neighborhood appeared that did not exist back then. It had been a downright grungy area at the time. Now cafés, restaurants, bookstores, and pretty shops lined the street on both sides gleaming with a clean crisp look. The date was December 21, the Winter Solstice, the second day of Hanukkah and four days before Christmas. Students, professors, children and families were milling about purchasing gifts in a toyshop called "Sweet Dreams" as well as in a stationery store with its bright holiday cards and other paper products. A wellness/fitness shop, LaFoot, was filled with people trying on an array of running shoes and sporting gear. Next door a shoe store featured a small Christmas tree in the window decorated with tiny shoe ornaments as well as a silver Hanukkah menorah with three lit electric candles. Everyone appeared to be enjoying themselves in the bright afternoon. A young busker dressed in rainbow-colored leotards with a round neon-light beanie on his head and sequined red clown-like shoes was strumming tunes on his guitar. My mood grew lighter as I surveyed this joyous scene. Earlier in the day Andrey had called an old friend from his grad school days to confirm a get together. This friend had left Berkeley too after he received his PhD and had taught in math departments on many campuses around the world. He had decided to return to Berkeley and has been there ever since.

We were invited to his home for a holiday dinner the following evening.

The next morning, I woke up feeling refreshed and quite well. Maybe it had only been a 48-hour virus. Or maybe it had just been a physical response to my anxiety. In any case I had a hearty breakfast in the dining room and I noticed, truly noticed, its loveliness for the first time. I was ready to start the sabbatical! We both had work to do. I needed to get articles written and sent off to academic journals for publication. My husband had a research project planned with a colleague on campus, so he sailed out the door and on to the UC campus. I knew he would be passing the Sather Tower (the third-tallest bell clock-tower in the world) sleek and majestic against the Berkeley Hills, to an office in Evans Hall. The clock tower is colloquially called the Campanile because it was modelled after the Campanile di San Marco in Venice. I could see it against the backdrop of the Berkeley hills from the window of our room. It's the most famous symbol of the university, an icon. As it chimed out its song every hour, my heart began to feel a little lighter.

I carried a pot of strong black tea sweetened with pure honey from the dining room into the majestic wood-paneled library on the second floor of the Berkeley City Club. I noticed for the first time the enormous crimson and royal-blue Persian rug on the floor and the black, lacquered grand piano at one end of the huge room as well as an antique desk in a recessed corner facing a leaded glass window at the other end of the room. Floor-to-ceiling bookshelves lined the walls. This library was a space of grandeur with a gloriously decorated rosette in the middle of its high ceiling, and a Victorian English Rococo style chandelier hanging from it. Had I landed in some kind of intellectual fairyland?

I had my laptop and notes with me and sat down at the desk where I began to write. I wrote like the wind. Hours flew by. Words poured out of me like a waterfall. And then in my mind's eye I caught a glimpse of the friendly muses that seemed to be lurking all about in this noble library, announcing a sense of tradition. As my eyes wandered again over the spacious room this thought emerged: *What is a little child of refugees doing in a place of such great privilege?*

I sat alone, my laptop computer on the desk. Through the leaded diamond-glass window, I saw an imposing Victorian house painted canary yellow with white trim shone against an aquamarine sky. Trees swayed in the wind like graceful dancers. The yellow house stood tall on the tree-lined street, adorned with a lapis-colored roof and turret, and a Wedgwood-like decoration on its attic face. I was enchanted by the sunny glow around that particular building. Oh, this California sunlight, forever filled with the promise of a bright tomorrow, forever filled with hope. And as I stared out again through the window I realized how fitting it was that here, in this bastion of mainstream privilege, I was beginning to write a chapter about the first time my father took me to the Gatineau Public Library in Montréal – about my entry into the extraordinary world of reading.

When I took a break for lunch I put on my red wool cardigan with its inner fleece lining because it looked a little cool outside – although it was certainly balmy compared to the winter weather we had left in Toronto. I carried a notepad and walked down some flights of stairs and out into the street. For lunch I strolled over to a bistro nearby which doubled as a classical music CD shop. Next door was a bookshop with the logo *Ten Thousand Minds On Fire*. It caught my attention and after lunch I ambled inside. I walked to the back of the store while perusing the shelves housing books of various academic disciplines as well as best sellers. When I got to the back room I sat down in one of the plush upholstered chairs around a large oblong table hosting the latest journal publications. In front of me, some few yards away, I noticed steps leading up to a second level where more books could be found; some were quite antique and valuable, some even first editions. I got up and walked over to the glass back door and saw the pretty garden patio. No one else was there at that moment. I opened the door and sat myself down on one of the patio chairs next to a small round wooden table. The sun was warm and I turned my face toward its sheer radiance.

Was this the Berkeley to which I had vowed never to return? I began to feverishly write thoughts down in my little notebook. Ideas flourished in me like the flowers and the shrubs which were lined up on the grass. Now nothing could hold me back. It was as if a good witch had cast her magic spell. It was the Winter Solstice after all. I left the bookstore after a time and took a long stroll weaving in and out among groups of boisterous students on the street. My feelings seemed unrecognizable from those of the past. Then I would turn a corner and without warning catch a glimpse of myself in memory: a little girl exhausted, frightened, lost. I would experience such an intense desire to take that sad child and hold her in my arms.

"First you have to feel the pain before you can feel the joy – or any other emotion," Dr. Michaels had told me early on when all I could sense then was a dread so profound that I would sometimes feel like I was at the abyss staring into its black void. "I never promised you a rose garden," he would say. "However, you will see that as you go forward in your recovery, the path will become less dark, less tangled with brambles and you will walk onto a wide meadow with bright flowers and tall green grass." It sounded like a fairy tale at the time, but he wasn't kidding. Was I being offered the gift of collecting up all the parts of myself that I had been forced to discard way back then? Was I now being given the opportunity to bring them back into my present life, one at a time, and into a life that was now whole enough to be able to accept these abandoned treasures?

Berkeley had definitely changed too. It had become calmer. Upscale cafés and restaurants were ubiquitous – with even a few decent ones on the main strip of Telegraph Avenue. The names of important chefs graced menus in many other parts of town. Fraternities and sororities were back in vogue. Some of the students looked downright preppy. To be sure, street people still hung around Telegraph Avenue which in many spots was still as dirty and skanky as always. Some people in wacky outfits still stood at Sproul Plaza spouting outlandish theories on soapboxes believing they were messiahs. The exact same Hare Krishna types in flowing off-white tunics still chanted to the beat of their drums. A powerful vibe caught my attention, a glimpse of free-spiritedness, warm and intimate. Had it always been there and I just couldn't feel it? I wondered when the second shoe would drop. A transformation this miraculous couldn't last. I trod lightly and cautiously.

At the corner of Telegraph Avenue and Bancroft Street, a Latino street vendor drew me with the power of his dark eyes and his wares: a t-shirt embroidered with an image of *La Virgen de Guadelupe,* and a pair of sterling silver earrings in the shape of the trickster coyote in Huehecóyotl Aztec folklore. The vendor had long straight black hair in a ponytail. As we spoke I told him that I had lived in Berkeley long ago and that I had hated it then because of all its chaos. "I was a young girl then and felt completely overwhelmed." His eyes penetrated my thoughts as he said, "You weren't prepared for what was happening here at that time. Forgive yourself. Hold the vision of a Berkeley that can now embrace you. And trust the process."

Startled, I stared at him as if he were a visionary. I felt as if he should have been sitting at one of the fortunetelling tables nearby. I continued my promenade on Bancroft Avenue with the sight of International House and its Spanish architecture in the distance. All those social gatherings in I-House where I felt like an outsider because I hadn't been a full-fledged student. It took me weeks into the sabbatical before I could enter that place and not be overcome by pangs of loss as I watched the students inside milling around, engaged in their world – the world from which I had been excluded by circumstance back then.

And then the Caffe Strada appeared; its spacious patio and tables with umbrellas filled with the truly fortunate of this earth – those who could spend time in a college town with its special reputation and its magnificent westward view of the Golden Gate Bridge in the San Francisco Bay and of the Berkeley hills toward the east. Many students were deep in their youthful conversations, sipping their coffees, or writing up class assignments on their laptops. Some looked self-assured and at ease; others seemed more stressed, an aura of being over-extended hanging over their heads.

Perhaps some ached at being far from home for the first time; perhaps they were lonely, afraid of failing their courses. Professors too congregated at Caffe Strada, enjoying assorted discussions – many of them indulging in extremely arcane topics – and speaking with that extravagant confidence I had always longed for.

I remember well how much more of an emotional effort I had to expend figuring out the "system" as an undergraduate student at McGill than did my peers whose parents had been to college. And this became even more evident to me after I became a university professor. What was it that had stood in my way? Anton Chekhov nailed it perfectly in his remark to his brother: "What the aristocrats take for granted, we pay for with our youth." I had to learn, from scratch, that sophistication, that easy confidence which most of my peers had inherited – knowing already how it all works, as if they had been in on the story right from the beginning.

That evening we went over to Steve's (Andrey's old grad school friend) home for dinner. It was our first Christmas in Berkeley. And what a splendid time we had. For gifts we brought a wall calendar for the New Year with each month sporting a different Canadian scene. Also, we brought a big bottle of Québec maple syrup (hands down the best maple syrup in the world!) and a linen dish cloth with a Canadian map embroidered on it. At first, everyone sat near the glowing warmth of the living room fireplace with hot mulled wine in hand, gazing upon a tall fresh pine tree decorated with ornaments that harkened back to Mary's (Steve's partner's) childhood: little shiny snowmen, *papier maché* reindeers, snowflake crystal balls in bright reds and whites, candy canes and many other delights. The *pièce de resistance* was at the top of the tree: a lovely Victorian antique-looking angel with gold metallic wings embellished with shiny stars and a tinsel halo on her head – evoking memories of the long ago Christmas tree of my dear childhood friend, Françoise.

Then we moved into the dining room and enjoyed a meal of homemade pasta and hearty meatballs with sweet tomato basil sauce and a huge mixed salad. (Mary is Italian-American.) We all requested seconds and thirds and there were still left overs for us to take home. After the meal, we returned to the living room and began munching on mouthwatering Christmas biscotti which Mary's mother had sent her from Boston: almond and cinnamon cookies with white icing and red and green sprinkles. They came in a red tin box designed with snowmen and rotund Santas. Each cookie led to another. I became an instant addict. In between bites, we all chatted about what we do.

There was couple there, Emma and Joe, who were in the midst of building a house on several acres of land near Garberville, several hours north of San Francisco. Emma explained that she had lived a hippie existence for five years "in the good old days" on Hydra (the island closest to Athens) with her boyfriend who became her first husband. I commented, "You probably don't regret it." She replied: "No, I don't," with a twinkle in her ocean-blue eyes. Leonard Cohen had actually been a neighbor of hers! "The only thing I regret is that I refused Leonard's offer to sing at my wedding," she said. "I thought at the time that his songs were too depressing. This was before he became world famous." Now her hair was white and her face had some wrinkles, but I could visualize her as a young flower child, her long flowing blond tresses filled with the light of a gentler sun. *Those were the days, my friend*, as the song went. And here I was in Berkeley now, finally beginning to savor a taste of those days. Better late than never.

There was also Beth, another of Mary's friends. She explained how she was creating a pond in her backyard. There was much discussion about canvas bags and cement and about plants and berries and a balcony where she had allowed a (teenage) street person to make it his home until his sister from Missouri could come to get him. He was a runaway. His sister was a good friend of Beth's. It was all so "Berkeley." So refreshingly alternative. Beth grinned like a Cheshire cat as she told us that she had lived on a hippie commune in Marin County in the late-1960s and early-1970s and had hooked up with (of all cultures!) a French-Canadian guy from Montréal.

She reminisced about her days in the commune: "We shared chores; we made meals together; we took care of each other's babies. We lived our lives together. My daughter Rose was born on the commune and she grew up with all the other babies." Beth looked like an "earth mother" with her broad clear olive-skinned face, expressive dark eyes and ample figure. She had a tattoo on her arm, an exquisite purple rose with pink edges. I could picture her in a long skirt and shawl, dark hair falling down to her waist with a baby on her hip. She continued: "Of course, there were interpersonal problems. Sometimes someone blew their stack. It wasn't always easy being so close together all the time. Some people left of their own volition or were told to leave. Communal living is not for everyone."

I recognized how Beth's description of her commune resembled the lifestyle of the kibbutz, except that the kibbutz was more organized and not "hippie." Now a massage therapist, and married to a computer programmer (not the French-Canadian guy), she sighed and murmured: "If I had to do it all over again I would do exactly the same thing. I miss those times."

It was as if I had tuned into a different channel on the radio. So great to be where people just "are." I took it all in like a hungry orphan at a gala banquet.

One afternoon a few days later something truly incredible happened as I was walking along Telegraph Avenue. Several blocks down the street I noticed a brightly colored display of bilingual Spanish-English children's books in the window of the used bookstore Shakespeare & Company. I walked into the store hoping to find "dual-track" children's books as materials for the literacy project I was conducting with colleagues on campus. At the back of the shop, I joyously leafed through stacks of bilingual books in Chinese/English, Arabic/English, Spanish/English as well as African-American stories, Asian Cinderella stories, Native-American tales, and so on.

Tucked under one of these piles lay a humble book with the unassuming title *Little Stories for Little Children*. I picked it up, completely unprepared for the shock to follow. The words that peered out at me from its back cover were printed in both Yiddish and English! This book had originally been published in 1922 in St.

Petersburg, Russia and in it were ten short stories for children about Jewish *shtetl* life. English text had been added for the American edition years later. As I started to turn the pages of this unexpected treasure my eyes began to blur. I was taken aback because I had read this same book as a child in my after-school Yiddish classes. How I hated those classes at the time! The teacher seemed ancient and exhausted as we pupils stared out the window. I raised such a tantrum at home that my parents finally took me out. Yet, in the stillness of night, I often felt guilty for having abandoned my Yiddish. I tried hard to hold onto the Hebrew alphabet as I drifted off to sleep. As months went by, the letters became fainter and fainter...

There I stood, so many years later, re-reading this same children's book in the improbable location of a bookstore on Telegraph Avenue. And all I could hear – once again – was the screaming of children in Auschwitz. Perhaps some of them were carrying this very book with them when they entered the gates of hell. When I got back to my hotel room I quickly tucked this book into my valise, as if it were an unearthed relic meant to be inspected at a later date. When I eventually returned to Toronto months later, I brought *Little Stories for Little Children* to show to the students in my children's literature graduate course and I told them about how I had found this book. I would tell this story each time I would teach that course.

Andrey and I began to housesit for friends in Berkeley every chance we got. We came at least once and often twice a year. Our social and cultural lives there kept growing. I was even invited to attend sessions of a Berkeley community chorus as a soprano. We recovered old friendships and created many new ones. One highlight was the Friday night "math" dinners hosted by Andrey's former professors and peers from his PhD days (including Steve who had originally invited us to these Friday night dinners). The weekly dinner became a tradition and usually took place at a favorite Chinese restaurant, The Great China. We all sat around a large round table and chatted while devouring mouth-watering dishes. I'll never forget the warm and welcoming feeling of those

Friday evenings, like a cozy family gathering in which every member was so happy to be there. Visit after visit, Andrey and I were finally able to enjoy Berkeley together. A new chapter in our lives opened. But for me anxiety was never far behind. We would return from parties and dinners and I would begin to worry about some pain or other. Maybe I had a terminal illness and all this newfound social life would vanish? This may sound outlandish, but that is how afraid I was that I would be punished for all this socializing. "How dare you?" was the constant recurring refrain that would assault my brain and diminish my happiness. I kept plodding on.

During one visit, I had an experience that shot back a warning to be on guard against the dark forces of my childhood. We were housesitting for two months one spring. Andrey needed to return to Toronto for some university meetings and so I was on my own for a week taking care of a cat named Trudy who had to remain in the garden because of my cat allergies. Trudy had a boyfriend named Boris (aka Bully Boy because he always tried to grab food from her bowl – so maybe not really a boyfriend). The house we were in, an arts and crafts style, with its low-pitched gabled roof and broad eaves, large front porch, and exposed Redwood shingles, was located in the gentrified neighborhood (the Elmwood area) that we had discovered on that first visit back to Berkeley. I said goodbye to Andrey early in the morning and looked forward to some quiet time for writing. I spread out all my notes and books and placed my laptop on the teak dining room table. My goal in Berkeley was to complete one academic article and begin another although I vowed to also make time to see friends and take time for myself.

I had an early dinner with friends at a bistro in the neighborhood. They had just returned from a week-long retreat at a Zen Buddhist monastery in Marin county and regaled me with stories about their sessions in meditation. Afterward I took a walk. The streets offered a potage of ingredients. The scent of eucalyptus and jasmine pervaded the air. Persimmon, trumpetvine, bougainvillea and bottlebrush trees, wisteria, as well as Redwoods, live oaks, sequoias and palm trees surrounded homes with interesting architectural designs, arts and craft, Spanish hacienda, the craftsman bungalows of stucco and Redwood shingles.

I returned to the house and had a phone chat with Andrey who had just touched down in Toronto. I lay down to read on the couch in the living room and took a nap. I woke up to a darkness that suddenly frightened me. I heard a scratching at the kitchen door and it sounded menacing. Why was I so afraid? It was obviously Trudy, the little tabby cat. Panic stalked me and I couldn't move. I began to worry about someone breaking into the house. There was no alarm system. I forced myself into the dining room where the window had been left open, its curtains flying furiously in a wind that had arisen. I hurried to shut the window, hands shaking. I noticed that the lights in the house next door were on. "I could always run over there if I need to," were words that sprang into my mind.

I decided that perhaps writing down my feelings would dispel the gloom. I sat down at the dining table. I wrote words down by hand in a notepad instead of on the computer. I needed to feel the words in my fingers, in my bones. As I wrote, I began to realize that I had reverted to my childhood self who had been abandoned in a dark, empty apartment by her parents on moving day. I could barely make her out – that little girl who had probably sensed that, whether or not her parents came to get her, there would be no safe harbor. Maybe that's why she had rocked herself back and forth in chaotic silence.

The wind was calming down outside and slowly, slowly I spied the leaves on the treetops through the window swaying elegantly in the silvery breeze. Then I remembered Dr. Michaels' words: "You will have to slay many dragons and dig deep in your soul to face the pain. You have the courage to do it." The sense of loss in that moment was almost unbearable and I couldn't help but wonder, *why did it have to take me so long to get to this point? Why did I have to be robbed of so much so early?* Then almost immediately I felt ashamed of myself. Because in spite of everything, I did get away. I have lived to see my liberation, imperfect as it may be. I thought of the quote from George Eliot, "It is not too late to be who you were meant to be."

I straightened up and walked into the kitchen. I opened the light and put the kettle on to boil. As I sat at the table with a steaming sweet spicy tea the scratching noise at the door resumed. I kept the second screened-in door closed as I opened the first (the kitchen had a double door). Indeed, little Trudy stared at me with her saucer-sized green eyes and meowed loudly. "Sorry, dear one," I apologized to her, "I wish I could let you in. But you know I am allergic to your dander. And the garden is lovely and it's not really cold out." (Our friends had placed a cozy felt bed in a crate for Trudy outside in their garden, to use if she was so inclined.) "Good night, little one," I waved to her. Truly, I think Trudy understood as she scuttled away from the door. I closed the inner door, turned off the kitchen light and, invigorated, bounded up the flight of stairs two steps at a time, undressed and got into bed with a book. A few hours later I awoke with a start. I had dreamt of a drama teacher who criticized me viciously as I stood on stage auditioning for a role I greatly coveted. She advised me never to try out for a drama production again. Hatred blazed from her coal-black eyes. Just before my audition a younger aspiring student had botched her lines and the same teacher had been quite forgiving. I was mystified at her behavior toward me and felt undone. Thankfully I fell back asleep almost immediately.

The next morning a cacophony of birdsong woke me. I jumped up and wrote out the dream in my journal notebook. Once the words were down on paper a wave of relief washed over me and I was ready to take on a fresh day. I had breakfast and worked all morning and then decided to take a long walk on College Avenue in the direction of Oakland. I walked all afternoon. All those vivid flowers and trees as well as folks around me enjoying the day. Several hours later I stopped in front of a chic looking women's boutique. I wandered inside. The woman at the counter had a mocha complexion, greenish eyes and a very warm smile. She chose a few items for me to try on. A great pair of flowing black silky pants and a red fitted jacket embroidered in a chinoiserie motif. I came out of the dressing room ready to look at the mirror. "It looks lovely on you," she announced. "I think it's too tight," I muttered. "What are you talking about?" she responded in amazement. "It fits perfectly and you look so sexy."

Another saleswoman came out from the back storeroom and the first one asked her opinion as I looked askance at the outfit in the full-sized mirror. The first woman's name was Claudette and she was tall and elegant with a Jamaican accent. The second woman, Joy, was from New York, darker and more petite. It turned out they were co-owners of the shop. "Girl, you'd better realize how stunning you are, with those big, dark eyes and luscious hair. You need to get this outfit and shine like a star," Joy asserted emphatically. Her words devastated me. I remembered what torture it had been to go shopping for clothes with my mother way back. "You look like a herring. Nothing looks good on you," reverberated in my brain. I also remembered the dream I had the night before. I was doing to myself what had been done to me. I froze. "I have to sit down for a moment," I said shakily.

"Sorry, my dear, did I say something wrong?" Joy asked. "No, you said something right." I sighed deeply as Joy spoke like a psychic. "I see such sadness in your eyes. Your eyes express it all. Whatever it is, you need to let it go." A cup of hot peppermint tea materialized in front of me. The shop owners sat down in overstuffed armchairs around me. Nobody else was in the store. Such a caring atmosphere with a bright red and yellow carpet on the floor. I told them both about my mother's shopping tirades, how she criticized me endlessly, and how I hated shopping after that – even now years afterward. Claudette took my hand and softly added: "There's nothing wrong with self-preservation. There comes a time when you have to live. Choose life. The force is in you. You have to own it. You have to be a good marine and get to the other side any way you can. You can't carry your mother's stuff anymore. Lay that burden down, girl."

"You're a good-looking woman; you gotta see that!" Joy nodded vigorously. "I also had a mother who couldn't be a mother. And I had to leave New York in order to survive. She is dead now and we could never manage to have any kind of positive relationship. Some things are beyond repair. But I see her more clearly now and with less anger." She continued as I sipped the warm tea. "Life is a miracle and you have it!" she exclaimed. "Let your little light shine, like in the bible song. Don't hide your light under a bushel. You can't be in this conspiracy of pain anymore. Get outta there in your mind."

I was grateful for Joy's and Claudette's words. Maybe I could finally feel for what my mother was forced to endure in her early years: first, a life of unrelenting poverty and then much worse in the concentration camp. And I thought to myself: *who knows what happened to her in the concentration camp?* She was only a teenager. She would tell how one of the Nazi officers always reminded her (in German): "You, my exotic Mediterranean beauty, you're going to be sent off to Treblinka on the next transport!" German is close enough to Yiddish that she understood what he had said. And I guess you didn't need language to figure it out. Even in her shabby prisoner's clothes, she must have made an impression. Who knows what he did to her. It was never, ever mentioned in my home. And yet, I did feel dirty and vulnerable when I heard that story. I must have sensed that she felt tainted. Emotionally, this would emerge as wanton rage on her part. I understand it now. As a child it was not possible for me to understand. Instead, I blamed myself for her wild mood swings.

I finished my tea and went into the dressing room to take off the outfit and return to my street clothes. "I'm buying all of it, the top, the pants, the skirt, the blazer," I exclaimed suddenly euphoric as I handed the items to Claudette and Joy. They both smiled. We walked up to the cash at the front of the store and these two lovely women threw in a gossamer rose-colored scarf and a cherry-red wool beret as gifts to me. They wrapped everything lovingly. I thanked them not only for the clothing, but especially for the extraordinary conversation.

When I returned to the house I stood on the porch for a while and watched the fog roll in while looking up toward the Berkeley hills. The scene was ethereal, like a fairytale with shiny lights from houses on the hills beginning to pop out through the milky sky. I felt a twinge of anxiety that all this would be taken away from me when I would have to leave Berkeley to return to Toronto. Then I heard the train whistle in the distance. Oh, how I love the sound of the train that passes through Berkeley every night like a spritely spirit. The sound of moving on and moving forward. And I understood for the first time that freedom is not a place; freedom is a feeling.

33

PHOTOS FROM POLAND

I woke up one January morning some years ago from the kind of dream that promises a new beginning. In this dream I had been traveling on a long and anxiety-filled bus ride on my way to give a lecture. I felt lost and uncertain as to where I needed to get off. Suddenly someone took me by the hand and escorted me to the right street and to the right building. Everyone clapped their hands as I walked into the lecture hall. And then I woke up.

It was wintertime – a fresh new year. In the kitchen I made myself a cup of sweet black tea. Thus energized, I headed to the basement and began to clean out the mess of boxes that were filled with torn books and curriculum materials from my long-ago elementary school teaching years. It was a task I had been putting off for years – for decades even. Now I was finally ready to sort through the boxes and to throw away whatever was just clutter. It was back-breaking work. After a few hours of this I went upstairs, made another cup of tea, and then again trod carefully down the rickety stairs to the basement, the cup of tea firmly in hand. I sat down on a stool while inhaling the mustiness of the basement air and gazed out of a window overhead at the ascending morning light. All was quiet. All was calm.

And then I saw the manila envelope. The one with the photos

from Poland inside. This time I couldn't look away. Some years had passed since they were mailed to me by my cousin Emilia. I had not known of the existence of these photos or of the letters that accompanied them until I encountered Emilia in Montréal at a funeral. (A friend had once told me that funerals often bring amazing events to bear.) I had not seen my cousin for a good many years owing to the abysmal state of my family situation. We were both grateful to finally be reunited. After the funeral, we had made plans to meet the following day. Emilia and I ended up at a coffee shop chatting for many hours over warm apple pie with vanilla ice cream. At some point she casually mentioned the letters and the photos as we reminisced about her mother (who was my aunt) and my father (who was her uncle). I was taken aback. "What pictures? What letters?" I asked. "The ones that went between Częstochowa and Montréal," she said as she stared at my blank expression. "Didn't you know?" "I did not," I answered, stunned.

Apparently, there had been a full correspondence between my aunt in Montréal and her family in Poland in the late-1920s and 1930s before the war broke out. Emilia promised to send me copies of the letters and photos as soon as possible. When the package arrived in my mailbox at home not long afterward, it felt rather sudden and yet, it also seemed as if I had been waiting for that moment all of my life. At the time my hands trembled as I clutched the package. I was not able to open it. I hurriedly carried it downstairs and put it away. Then on that morning in the basement, I finally opened the package and took out the photos. I placed them on a counter nearby. I felt light-headed, as if hovering in some in-between space. The photos all had names on them and some also had dates handwritten at the bottom. I handled them gently as if they were made of fragile glass...

There is a tinted portrait of my aunt Karolina and her baby son, Jurek, with their eyes, bright as stars. She is wearing a velvet blouse adorned by a lace collar. Her son is dressed in a white jumper embroidered with flowers on a gray woolen sweater. In the photo Karolina has the air of a well-groomed woman with turquoise eyes and a lush mouth. She looks beautiful. (I remember how my father and aunt used to mention how lovely she was.) Karolina and Jurek are in a sweet embrace, much like in an image I had seen of the Madonna and Child.

Other pictures followed – of various aunts and uncles, at home and away, on holiday in the mountains, in a garden, and at parties. There is also a photo of my father's mother, Bracha, with permed gray-specked hair in a dark tailored suit with a round white collar. With eyes so much like those of my father and my aunt. And a splendid portrait photo of my father's three oldest sisters: my *ciocias* Helenka (the one who moved to Montréal, and the only one who survived), Dorota, and Karolina who was the youngest. Helenka is wearing an off-the-shoulder patterned dress with frills on its short sleeves. Dorota also has frilled sleeves and a scooped neckline. In this photo, Karolina wears a tailored sailor blouse. Their hairstyles appear to reflect the latest fashion of the 1920s and 1930s. The background wall is papered in a flowery design and on the wall hangs a picture of a woman (probably of a relative or friend) sitting on a horse in the countryside. The picture is inscribed: Częstochowa, 1923. A vacation photo. I know that they came from a very modest background so these photos must have set them back economically. But there they are for posterity.

My tears begin to flow when I come across the formal wedding photo of my youngest aunt, Agnieszka, at the bottom of the pile. This picture had been taken in my grandparents' home, in a large room with a dark wood floor, and high windows with white curtains framing them. There are 46 relatives in this wedding picture. I count them again carefully just to be sure. So many relatives! A real extended family. My father is in it as well, standing there with a youthful face, wearing a Polish Army uniform. He was the youngest child of the family and would have been 18 years old at the time this photo was taken in 1932. He was born in 1914.

I take another sip of sweet black tea as the ghosts in those photos stare out at me. What do they want of me? I turn and gaze out of the window again at the soft clouds of the silvery morning sky. The clouds are moving swiftly as if being pulled by some heavenly current and I begin to feel strangely connected to a much larger part of the universe. I stare down again at the silent photos. Am I waiting for some revelation, for a sign, for some message? All I can feel is a disconcerting absence because I did not have these relatives in my life. They were part of the Great Nightmare that had governed my family. *Deported in 1942. Murdered in Treblinka.* These words are seared in my brain forever.

If there had been no genocide of the European Jews in World War II, I would have known the people in these pictures intimately, my paternal extended family. Grandmother Bracha, Grandfather Itzhak (who died of a heart attack before the Nazis invaded Poland), Aunt Karolina, Aunt Dorota, Aunt Agnieszka, and Aunt Helenka – the oldest (the one who moved to Canada and whom I knew), Uncle Stashek, Uncle Moniek (who died from a childhood illness also before the war) and my cousin Jurek, Karolina's son. I've never written out all of their names in this way before. There is no doubt that some powerful force is in charge. What an awesome gift. It is as if I am holding a baby girl that had been presumed dead all these years and is suddenly in my arms fully and passionately alive – and smiling. Rescued from some hidden place in order to love and be loved. She is my little girl and I hers. She has been resurrected – just as have the people in these photos. I once read somewhere that the act of personal witness is an act of love. But what does that really mean?

I have hesitated to write about these photos. It seems almost profane. They are a private suffering – and in any case there is no way by which anyone can create an authentic perspective of the Holocaust. There is no catharsis to be found. No consolation possible. All of the other parts of my story have been fueled by hope and love and transformation. This part is different; it will remain haunted. It is my Kaddish, my prayer for the dead. I must find some way to have compassion for being the one who came after the Apocalypse and now has the obligation (or do I really?) to share such shattered pieces as remain. This seems to me the only possible way to honor their souls. It is not about memory, but about re-memory, about remembrance. These photos are not about the horrors; they are about ordinary lives lived before the war. Is this what the ghosts want me to share? To say aloud that they were not just emaciated skeletons, anonymous corpses in stinking open pits with Nazi vultures swarming around or in the smoke snaking up from the furnaces of the crematoria. To say that they were just like any other human beings in their everyday existence with all its ups and downs, successes and failures. Not just digits tattooed on forearms.

The images in these photos call to me softly from across the Great Divide telling me of their desires, their loves, their work, their dreams, their anxieties and disappointments, their joys and sorrows. They say to me that they made love, raised families, had friendships of all sorts. They celebrated birthday and engagement and wedding parties. They were people just like the ones that I wrote about in my stories about French-Canadian families, only they were my real family. In Poland. I am now able to *see* them in all their aliveness.

A question from deep arises: Where do I fit in relation to these relatives who had been endlessly whispered about, incessantly cried over – their deaths the eternal torment of my parents? Survivors cannot help but remember. Yet, what is the responsibility of the children of the survivors who imbibed their parents' traumas which then became their own? How are we to transcend the emptiness and the void, the anonymity and the ultimate rendering of facelessness? No graves to visit. No family gatherings to attend. No comforting conversations to be had. Our parents were sentenced to live in that hell forever. What about us, their children? Many children of survivors hear only silence, feel only shame and loss, haunted by whispered stories of lives that ended in humiliating deaths. Other children of survivors are subjected to the hysterical shrieks of their parents which can occur suddenly and at any time of the day or night. Still others keep hearing the screams of children torn away from their mothers. What, then, are we called upon to do?

In the Jewish tradition it is stated that all destinies are intertwined. Perhaps what we are called upon to do is continue to search for the thread in the labyrinth which might show us the way toward a ray of light. That sounds too simple, doesn't it? How can there be any solace after such horror? Staring at the photos for a long time, I finally come up with a very personal response to the utter darkness of this dilemma which plagues every child of survivors, whether they realize it or not. I can bear witness to the legacy handed to me by putting it down on paper. Certainly, the act of writing has offered me much comfort. It may even carry some redemptive value.

As I gaze upon the photos yet again, my mind wanders and I see myself as a child, but this time I am filled with the gift of home, and place, and belonging. I remember what my father and his only surviving sister, my *ciocia* Helenka, would often say sorrowfully to each other in Montréal when I was young. "Someday we will return again to Our Father's house."

I see a little girl knocking at the gleaming door – huge and dazzling – as in a trance. When the door opens wide, a powerful light shines forth and there they all are. Waiting for her. They embrace her, one by one, and then all together. She is their long-lost granddaughter, their niece, and their cousin. Everybody is crying and laughing at the same time. "In Our Father's house" where there will always be Love.

EPILOGUE

I am in a place where I have never been before. A place of inner solace. It is not the joy of a fresh spring, nor the warmth of a ripened summer. It is not even the flaming beauty of autumn leaves. In fact it is the beginning of a luminous day in early winter. Just as it was that winter in Montréal when I first noticed the frozen crystalline patterns on the windowpanes of our apartment. The designs of Life.

"Hold on! Hold on!" Faint but enduring came those words in a time when the sun shone only for others. Peace might have been hiding somewhere, but not for me. I had been forgotten. Yet, some unknown Presence kept saying: "Hold on! Hold on!" I held out my small hands and I waited. Only now do I understand that behind that emptiness lay a radiance so bright that I cannot find the words to describe it. Now what I see is a strong woman, scarred and wounded to be sure, but blessed and free. A woman with purpose. A teacher who loves to teach about language and culture and liberation, to write about it, to sing about it.

Perhaps this entire book has been my attempt to recapture that one moment of revelation when I first met the winter light of Montréal, offering me the chance to be reborn. I cannot reverse all of the damage that was done nor can I undo the intervening "blindness" that ensued. But the light allowed me a glimpse at the grandeur of things – the potential of a larger life, the possibility of doing something of value.

All I can say is that I have tried my best to live a life not destroyed by despair. And I'll keep trying as long as I live. As a child I moved forward in the only way I could, inventing a life in a different world – first in the language and culture of my French-Canadian neighbors and then, later on, in other languages and other cultures as well. I discovered my shelter in the shade of the great tree of language and literature at university and it offered me sustenance beyond measure. I feel extremely fortunate to have been able to create all the trappings of success and industry and joy as a teacher and researcher. And to have been given the greatest blessing – that of finding my soulmate, my husband Andrey. We saved each other right from the first day we met back in Berkeley when we were so young. I am in awe of all the light and joy that arrived miraculously and rescued us in spite of the shadows of death that have always haunted us both in different ways.

I have had to muster the courage to look back at all the light that I had to let pass by. I know that I am only one of many on this earth who have been maimed by the aftermath of devastating loss. Memory can break our hearts, but it can also save our lives. I hope that the telling of these stories of my life may connect with the larger story of how we must all try to discover the means to triumph over adversity. In the final analysis, the human condition is an equal opportunity employer. We all face mortality, but we must keep working to make things better while we can. We must keep striving for love and hope in the places where light has not yet entered.

ALSO BY GRACE FEUERVERGER

Oasis of Dreams: Teaching and Learning Peace in a Jewish-Palestinian Village in Israel

Teaching, Learning and Other Miracles

ACKNOWLEDGMENTS

This work has been a labor of love – a voyage of discovery, both excruciating and exhilarating. It is about devastating loss but also about extraordinary good fortune.

Two locations played starring roles in the writing of this book. First, I was fortunate to have been able to spend time in the serene atmosphere of the Berkeley City Club where I wrote many drafts of this book. Writing in its tranquil and magnificent library was other-worldly, and I am convinced that the spirit of its architect, Julia Morgan, was right there beside me as I sat at an exquisite antique desk with my laptop.

But it is the second location – the Montréal in which I was born and raised – that will live forever in my heart. In part, this book is a gift to my hometown, one of the great cities of the world, and one which in so many ways saved my life. In writing and rewriting this memoir I visited Montréal many times. I wandered through its streets as in a dream. Each visit spurred me on to keep writing. During each of these visits, my beloved Montréal offered me shelter and hope – just as it had done right from the beginning of my life.

This book is also a way for me to "give back" to an institution that offered me so much sustenance: School, my place of safety and of comfort. I am filled with gratitude for those teachers of my childhood years who bore silent witness and helped me find a path toward the life force.

To my next-door neighbor Françoise and her family of so long ago, I would like to say: *Je vous remercie de m'avoir donné un premier chemin vers la vie, vers la joie, vers la beauté de la culture canadienne-française.*

I also want to thank the children of all my classrooms who taught me more than I ever dreamt possible, and especially to my young Grade Five student Mandy whose words "Express yourself, Mrs. Feuerverger, you have a right to," became a part of my mantra forever.

I was also blessed to have been given the opportunity to teach, and to be nourished by my bright and devoted graduate students at the University of Toronto. They have given me so much more than I could ever have given them.

My thanks to the Social Sciences and Humanities Research Council of Canada (SSHRCC) for their generous support over the course of my academic career. Also it has been an honor to serve at the Canadian Commission for UNESCO for so many years, and to be a member of Delta Kappa Gamma International.

I will never forget the kindness and understanding that the late Cardinal Jean-Marie Lustiger, Archbishop of Paris, had shown me by listening to my feelings about childhood with my parents. He himself was a Holocaust survivor. *"Écris tout lorsque tu seras prête à le faire. C'est ton devoir,"* he told me.

And I will always remember the Mother Superior at the convent of *Les Soeurs de Notre Dame de L'Arche de L'Alliance*, and Père Paul, the former abbot of the Latrun Monastery – both near Jerusalem. Their compassion for my suffering as a child of Holocaust survivors was so comforting.

I also owe so much to the residents of the co-operative village of *Neve Shalom/Wahat Al-Salam* whose examples of hope and reconciliation in the midst of all their emotional pain helped me to find my own voice and begin to speak and write about my own traumas. Very special thanks to Bob Mark and Rayek Rizek of the village. And deep gratitude to the late Father Bruno Hussar and to the late Anne LeMeignen whose vision of peaceful coexistence brought this village into being.

I am grateful to Evelin Lindner who many years ago invited me to join her Human Dignity and Humiliation Studies group which met annually at Columbia University in New York; what a wonderful and brilliant bunch of participants from all over the world.

My Oakland Writers' Group offered enormous support as I rewrote and revised the manuscript according to their incisive comments: thanks to Joanna Biggar, the late Antoinette Constable, Anne Esmonde, Ann Harleman, the late Barbara Milman, Claudia Monpère, and Molly Walker.

Many thanks go to Adam Hochschild who allowed me to audit his "Writing the Non-Fiction Book" course in the Graduate School of Journalism at UC Berkeley one spring semester several years ago. The discussions in that class (with its fascinating students, all less than half my age) were inspiring and moved me forward in all sorts of ways.

I thank Lynn Freed who was one of my teachers at the Squaw Valley Writers' Workshop almost a decade ago. Her appreciation of my work in her class gave me an extra boost of confidence right at the beginning of the writing of this memoir.

I am so fortunate to know Roseann Runte, a dear friend and colleague for many years. Her wisdom, insight and compassion have been a blessing. She was always there to cheer me during the writing and rewriting of my memoir and that certainly helped me to cross the "finish line."

I shall also never forget the trip I took with my colleagues, Carol Pfaff and Normand Labrie to the Sachsenhausen concentration camp many years ago. They offered me solace in the midst of the emotional storm I felt during those hours in that place of hellish memories.

I would like to give my thanks to many others: Sandra Acker, Mary Lee Ackerman, Zvi Bekerman, Norman Bookstein, Laurie and David Brillinger, Shirley Brower, Sharon Burde, Elizabeth Campbell, Franka Cautillo, the late Kim Chernin, Jeanie Cohen, Jutta and Wayne Collins, the late David Corson, Jim Cummins, Miriam David, Freema Elbaz, Marcia Falk, Paula Fass, the late Jack Feldman, Richard Ford, Frieda Forman, Alta Gerrey, Rose Glickman, Nora Gold, Foster Goldstrom, Lyndon Harris, Linda

Hartman, Ruth Hayhoe, Eva Hoffman, the late Arlene and Wolf Homburger, Tom Hunt, the late Ann Ireland, Karen Jacobs, Joyce Jenkins, Marek Kanter, Joyce and Harvey Kolodny, Susi Kosower, Siggy Krajden, Gillian Kuehner, Alf and Gayle Kwinter, Dave Kwinter, Allyson Latta, Marie Lauzier, Merle Lefkoff, Jack Lesch, Linda Levy, Pina Marchese, Lilian Mast, Mariana Masterson, Shirley McNeal, Anne Michaels, Jack Miller, Karen Mock, Linda Joy Myers, Carol Mullen, Becky and Mike O'Malley, Sylvia Paull, the late Michelangelo Picone, John Pilkington, Fran Quittel, Anna Rabkin, Pat Roberto, Richard Rodriguez, Elizabeth Rosner, the late Robert Ruddell, Naomi Seidman, Linda Siegel, Richard Silberg, the late Roger Simon, Dennis Thiessen, Hesh Troper, the late Roly Ward, David Weiss, Karen and Eli Yablonovitch. They all buoyed me up and helped me to move forward in so many different ways.

I was lucky to meet Lord Daniel Finkelstein of the House of Lords UK Parliament, who appreciated my memoir in terms of the different voice it presented as a child of Holocaust survivors.

I am greatly indebted to Liesbeth Heenk of Amsterdam Publishers for making the publication of this book such a joyful experience. How fortunate it is that I have found her.

I am grateful to my publicists Sylvia Paull and Heather Wood for their guidance.

Very special thanks go to Michael Connelly who opened a new professional door for me when he hired me into the Joint Centre for Teacher Development at OISE of the University of Toronto so many years ago. I walked through that door into an extraordinary narrative journey that transformed my life.

I will forever be grateful to the late Benjamin Geneen who taught me the true meaning of faith, love and compassion. He was and always will be *in loco parentis* for me.

Finally, words cannot express the feelings in my heart for my husband Andrey, the greatest of all the great good fortunes of my life. He also happens to be an exceptional editor with a linguistic sense of nuance beyond compare.

NOTES

4. The Poland They Knew

1. This piece of Canadian history was later unearthed by two social historians, Irving Abella and Harold Troper, who discovered letters in the archives from an official in the then Minister of Mines and Immigration to then Prime Minister William Lyon MacKenzie King displaying vicious antisemitic tone and content. Their book, *None is Too Many,* whose title alludes to a sentence in one of these letters that "even letting one Jew into the country would be too many," caused an uproar when it came out in 1982. It rankled the non-Jewish Anglo-Saxon population who did not want to see the reputation of 'Canada the peacemaker' sullied. But Canada was only one of many countries, including the United States, who cared nothing for the Jews thus allowing Hitler to carry out his Final Solution. How does the expression go? "For evil to happen, it is enough for good people to do nothing."

7. Fiasco in Kindergarten

1. The educational system of Québec was a confessional one – that is, religiously based – and it reflected the original historical realities of England's and France's hostilities in the New World. The *Quebec Act*, which had been drawn up by the English "victors" of the 1759 battle on the Plains of Abraham, divided education into Catholic for the French, in order that they be permitted to maintain their language and religion, and into Protestant (the Protestant School Board of Greater Montreal) for the English. Immigrant non-French kids who were Catholic attended separate English-speaking Catholic schools because English was the language of power. By the late-1800s, and especially in the early-1900s, immigration brought Jews to Québec and this became an issue for the province's confessional (i.e., Christian) educational model. In order for Jews to have a place in the schools, a by-law was created in the early-1900s which allowed Jews to be considered as Protestants "for educational purposes."

ABOUT THE AUTHOR

Grace Feuerverger was born and raised in her beloved city of Montréal surrounded by a multitude of languages and cultures inside and outside her home. She is professor emerita of education and ethnography at the University of Toronto, and taught courses on language, culture and identity as well as peace education for many years.

Grace was educated at McGill University, the *Università per Stranieri* in Perugia, Italy, the University of California at Berkeley, the Hebrew University in Jerusalem and the University of Toronto. She has also been an invited member of the Canadian Commission for UNESCO for many years.

Among her many publications are two award-winning books: *Oasis of Dreams* (about a cooperative Jewish-Palestinian village in Israel) and *Teaching, Learning and Other Miracles* (about education as a sacred life journey). Although now retired, her heart will always be in the classroom with her students. Grace and her husband divide their time between Berkeley and Toronto.

"A beautifully written quest for meaning through teaching, this narrative imparts a glow and significance to the relation between teachers and learners that can only arise in an awareness of a darkness ordinarily denied. A fine and unusual book, authentic and wise." –**Maxine Greene, Teachers College, Columbia University**

"A splendid meditation on education, Feuerverger reminds us of the deepest consolation of the classroom." –**Richard Rodriguez, author of** *Hunger of Memory: The Education of Richard Rodriguez*

AMSTERDAM PUBLISHERS
HOLOCAUST LIBRARY

The series **Holocaust Survivor Memoirs World War II** consists of the following autobiographies of survivors:

Outcry. Holocaust Memoirs, by Manny Steinberg

Hank Brodt Holocaust Memoirs. A Candle and a Promise,
by Deborah Donnelly

The Dead Years. Holocaust Memoirs, by Joseph Schupack

Rescued from the Ashes. The Diary of Leokadia Schmidt, Survivor of the
Warsaw Ghetto, by Leokadia Schmidt

My Lvov. Holocaust Memoir of a twelve-year-old Girl, by Janina Hescheles

Remembering Ravensbrück. From Holocaust to Healing, by Natalie Hess

Wolf. A Story of Hate, by Zeev Scheinwald with Ella Scheinwald

Save my Children. An Astonishing Tale of Survival and its Unlikely Hero,
by Leon Kleiner with Edwin Stepp

Holocaust Memoirs of a Bergen-Belsen Survivor & Classmate of Anne
Frank, by Nanette Blitz Konig

Defiant German - Defiant Jew. A Holocaust Memoir from inside the Third
Reich, by Walter Leopold with Les Leopold

In a Land of Forest and Darkness. The Holocaust Story of two Jewish
Partisans, by Sara Lustigman Omelinski

Holocaust Memories. Annihilation and Survival in Slovakia,
by Paul Davidovits

From Auschwitz with Love. The Inspiring Memoir of Two Sisters' Survival, Devotion and Triumph Told by Manci Grunberger Beran & Ruth Grunberger Mermelstein, by Daniel Seymour

Remetz. Resistance Fighter and Survivor of the Warsaw Ghetto, by Jan Yohay Remetz

My March Through Hell. A Young Girl's Terrifying Journey to Survival, by Halina Kleiner with Edwin Stepp

Roman's Journey, by Roman Halter

Beyond Borders. Escaping the Holocaust and Fighting the Nazis. 1938-1948, by Rudi Haymann

The Engineers. A memoir of survival through World War II in Poland and Hungary, by Henry Reiss

Spark of Hope. An Autobiography, by Luba Wrobel Goldberg

Footnote to History. From Hungary to America. The Memoir of a Holocaust Survivor, by Andrew Laszlo

The series **Holocaust Survivor True Stories**
consists of the following biographies:

Among the Reeds. The true story of how a family survived the Holocaust,
by Tammy Bottner

A Holocaust Memoir of Love & Resilience. Mama's Survival from
Lithuania to America, by Ettie Zilber

Living among the Dead. My Grandmother's Holocaust Survival Story of
Love and Strength, by Adena Bernstein Astrowsky

Heart Songs. A Holocaust Memoir, by Barbara Gilford

Shoes of the Shoah. The Tomorrow of Yesterday, by Dorothy Pierce

Hidden in Berlin. A Holocaust Memoir, by Evelyn Joseph Grossman

Separated Together. The Incredible True WWII Story of Soulmates
Stranded an Ocean Apart, by Kenneth P. Price, Ph.D.

The Man Across the River. The incredible story of one man's will to survive
the Holocaust, by Zvi Wiesenfeld

If Anyone Calls, Tell Them I Died. A Memoir, by Emanuel (Manu) Rosen

The House on Thrömerstrasse. A Story of Rebirth and Renewal in the
Wake of the Holocaust, by Ron Vincent

Dancing with my Father. His hidden past. Her quest for truth. How Nazi
Vienna shaped a family's identity, by Jo Sorochinsky

The Story Keeper. Weaving the Threads of Time and Memory - A Memoir,
by Fred Feldman

Krisia's Silence. The Girl who was not on Schindler's List, by Ronny Hein

Defying Death on the Danube. A Holocaust Survival Story,
by Debbie J. Callahan with Henry Stern

A Doorway to Heroism. A decorated German-Jewish Soldier who became an American Hero, by Rabbi W. Jack Romberg

The Shoemaker's Son. The Life of a Holocaust Resister, by Laura Beth Bakst

The Redhead of Auschwitz. A True Story, by Nechama Birnbaum

Land of Many Bridges. My Father's Story, by Bela Ruth Samuel Tenenholtz

Creating Beauty from the Abyss. The Amazing Story of Sam Herciger, Auschwitz Survivor and Artist, by Lesley Ann Richardson

On Sunny Days We Sang. A Holocaust Story of Survival and Resilience, by Jeannette Grunhaus de Gelman

Painful Joy. A Holocaust Family Memoir, by Max J. Friedman

I Give You My Heart. A True Story of Courage and Survival, by Wendy Holden

In the Time of Madmen, by Mark A. Prelas

Monsters and Miracles. Horror, Heroes and the Holocaust, by Ira Wesley Kitmacher

Flower of Vlora. Growing up Jewish in Communist Albania, by Anna Kohen

Aftermath: Coming of Age on Three Continents. A Memoir, by Annette Libeskind Berkovits

Not a real Enemy. The True Story of a Hungarian Jewish Man's Fight for Freedom, by Robert Wolf

Zaidy's War. Four Armies, Three Continents, Two Brothers. One Man's Impossible Story of Endurance, by Martin Bodek

The Glassmaker's Son. Looking for the World my Father left behind in Nazi Germany, by Peter Kupfer

The Apprentice of Buchenwald. The True Story of the Teenage Boy Who Sabotaged Hitler's War Machine, by Oren Schneider

Good for a Single Journey, by Helen Joyce

Burying the Ghosts. She escaped Nazi Germany only to have her life torn apart by the woman she saved from the camps: her mother, by Sonia Case

American Wolf. From Nazi Refugee to American Spy. A True Story, by Audrey Birnbaum

Bipolar Refugee. A Saga of Survival and Resilience, by Peter Wiesner

In the Wake of Madness. My Family's Escape from the Nazis, by Bettie Lennett Denny

Before the Beginning and After the End, by Hymie Anisman

I Will Give Them an Everlasting Name. Jacksonville's Stories of the Holocaust, by Samuel Cox

Hiding in Holland. A Resistance Memoir, by Shulamit Reinharz

The Ghosts on the Wall. A Grandson's Memoir of the Holocaust, by Kenneth D. Wald

The series **Jewish Children in the Holocaust** consists of the following
autobiographies of Jewish children
hidden during WWII in the Netherlands:

Searching for Home. The Impact of WWII on a Hidden Child,
by Joseph Gosler

Sounds from Silence. Reflections of a Child Holocaust Survivor,
Psychiatrist and Teacher, by Robert Krell

Sabine's Odyssey. A Hidden Child and her Dutch Rescuers,
by Agnes Schipper

The Journey of a Hidden Child, by Harry Pila and Robin Black

The series **New Jewish Fiction** consists of the following novels, written by Jewish authors. All novels are set in the time during or after the Holocaust.

The Corset Maker. A Novel, by Annette Libeskind Berkovits

Escaping the Whale. The Holocaust is over. But is it ever over for the next generation? by Ruth Rotkowitz

When the Music Stopped. Willy Rosen's Holocaust, by Casey Hayes

Hands of Gold. One Man's Quest to Find the Silver Lining in Misfortune, by Roni Robbins

The Girl Who Counted Numbers. A Novel, by Roslyn Bernstein

There was a garden in Nuremberg. A Novel, by Navina Michal Clemerson

The Butterfly and the Axe, by Omer Bartov

To Live Another Day. A Novel, by Elizabeth Rosenberg

A Worthy Life. Based on a True Story, by Dahlia Moore

The Right to Happiness. After all they went through. Stories, by Helen Schary Motro

The series **Holocaust Heritage** consists of the following memoirs by 2G:

The Cello Still Sings. A Generational Story of the Holocaust and of the Transformative Power of Music, by Janet Horvath

The Fire and the Bonfire. A Journey into Memory, by Ardyn Halter

The Silk Factory: Finding Threads of My Family's True Holocaust Story, by Michael Hickins

Winter Light. The Memoir of a Child of Holocaust Survivors, by Grace Feuerverger

Out from the Shadows. Growing up with Holocaust Survivor Parents, by Willie Handler

Stumbling Stones, by Joanna Rosenthall

The Unspeakable. Breaking decades of family silence surrounding the Holocaust, by Nicola Hanefeld

Hidden in Plain Sight. A Journey into Memory and Place, by Julie Brill

The series **Holocaust Books for Young Adults** consists of the following novels, based on true stories:

The Boy behind the Door. How Salomon Kool Escaped the Nazis. Inspired by a True Story, by David Tabatsky

Running for Shelter. A True Story, by Suzette Sheft

The Precious Few. An Inspirational Saga of Courage based on True Stories, by David Twain with Art Twain

Dark Shadows Hover, by Jordan Steven Sher

The Sun will Shine on You again one Day, by Cynthia Monsour

The series **WWII Historical Fiction** consists of the following novels, some of which are based on true stories:

Mendelevski's Box. A Heartwarming and Heartbreaking Jewish Survivor's Story, by Roger Swindells

A Quiet Genocide. The Untold Holocaust of Disabled Children in WWII Germany, by Glenn Bryant

The Knife-Edge Path, by Patrick T. Leahy

Brave Face. The Inspiring WWII Memoir of a Dutch/German Child, by I. Caroline Crocker and Meta A. Evenbly

When We Had Wings. The Gripping Story of an Orphan in Janusz Korczak's Orphanage. A Historical Novel, by Tami Shem-Tov

Jacob's Courage. Romance and Survival amidst the Horrors of War, by Charles S. Weinblatt

A Semblance of Justice. Based on true Holocaust experiences, by Wolf Holles

This Grey Place, by Katie O'Connor

Amsterdam Publishers Newsletter

Subscribe to our Newsletter by selecting the menu at the top (right) of **amsterdampublishers.com** or scan the QR-code below.

Receive a variety of content such as:

- A welcome message by the founder
- Free Holocaust memoirs
- Book recommendations
- News about upcoming releases
- Chance to become an AP Reviewer.